HUTCHINSON

On This Day

Titles in this series

Dictionary of Abbreviations
Dictionary of Biology
Dictionary of Chemistry
Dictionary of Classical Music
Dictionary of Computing and Multimedia
Guide to Countries of the World
Dictionary of Geography
Dictionary of Mathematics
Dictionary of Physics
Dictionary of Science
Dictionary of World War I
Dictionary of World War II
Dictionary of 20th Century World History
Dictionary of Battles
On This Day
Chronology of World Events

Family Encyclopedia

HUTCHINSON

On This Day

BROCKHAMPTON PRESS
LONDON

Helicon Publishing Ltd
42 Hythe Bridge Street
Oxford OX1 2EP

Printed and bound in Great Britain by
Mackays of Chatham Plc,
Chatham, Kent

This edition published 1997 by
Brockhampton Press Ltd
20 Bloomsbury Street
London WC1B 3QA
(a member of the Hodder Headline PLC Group)

ISBN 1-86019-580-6

British Cataloguing in Publication Data

A catalogue record for this book is available
from the British Library

Introduction

Most of us have an interest in anniversaries. We may be seeking important information for specific purposes or just enjoying the pleasure of browsing through facts and coincidences.

In this book are important dates of the famous and infamous and notable events throughout history for every day of the year. Within the limitations of space, we have aimed to achieve a balanced range of entries – historical, political, popular culture, and serendipity. So the reader can find, for example, that Jerusalem was destroyed under Titus on 1 September in AD 70, that the first episode of the BBC television soap opera 'East Enders' was transmitted on 19 February 1985, and that Nelson Mandela was released on 11 February 1990.

The presentation for each day is divided into four parts: the entry starts with feasts that are traditionally celebrated on that day; followed by a section of notable events; then births of significant people; and deaths.

Happy browsing!

Editorial director
Michael Upshall

Contributors
Jane Anson
Anna Farkas

Project editor
Sheila Dallas

Design and page make-up
TJ Graphics

Production
Tony Ballsdon

On This Day

JANUARY ████████

1 New Year's Day, and the national day of Cuba, Sudan, and Haiti. Feast day of St Felix of Bourges, St Almachius, St William of Dijon, St Eugendus or Oyend, St Peter of Atroa, St Odilo, and St Fulgentius of Ruspe.

1785 London's oldest daily paper *The Daily Universal Register* (renamed *The Times* in 1788) was first published. **1801** Italian astronomer Giuseppe Piazzi became the first person to discover an asteroid; he named it Ceres. **1887** Queen Victoria was proclaimed empress of India in Delhi. **1894** The Manchester Ship Canal was officially opened to traffic. **1901** The Commonwealth of Australia was formed. **1909** The first payments of old-age pensions were made in Britain, with persons over 70 receiving five shillings (25p) a week. **1958** The European Community came into existence. **1959** Fidel Castro overthrew the government of Fulgencio Batista, and seized power in Cuba. **1993** Czechoslovakia split into two separate states, the Czech Republic and Slovakia; the peaceful division had been engineered in **1992**.

Lorenzo de' Medici (The Magnificent), Florentine ruler, **1449**; Paul Revere, US patriot, **1735**; E M Forster, English novelist, **1879**; William Fox, US movie mogul, **1879**; J Edgar Hoover, director of the FBI, **1895**; J D Salinger, US author, **1919**; Joe Orton, English dramatist, **1933**.

William Wycherley, English dramatist, **1716**; James Stuart, the Old Pretender, **1766**; Heinrich Hertz, German physicist, **1894**; Edwin Landseer Lutyens, English architect, **1944**; Maurice Chevalier, French actor and singer, **1972**; L Ron Hubbard, US science-fiction writer and founder of Scientology, **1986**.

---

2 Feast day of St Seraphim of Sarov, St Basil, St Gregory Nazianzen, St Munchin, St Adalhard or Adelard, St Caspar of Bufalo, St Macarius of Alexandria, St Vincentian, and the Holy Name of Jesus.

1492 Granada, the last Moorish stronghold in Spain, surrendered to the Spaniards. **1635** Cardinal Richelieu established the Académie Française. **1839** French photographer

Louis Daguerre took the first photograph of the moon. **1946** King Zog of Albania, who had been residing in England since 1939, was deposed. **1959** The Russian uncrewed spacecraft Luna I, the first rocket to pass near the moon, was launched. **1971** A barrier collapsed at the Ibrox Park football stadium in Glasgow, crushing 66 fans to death. **1979** The trial of Sid Vicious, the Sex Pistols' singer accused of murdering his girlfriend Nancy Spungen, began in New York.

James Wolfe, British general, **1727**; George Murray, English classical scholar, **1866**; Michael Tippett, English composer, **1905**; Isaac Asimov, US biochemist and science-fiction writer, **1920**; Roger Miller, US singer and composer, **1936**; David Bailey, English photographer, **1938**.

Ovid, Roman poet, **17**; Livy, Roman historian, **17**; George Airy, English Astronomer Royal, **1892**; Emil Janning, US film actor, **1950**; Tex Ritter, US stage and screen singing cowboy, **1974**; Dick Emery, English comedian, **1983**.

3

Feast day of St Peter Balsam, St Bertilia of Mareuil, St Antherus, pope, and St Genevieve or Genovefa.

1521 Pope Leo X excommunicated Martin Luther. **1777** The Battle of Princeton took place in the War of Independence, in which George Washington defeated the British forces, led by Cornwallis. **1924** English explorer Howard Carter discovered the sarcophagus of Tutankhamen in the Valley of the Kings, near Luxor, Egypt. **1959** Alaska became the 49th of the United States. **1962** Pope John XXIII excommunicated Cuban prime minister Fidel Castro. **1991** The British government announced that seven Iraqi diplomats, another embassy staff member and 67 other Iraqis were being expelled from Britain. **1993** US President George Bush and Russian President Boris Yeltsin signed the second Strategic Arms Reduction Treaty (START) in Moscow.

Marcus Tullius Cicero, Roman orator and statesman, **106 BC**; Clement Attlee, British statesman, **1883**; J R R Tolkien, English writer, **1892**; Ray Milland, US film actor, **1907**; Victor Borge, Danish musician and comedian, **1909**; John Thaw, British actor, **1942**.

Josiah Wedgwood, English potter, **1795**; Pierre Larousse, French editor and encyclopedist, **1875**; Jaroslav Hasek, Czech novelist, **1923**; Conrad Hilton, US hotel magnate, **1979**; Joy Adamson, British naturalist and author, **1980**.

4 The national day of Myanmar. Feast day of St Gregory of Langres, St Roger of Ellant, St Elizabeth Bayley Seton, St Pharaïdis, and St Rigobert of Reims.

1884 The socialist Fabian Society was founded in London. **1885** The first successful surgical removal of an appendix was performed, in Iowa, USA. **1936** The first pop-music chart was compiled, based on record sales published in New York in Billboard. **1944** The attack on Monte Cassino was launched by the British Fifth Army in Italy. **1972** Rose Helibron became the first woman judge in Britain at the Old Bailey, London. **1981** The Broadway show Frankenstein lost an estimated 2 million dollars, when it opened and closed on the same night. **1991** The UN Security Council voted unanimously to condemn Israel's treatment of the Palestinians in the occupied territories.

Louis Braille, French deviser of an alphabet for the blind, **1809**; Augustus John, Welsh painter, **1878**; Floyd Patterson, US boxer, **1935**; Grace Bumbry, US opera singer, **1937**; Dyan Cannon, US actress, **1939**; John McLaughlin, British blues and jazz guitarist, **1943**.

Ralph Vaughan Williams, English composer, **1958**; Albert Camus, French novelist and dramatist, **1960**; T S Eliot, US poet and critic, **1965**; Brian Gwynne Horrocks, British general, **1985**; Christopher Isherwood, English novelist and dramatist, **1986**.

5 Feast day of St Simeon Stylites, St Gerlac, St Dorotheus the Younger, St Apollinaris, St Convoyon, St Syncletica, and St John Nepomucene Neumann.

1477 Charles the Bold, King of France, was killed at the Battle of Nancy. **1896** German physicist Röntgen gave the first demonstration of X-rays. **1938** Billie Holiday recorded 'When You're Smiling (the Whole World Smiles with You)' in New York. **1964** The London Underground's first automatic ticket barrier was installed, at Stamford Brook. **1964** On his tour of the Holy Land, Pope Paul VI met Patriarch Athenagoras I, the first meeting between the heads of the Roman Catholic and Orthodox Churches in over 500 years. **1976** French premier Giscard d'Estaing promulgated a law making French the only language permitted in advertising in France.

Konrad Adenauer, German statesman, **1876**; Stella Gibbons, English poet and novelist, **1902**; Alfred Brendel, Austrian concert pianist, **1931**; Robert Duvall, US film actor, **1931**; Juan Carlos, King of Spain, **1938**; Diane Keaton, US film actress, **1946**.

English king Edward the Confessor, **1066**; Catherine de' Medici, Queen of France, **1589**; Count Radetzky, Austrian soldier, **1858**; Henry Shackleton, Irish Antarctic explorer, **1922**; Calvin Coolidge, 30th US president, **1933**; Amy Johnson, English aviator, **1941**.

6

Epiphany. Feast day of St John de Ribera, St Erminold, St Wiltrudis, St Guarinus

871 English king Alfred defeated the Danes at the Battle of Ashdown. **1540** King Henry VIII was married to Anne of Cleves, his fourth wife. **1720** The Committee of Inquiry on the South Sea Bubble published its findings. **1838** The first public demonstration of the electric telegraph was given by its inventor, Samuel Morse. **1928** The River Thames flooded, drowning four people, and severely damaging paintings stored in the Tate Gallery's basement. **1945** The Battle of the Bulge, or Ardennes offensive, ended, with 130,000 German and 77,000 Allied casualties. **1988** La Coupole, the Parisian brasserie made famous by generations of notable artists and writers who frequented it, was sold for £6 million to be converted into an office block.

King Richard II of England, **1367**; St Joan of Arc, **1412**; Gustave Doré, French artist and illustrator, **1833**; Carl Sandburg, US poet, **1878**; Loretta Young, US film actress, **1913**; Rowan Atkinson, English actor and comedian, **1957**; Kapil Dev, Indian cricketer, **1959**.

JAN FEB MAR APR MAY JUN JUL AUG SEP OCT NOV DEC

D Fanny Burney, English novelist and diarist, **1840**; Gregor Mendel, Austrian monk and biologist, **1884**; Theodore Roosevelt, 26th US president, **1919**; Archibald Joseph Cronin, Scottish novelist, **1981**; Rudolf Nureyev, Russian dancer, **1993**; Dizzy Gillespie, US jazz trumpeter, **1993**.

7 Christmas Day in the Orthodox Church. Feast day of St Valentine, St Raymund of Peñafort, St Aldric, St Lucian of Antioch, St Tillo, St Canute Lavard, and St Reinold.

1558 Calais, the last English possession on mainland France, was recaptured by the French. **1610** Italian astronomer Galileo discovered Jupiter's four satellites, naming them Io, Europa, Ganymede, and Callisto. **1785** The first aerial crossing of the English Channel was made by Jean Pierre Blanchard and Dr John Jeffries, in a hot-air balloon. **1927** The London–New York telephone service began operating, a three-minute call costing £15. **1975** OPEC agreed to raise crude oil prices by 10%, which began a tidal wave of world economic inflation. **1990** The Leaning Tower of Pisa was closed to the public, as its accelerated rate of 'leaning' raised fears for the safety of its many visitors.

B Joseph Bonaparte, King of Naples, **1768**; Carl Laemmle, US film producer, founder of Universal Pictures, **1867**; Adolph Zukor, US film magnate, **1873**; Charles Péguy, French poet and socialist, **1873**; Francis Poulenc, French composer, **1899**; Gerald Durrell, British author and naturalist, **1925**.

D Catherine of Aragon, first wife of Henry VIII, **1536**; Nicholas Hilliard, English miniaturist painter, **1619**; André Maginot, French politician, **1932**; Trevor Howard, British actor, **1988**; Michinomiya Hirohito, Emperor of Japan, **1989**.

8 Feast day of St Severinus of Noricum, St Severinus of Septempeda, and St Wulsin.

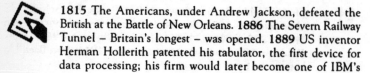

1815 The Americans, under Andrew Jackson, defeated the British at the Battle of New Orleans. **1886** The Severn Railway Tunnel – Britain's longest – was opened. **1889** US inventor Herman Hollerith patented his tabulator, the first device for data processing; his firm would later become one of IBM's founding companies. **1916** The final withdrawal of Allied troops from Gallipoli took place. **1921** David Lloyd George became the first prime minister tenant at Chequers Court, Buckinghamshire. **1959** French general Charles de Gaulle became the first president of the Fifth Republic. **1993** Bosnian President Izetbegovic visited the USA to plead his government's case for Western military aid and intervention to halt Serbian aggression.

Wilkie Collins, English novelist, **1824**; Elvis Presley, US rock singer, **1935**; Shirley Bassey, Welsh-born singer, **1937**; Stephen Hawking, English physicist and mathematician, **1942**; David Bowie, English rock singer and actor, **1947**; Calvin Smith, US athlete, **1961**.

Galileo Galilei, Italian astronomer, **1642**; Eli Whitney, US inventor of the cotton gin, **1825**; Paul Verlaine, French poet, **1895**; Zhou Enlai, Chinese leader, **1976**; Gregori Maximilianovich Malenkov, Soviet leader, **1988**; Terry-Thomas, English film comedy actor, **1990**.

9

Feast day of Saints Julian and Basilissa, St Berhtwald of Canterbury, St Peter of Sebastea, St Waningus or Vaneng, and St Marciana of Rusuccur.

1799 British prime minister William Pitt the Younger introduced income tax, at two shillings (10p) in the pound, to raise funds for the Napoleonic Wars. **1902** New York State introduced a bill to outlaw flirting in public. **1969** The supersonic aeroplane Concorde made its first trial flight, at Bristol. **1972** The ocean liner *Queen Elizabeth* was destroyed by fire in Hong Kong harbour. **1972** British miners went on strike for the first time since 1926. **1991** US secretary of state Baker and Iraqi foreign minister Aziz met for 6½ hours in Geneva, but failed to reach any agreement that would forestall war in the Persian Gulf.

Gracie Fields, English singer, **1898**; George Balanchine, US choreographer, **1904**; Simone de Beauvoir, French novelist and critic, **1908**; Richard Nixon, 37th US president, **1913**; Gypsy Rose Lee, US striptease artist and actress, **1914**; Joan Baez, US singer, **1941**.

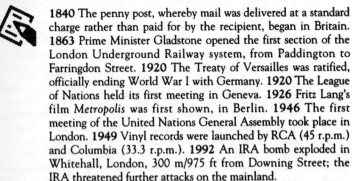

Caroline Lucretia Herschel, English astronomer, **1848**; Napoleon III, French emperor, **1873**; Katherine Mansfield, New Zealand writer, **1923**; Tommy Handley, English radio comedian, **1949**; Frederick Gibberd, British architect, **1984**; Robert Mayer, British philanthropist, **1985**.

10

Feast day of St Marcian of Constantinople, St William of Bourges, St Agatho, pope, St Dermot or Diarmaid, St Peter Orseolo, and St John the Good.

1840 The penny post, whereby mail was delivered at a standard charge rather than paid for by the recipient, began in Britain. **1863** Prime Minister Gladstone opened the first section of the London Underground Railway system, from Paddington to Farringdon Street. **1920** The Treaty of Versailles was ratified, officially ending World War I with Germany. **1920** The League of Nations held its first meeting in Geneva. **1926** Fritz Lang's film *Metropolis* was first shown, in Berlin. **1946** The first meeting of the United Nations General Assembly took place in London. **1949** Vinyl records were launched by RCA (45 r.p.m.) and Columbia (33.3 r.p.m.). **1992** An IRA bomb exploded in Whitehall, London, 300 m/975 ft from Downing Street; the IRA threatened further attacks on the mainland.

Michel Ney, French marshal, **1769**; Barbara Hepworth, English sculptor, **1903**; Paul Henreid, Austrian actor, **1908**; Galina Ulanova, Russian ballerina, **1910**; Johnny Ray, US singer, **1927**; Rod Stewart, English rock singer, **1945**.

Carolus Linnaeus, Swedish botanist, **1778**; Samuel Colt, US gunsmith, **1862**; Sinclair Lewis, US novelist, **1951**; Dashiell Hammett, US detective-story writer, **1961**; Coco (Gabrielle) Chanel, French fashion designer, **1971**; Anton Karas, Austrian composer, **1985**.

11

Feast day of St Salvius or Sauve of Amiens, and St Theodosius the Cenobiarch.

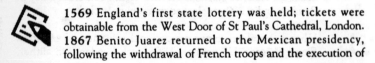

1569 England's first state lottery was held; tickets were obtainable from the West Door of St Paul's Cathedral, London. **1867** Benito Juarez returned to the Mexican presidency, following the withdrawal of French troops and the execution of

Emperor Maximilian. **1922** Leonard Thompson became the first person to be successfully treated with insulin, at Toronto General Hospital. **1963** The first disco, called the 'Whisky-a-go-go', opened in Los Angeles, USA. **1973** The Open University awarded its first degrees. **1977** Rolling Stone Keith Richards was tried in London for possession of cocaine, found in his car after an accident, and fined £750. **1991** An auction of silver and paintings that had been acquired by the late Ferdinand Marcos and his wife, Imelda, brought in a total of $20.29 million at Christie's in New York.

Ezra Cornell, US philanthropist, **1807**; Fred Archer, English jockey, **1857**; Henry Gordon Selfridge, US entrepreneur and founder of the London department store, **1864**; Alan Paton, South African author, **1903**; Rod Taylor, Australian film actor, **1929**; John Sessions, English actor and comedian, **1953**.

Hans Sloane, British physician and naturalist, **1753**; Thomas Hardy, English poet and novelist, **1928**; Alberto Giacometti, Swiss sculptor and painter, **1966**; Richmal Crompton, English author, **1969**; Padraic Colum, Irish poet, **1972**; Isidor Rabi, US physicist, **1988**.

12 Feast day of St Benedict or Benet Biscop, St Tatiana, St Margaret Bourgeoys, St Arcadius, St Caesaria, St Victorian, and St Eutropius.

1866 The Royal Aeronautical Society was founded in London. **1875** Kwang-su was made emperor of China. **1964** The Sultan of Zanzibar was overthrown, following an uprising, and a republic proclaimed. **1971** PLO terrorist Abu Davoud, leader of the Black September group responsible for the killing of 11 Israeli athletes at the Munich Olympics, was released from prison in France. **1970** The Boeing 747 aircraft touched down at Heathrow Airport at the end of its first transatlantic flight. **1991** US Congress passed a resolution authorising President Bush to use military power to force Iraq out of Kuwait. **1993** Sectarian violence continued for the eighth consecutive day in Bombay, India; 200 people died in nationwide clashes.

Johann Pestalozzi, Swiss educational reformer, **1746**; John Singer Sargent, US painter, **1856**; Jack London, US author,

JAN FEB MAR APR MAY JUN JUL AUG SEP OCT NOV DEC

1876; Hermann Goering, German Nazi leader, 1893; P W Botha, South African politician, 1916; Joe Frazier, US heavyweight boxer, 1944.

Maximilian I, Holy Roman Emperor, 1519; Jan Breughel the Elder, Flemish painter, 1625; Pierre de Fermat, French mathematician, 1665; Isaac Pitman, English teacher and inventor of shorthand, 1897; Nevil Shute, English novelist, 1960; Agatha Christie, English detective-story writer, 1976.

13

Feast day of St Hilary of Poitiers, St Agrecius, and St Berno.

1893 The British Independent Labour Party was formed by Keir Hardie. 1898 French novelist Emile Zola published *J'accuse/I Accuse*, a pamphlet indicting the persecutors of Dreyfus. 1910 Opera was broadcast on the radio for the first time – Enrico Caruso singing from the stage of New York's Metropolitan Opera House. 1964 Capitol records released the Beatles' first single in the USA; 'I Wanna Hold Your Hand' sold one million copes in the first three weeks. 1978 NASA selected its first women astronauts, 15 years after the USSR had a female astronaut orbit the Earth. 1991 Soviet troops killed 15 protesters in Vilnius, capital of Lithuania, in a crackdown on pro-independence forces. 1993 Former East German leader Erich Honecker, who had been awaiting trial on charges of manslaughter, was released from a Berlin prison because of ill health.

Sophie Tucker, US singer and vaudeville star, 1884; Johannes Bjelke-Petersen, Australian politician, 1911; Ted Willis, English dramatist, 1918; Robert Stack, US film actor, 1919; Michael Bond, English creator of the Paddington Bear stories for children, 1926.

Edmund Spenser, English poet, 1599; George Fox, English founder of the Society of Friends, 1691; Stephen Foster, US songwriter, 1864; James Joyce, Irish novelist, 1941; Hubert Humphrey, US politician, 1978.

14

Feast day of The Martyrs of Mount Sinai, St Barbasymas or Barbascemin, St Antony Pucci, St Datius, St Macrina the Elder, St Sava, St Felix of Nola, and St Kentigern or Mungo.

1858 Attempt on the life of Napoleon III, in Paris. 1900 Puccini's opera *Tosca* was first performed, in Rome. 1907 An earthquake killed over 1,000 people in Kingston, Jamaica, virtually destroying the capital. 1943 US President Roosevelt and British Prime Minister Churchill met at Casablanca. 1954 Baseball hero Joe DiMaggio married film star Marilyn Monroe. 1993 Amid increasingly intrusive coverage about the private lives of the British royal family, the government pledged to introduce legislation to criminalise invasions of privacy by the press.

Henri Fantin-Latour, French painter, 1836; Albert Schweitzer, French missionary surgeon, 1875; Cecil Beaton, British photographer and stage designer, 1904; Joseph Losey, US film director, 1909; Trevor Nunn, British stage director, 1940; Faye Dunaway, US actress, 1941.

Edmond Halley, English astronomer, 1742; Jean Auguste Dominique Ingres, French painter, 1867; Lewis Carroll, English mathematician and author, 1898; Humphrey Bogart, US film actor, 1957; Peter Finch, English actor, 1977; Anaïs Nin, US novelist and diarist, 1977.

15

Feast day of St Macarius the Elder, St Isidore of Alexandria, St Bonitus or Bonet, St Ita, and St John Calybites.

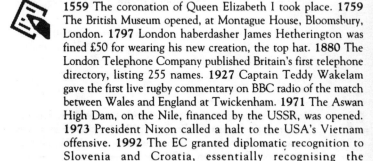 1559 The coronation of Queen Elizabeth I took place. 1759 The British Museum opened, at Montague House, Bloomsbury, London. 1797 London haberdasher James Hetherington was fined £50 for wearing his new creation, the top hat. 1880 The London Telephone Company published Britain's first telephone directory, listing 255 names. 1927 Captain Teddy Wakelam gave the first live rugby commentary on BBC radio of the match between Wales and England at Twickenham. 1971 The Aswan High Dam, on the Nile, financed by the USSR, was opened. 1973 President Nixon called a halt to the USA's Vietnam offensive. 1992 The EC granted diplomatic recognition to Slovenia and Croatia, essentially recognising the dismemberment of Yugoslavia.

Molière, French dramatist, 1622; Aristotle Onassis, Greek shipowner, 1906; Lloyd Bridges, US film actor, 1913; Gamal

Nasser, Egyptian leader, 1918; Martin Luther King, US civil-rights campaigner, 1929; Margaret O'Brien, US film actress, 1937.

Emma Hamilton, English courtesan, mistress to Lord Nelson, 1815; Matthew B Brady, US Civil War photographer, 1896; Rosa Luxemburg, German socialist, 1919; Jack Teagarden, US jazz musician, 1964; Sean MacBride, Irish politician, 1988; Sammy Cahn, US lyricist, 1993.

16

Feast day of St Henry of Cocket, St Marcellus, pope, St Berard and Others, St Fursey, St Priscilla, and St Honoratus of Arles.

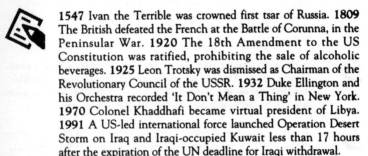

1547 Ivan the Terrible was crowned first tsar of Russia. 1809 The British defeated the French at the Battle of Corunna, in the Peninsular War. 1920 The 18th Amendment to the US Constitution was ratified, prohibiting the sale of alcoholic beverages. 1925 Leon Trotsky was dismissed as Chairman of the Revolutionary Council of the USSR. 1932 Duke Ellington and his Orchestra recorded 'It Don't Mean a Thing' in New York. 1970 Colonel Khaddhafi became virtual president of Libya. 1991 A US-led international force launched Operation Desert Storm on Iraq and Iraqi-occupied Kuwait less than 17 hours after the expiration of the UN deadline for Iraqi withdrawal.

Franz Brentano, German philosopher, 1838; André Michelin, French tyre-maker, 1853; Diana Wynyard, British actress, 1906, Alexander Knox, Canadian film actor, 1907; Ethel Merman, US singer and actress, 1909; Cliff Thorburn, snooker player, 1948.

Léo Delibes, French composer, 1891; Carole Lombard, US film actress, 1942; Arturo Toscanini, Italian conductor, 1957; Robert Van de Graff, US nuclear physicist, 1967; Mohammed Reza Pahlavi, former Shah of Iran, 1979; Florence Desmond, British actress, 1993.

17

Feast day of St Sabinus of Piacenza, St Julian Sabas, St Antony the Abbot, St Geulf or Genou, St Richimir, St Sulpicius II or Sulpice of Bourges, and Saints Speusippus, Eleusippus, and Meleusippus.

1377 The Papal See was transferred from Avignon back to Rome. 1773 Captain Cook's Resolution became the first ship to cross the Antarctic Circle. 1852 The independence of the Transvaal Boers was recognised by Britain. 1912 English explorer Robert Falcon Scott reached the South Pole; Norwegian Roald Amundsen had beaten him there by one month. 1959 Senegal and the French Sudan joined to form the Federal State of Mali. 1966 A B-52 carrying four H-bombs collided with a refuelling tanker, killing eight of the crew and releasing the bombs. 1977 US double murderer Gary Gilmore became the first to be executed in the USA in a decade; he chose to be executed by firing squad. 1992 An IRA bomb, placed next to a remote country road in County Tyrone, Northern Ireland, killed seven building workers and injured seven others.

B

Benjamin Franklin, US statesman and scientist, 1706; David Lloyd George, English statesman, 1863; Nevil Shute, English novelist, 1899; Al Capone, US gangster, 1899; Muhammad Ali, US boxer, 1942; Paul Young, English singer, 1956.

D

Tomaso Giovanni Albinoni, Italian composer, 1751; Quintin Hogg, English merchant and philanthropist, 1903; Francis Galton, English anthropologist and explorer, 1911; T W White, English writer, 1964; Ruskin Spear, British artist, 1990.

18

Feast day of St Prisca, St Peter's Chair, Rome, St Desle or Deicolus, and St Volusian.

1778 Captain Cook discovered the Sandwich Islands, now known as Hawaii. 1871 Wilhelm, King of Prussia from 1861, was proclaimed the first German Emperor. 1911 The first landing of an aircraft on a ship's deck was made by US pilot Eugene Ely, in San Francisco Bay. 1919 The Versailles Peace Conference opened. 1944 The German siege of Leningrad, which began Sept 1941, was relieved. 1972 Former Rhodesian prime minister Garfield Todd and his daughter were placed under house arrest for campaigning against Rhodesian independence. 1977 In Australia, a Sydney-bound train derailed, killing 82 people.

JAN FEB MAR APR MAY JUN JUL AUG SEP OCT NOV DEC

B Peter Mark Roget, English lexicographer, 1779; A A Milne, English author, 1882; Oliver Hardy, US comedian, 1892; Cary Grant, US film actor, 1904; Danny Kaye, US film actor and comedian, 1913; David Bellamy, English botanist, 1933.

D John Tyler, 10th US president, 1862; Rudyard Kipling, English author, 1936; Sydney Greenstreet, British film actor, 1954; Hugh Gaitskell, British statesman, 1963; Cecil Beaton, English photographer and designer, 1980; George Markstein, British author, 1988.

19 Feast day of St Canute IV of Denmark, Saints Abachum and Audifax, St Fillan or Foelan, St Albert of Cashel, St Charles of Sezze, St Germanicus, Saints Marius and Martha, St Messalina, St Henry of Uppsala, St Nathalan, and St Wulfstan.

1764 John Wilkes was expelled from the British House of Commons for seditious libel. 1793 King Louis XVI was tried by the French Convention, found guilty of treason and sentenced to the guillotine. 1853 Verdi's opera *Il Trovatore* was first staged in Rome. 1915 More than 20 people were killed when German zeppelins bombed England for the first time; the bombs were dropped on Great Yarmouth and King's Lynn. 1942 The Japanese invaded Burma (now Myanmar). 1966 Indira Gandhi became prime minister of India. 1969 In protest against the Russian invasion of 1968, Czech student Jan Palach set himself alight in Prague's Wenceslas Square. 1993 IBM announced a loss of $4.97 billion for 1992, the largest single-year loss in US corporate history.

B James Watt, Scottish inventor, 1736; Edgar Allan Poe, US author and poet, 1809; Paul Cézanne, French painter, 1839; Janis Joplin, US rock singer, 1943; Dolly Parton, US country singer, 1946; Stefan Edberg, Swedish tennis player, 1966.

D Hans Sachs, German poet and composer, 1576; William Congreve, English dramatist, 1729; Louis Hérold, French composer, 1833; Pierre Joseph Proudhon, French journalist and anarchist, 1865; Bhagwam Shree Rajneesh, Indian guru, 1990.

20 Feast day of St Sebastian, St Fabian, pope, St Euthymius the Great, and St Fechin.

1265 The first English parliament met in Westminster Hall, convened by the Earl of Leicester, Simon de Montfort. **1841** Hong Kong was ceded by China and occupied by the British. **1886** The Mersey Railway Tunnel was officially opened by the Prince of Wales. **1892** The game of basketball was first played at the YMCA in Springfield, Massachusetts. **1944** The RAF dropped 2,300 tons of bombs on Berlin. **1961** John F Kennedy was inaugurated as the 35th US president, and the first Roman Catholic to hold this office. **1981** Fifty-two Americans, held hostage in the US embassy in Teheran for 444 days by followers of Ayatollah Khomeini, were released. **1987** Terry Waite, the Archbishop of Canterbury's special envoy in the Middle East, disappeared on a peace mission in Beirut, Lebanon.

B Theobald Wolfe Tone, Irish nationalist, **1763**; George Burns, US comedian and actor, **1896**; Federico Fellini, Italian film director, **1920**; Patricia Neal, US film actress, **1926**; Edwin Aldrin, US astronaut, **1930**; Malcolm McLaren, British rock impresario, **1946**.

D John Soane, English architect, **1837**; John Ruskin, English art critic and writer, **1900**; King George V, **1936**; Johnny Weissmuller, US film actor and swimmer, **1984**; Barbara Stanwyck, US film actress, **1990**; Audrey Hepburn, British film actress, **1993**.

---

21 Feast day of St Agnes, St Fructuosus of Tarragona, St Patroclus of Troyes, St Alban or Bartholomew Roe, St Epiphanius of Pavia, and St Meinrad.

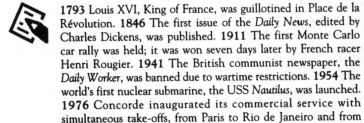

1793 Louis XVI, King of France, was guillotined in Place de la Révolution. **1846** The first issue of the *Daily News*, edited by Charles Dickens, was published. **1911** The first Monte Carlo car rally was held; it was won seven days later by French racer Henri Rougier. **1941** The British communist newspaper, the *Daily Worker*, was banned due to wartime restrictions. **1954** The world's first nuclear submarine, the USS *Nautilus*, was launched. **1976** Concorde inaugurated its commercial service with simultaneous take-offs, from Paris to Rio de Janeiro and from London to Bahrain.

John Charles Fremont, US explorer, **1813**; Thomas Jonathan

JAN FEB MAR APR MAY JUN JUL AUG SEP OCT NOV DEC

B ('Stonewall') Jackson, US Confederate general, **1824**; Christian Dior, French couturier, **1905**; Benny Hill, English comedian, **1924**; Jack Nicklaus, US golfer, **1940**; Placido Domingo, Spanish operatic tenor, **1941**.

D Elisha Gray, US inventor, **1901**; V I Lenin, Russian leader, **1924**; Lytton Strachey, English critic and biographer, **1932**; George Orwell, British novelist, **1950**; Cecil B De Mille, US film director, **1959**.

22 Feast day of St Dominic of Sora, St Berthwald of Ramsbury, St Anastasius the Persian, St Blesilla, St Vincent Pallotti, and St Vincent of Saragossa.

 1771 The Falkland Islands were ceded to Britain by Spain. **1879** British troops were massacred by the Zulus at Isandhlwana. **1905** Insurgent workers were fired on in St Petersburg, resulting in 'Bloody Sunday'. **1924** Ramsay MacDonald took office as Britain's first Labour prime minister. **1959** British world racing champion Mike Hawthorn was killed while driving on the Guildford bypass. **1972** The United Kingdom, the Irish Republic, and Denmark joined the Common Market. **1973** US boxer George Foreman knocked out Joe Frazier in Kingston, Jamaica, becoming the world heavyweight boxing champion. **1992** Rebel soldiers seized the national radio station in Kinshasa, Zaire's capital, and broadcast a demand for the government's resignation.

B Ivan III (the Great), Grand Duke of Muscovy, **1440**; Francis Bacon, English politician and philosopher, **1561**; Lord Byron, English poet, **1788**; D W Griffith, US film producer and director, **1875**; John Hurt, English actor, **1940**; George Foreman, US boxer, **1948**.

D William Paterson, Scottish financier, **1719**; David Edward Hughes, English inventor, **1900**; Queen Victoria, **1901**; Lyndon B Johnson, 36th US president, **1973**; Herbert Sutcliffe, English cricketer, **1978**: Arthur Bryant, British historian, **1985**.

23 Feast day of St Bernard of Vienne, Saints Clement and Agathangelus, St Asclas, St John the Almsgiver, St Emerentiana, St Maimbod, St Ildephonsus, and St Lufthidis.

1556 An earthquake in Shanxi Province, China, is thought to have killed some 830,000 people. **1571** The Royal Exchange in London, founded by financier Thomas Gresham, was opened by Queen Elizabeth I. **1849** English-born Elizabeth Blackwell graduated from a New York medical school to become the first woman doctor. **1924** The first Labour government was formed, under Ramsay MacDonald. **1943** The British captured Tripoli from the Germans. **1960** The US Navy bathyscaphe *Trieste*, designed by Dr Piccard, descended to a record depth of 10,750 m /35,820 ft in the Pacific Ocean. **1985** The proceedings of the House of Lords were televised for the first time.

Stendhal, French novelist, **1783**; Edouard Manet, French painter, **1832**; Sergei Mikhailovich Eisenstein, Russian film director, **1898**; Alfred Denning, British judge and former Master of the Rolls, **1899**; Jeanne Moreau, French actress, **1928**; HSH Princess Caroline of Monaco, **1957**.

William Pitt the Younger, British prime minister, **1806**; Anna Pavlova, Russian ballerina, **1931**; Edvard Munch, Norwegian painter, **1944**; Pierre Bonnard, French painter, **1947**; Paul Robeson, US actor and singer, **1976**; Salvador Dali, Spanish painter and sculptor, **1989**.

24 Feast day of St Francis of Sales, St Babylas of Antioch, St Felician of Foligno, and St Macedonius the Barley-eater.

1848 James Marshall was the first to discover gold in California, at Sutter's Mill near Coloma. **1916** The US Supreme Court ruled that income tax is unconstitutional. **1916** Conscription was introduced in Britain. **1935** Beer in cans was first sold, in Virginia, USA, by the Kreuger Brewing Company. **1962** French film director François Truffaut's *Jules et Jim* premiered in Paris. **1978** A Russian satellite crashed near Yellow Knife in Canada's Northwest Territory. **1991** More than 15,000 Allied air sorties were flown in the Gulf War, with 23 aircraft lost.

Hadrian, Roman emperor, **76**; Frederick the Great, King of Prussia, **1712**; Ernest Borgnine, US film actor, **1917**; Desmond Morris, English zoologist and writer, **1928**; Neil Diamond, US singer and songwriter, **1941**; Nastassja Kinski, German film actress, **1961**.

JAN FEB MAR APR MAY JUN JUL AUG SEP OCT NOV DEC

D Caligula, Roman emperor, assassinated, AD 41; Randolph Churchill, British politician, 1895; Amadeo Modigliani, Italian artist, 1920; Winston Churchill, British prime minister, 1965; George Cukor, US film director, 1983.

25 Feast day of Saints Juventinus and Maximinimus, the Conversion of St Paul, St Apollo, St Artemas, St Publius, St Dwynwen, St Poppo, and Saint Praejectus or Prix.

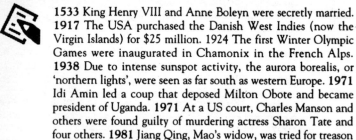

1533 King Henry VIII and Anne Boleyn were secretly married. 1917 The USA purchased the Danish West Indies (now the Virgin Islands) for $25 million. 1924 The first Winter Olympic Games were inaugurated in Chamonix in the French Alps. 1938 Due to intense sunspot activity, the aurora borealis, or 'northern lights', were seen as far south as western Europe. 1971 Idi Amin led a coup that deposed Milton Obote and became president of Uganda. 1971 At a US court, Charles Manson and others were found guilty of murdering actress Sharon Tate and four others. 1981 Jiang Qing, Mao's widow, was tried for treason and received a death sentence, which was subsequently commuted to life imprisonment.

B Robert Boyle, Irish physicist and chemist, 1627; Robert Burns, Scottish poet, 1759; William Somerset Maugham, English author, 1874; Virginia Woolf, English author, 1882; Wilhelm Furtwängler, German conductor, 1886; Edvard Shevardnadze, Russian politician, 1928.

D Marcus Cocceius Nerva, Roman emperor, AD 98; Lucas Cranach the Younger, German painter, 1586; Dorothy Wordsworth, English writer, 1855; Al Capone, US gangster, 1947; Ava Gardner, US film actress, 1990.

26 The national day of Australia and of India. Feast day of St Timothy, St Margaret of Hungary, St Alberic, St Paula, St Conan of Man, St Titus, St Eystein, and St Thordgith or Theorigitha of Barking.

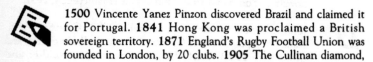

1500 Vincente Yanez Pinzon discovered Brazil and claimed it for Portugal. 1841 Hong Kong was proclaimed a British sovereign territory. 1871 England's Rugby Football Union was founded in London, by 20 clubs. 1905 The Cullinan diamond, weighing 1¼ lbs, was found by Captain Wells at the Premier Mine, near Pretoria, South Africa. **1939** In the Spanish Civil War, Franco's forces, with Italian aid, took Barcelona. **1950** India became a republic within the Commonwealth. **1965** Hindi was made the official language of India. **1992** Russian President Yeltsin announced that his country would stop targeting US cities with nuclear weapons.

Douglas MacArthur, US general, **1880**; Stephane Grappelli, French jazz violinist, **1908**; Jimmy Van Heusen, US popular composer, **1913**; Paul Newman, US film actor, **1925**; Eartha Kitt, US singer, **1928**; Roger Vadim, French film director, **1928**.

Edward Jenner, English physician, **1823**; Charles George Gordon, British general, **1885**; Nikolaus August Otto, German engineer, **1891**; Edward G Robinson, US film actor, **1973**; Nelson Rockefeller, US statesman, **1979**; José Ferrer, US actor, **1992**.

27 Feast day of St Julian of Le Mans, St Marius or May, St Angela Merici, and St Vitalian, pope.

1879 Thomas Edison patented the electric lamp. **1926** The first public demonstration of television was given by John Logie Baird, at his workshop in London. **1943** The US Air Force carried out its first bombing raid on Germany. **1967** Three US astronauts died in a fire which broke out aboard the spacecraft Apollo during tests at Cape Kennedy. **1973** The Vietnam cease-fire agreement was signed by North Vietnam and the USA. **1992** Former world boxing champion Mike Tyson went on trial for allegedly raping an 18-year-old contestant in the 1991 Miss Black America Contest.

Wolfgang Amadeus Mozart, Austrian composer, **1756**; Wilhelm II, Emperor of Germany, **1859**; Jerome Kern, US composer, **1891**; John Eccles, Australian physiologist, **1903**; Mordecai Richler, Canadian novelist and dramatist, **1931**; John Ogden, English pianist, **1937**.

John Audubon, US artist and naturalist, **1851**; Giuseppe Verdi, Italian composer, **1901**; Giovanni Verga, Italian novelist and dramatist, **1922**; Carl Mannerheim, Finnish soldier and statesman, **1951**; Mahalia Jackson, US gospel singer, **1972**; Thomas Sopwith, British aircraft designer, **1989**.

28 Feast day of St Thomas Aquinas, St Amadeus of Lausanne, St Peter Nolasco, St Peter Thomas, and St Paulinus of Aquileia.

1521 The Diet of Worms began, at which Protestant reformer Luther was declared an outlaw by the Roman Catholic church. **1807** London became the world's first city to be illuminated by gas light, when the lamps on Pall Mall were lit. **1871** In the Franco-Prussian War, Paris fell to the Prussians after a five-month siege. **1935** Iceland became the first country to introduce legalised abortion. **1942** The British Eighth Army retreated to El Alamein. **1986** The US space shuttle *Challenger* exploded shortly after lift-off from Cape Canaveral, killing five men and two women on board. **1993** Solicitors for British prime minister John Major issued writs for libel against the New Statesman and Scallywag for publishing stories detailing rumours of an affair between Major and Clare Latimer, a caterer.

B Henry Morton Stanley, British journalist and explorer, **1841**; Auguste Piccard, Swiss balloonist and deep-sea explorer, **1884**; Ernst Lubitsch, US film director, **1892**; Jackson Pollock, US artist, **1921**; Alan Alda, US film actor and director, **1936**; Mikhail Baryshnikov, Russian ballet dancer, **1948**.

D Charlemagne, Holy Roman emperor, **814**; Francis Drake, English buccaneer and explorer, **1596**; Thomas Bodley, English scholar and diplomat, **1613**; Vicente Blasco Ibáñez, Spanish writer and politician, **1928**; W B Yeats, Irish poet, **1939**; Klaus Fuchs, German spy, **1988**.

29 Feast day of St Sainian of Troyes, St Sulpicius 'Severus', and St Gildas the Wise.

1728 John Gay's *The Beggar's Opera* was first performed at Lincoln's Inn Fields Theatre, London. **1848** Greenwich Mean Time was adopted by Scotland. **1856** Britain's highest military decoration, the Victoria Cross, was founded by Queen Victoria. **1886** The first successful petrol-driven motorcar, built by Karl Benz, was patented. **1916** Paris was bombed by German zeppelins for the first time. **1942** The BBC Radio 4 programme

'Desert Island Discs', devised and presented by Roy Plomley, was first broadcast. **1978** The use of environmentally damaging aerosol sprays was banned in Sweden. **1991** In the Gulf War, Iraq began its first major ground offensive into Saudi Arabia.

Thomas Paine, English political writer and reformer, **1737**; W C Fields, US film actor and comedian, **1880**; Victor Mature, US film actor, **1915**; Paddy Chayefsky, US writer, **1923**; Germaine Greer, Australian feminist and author, **1939**; Katharine Ross, US film actress, **1943**.

King George III, **1820**; Alfred Sisley, English painter, **1899**; Douglas Haig, British field marshal, **1928**; Fritz Kreisler, US violinist, **1962**; Alan Ladd, US film actor, **1964**; Jimmy Durante, US comedian, **1980**.

30 Feast day of St Martina, St Bathildis, St Adelelmus or Aleaume, St Aldegundis, St Barsimaeus, and St Hyacintha Mariscotti.

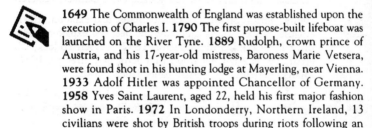

1649 The Commonwealth of England was established upon the execution of Charles I. **1790** The first purpose-built lifeboat was launched on the River Tyne. **1889** Rudolph, crown prince of Austria, and his 17-year-old mistress, Baroness Marie Vetsera, were found shot in his hunting lodge at Mayerling, near Vienna. **1933** Adolf Hitler was appointed Chancellor of Germany. **1958** Yves Saint Laurent, aged 22, held his first major fashion show in Paris. **1972** In Londonderry, Northern Ireland, 13 civilians were shot by British troops during riots following an illegal march – known as 'Bloody Sunday'.

Anton Chekhov, Russian dramatist and writer, **1860**; Franklin D Roosevelt, 32nd US president, **1882**; Gene Hackman, US film actor, **1932**; Vanessa Redgrave, English actress, **1937**; Boris Spassky, Russian chess champion, **1938**; Phil Collins, English pop singer and drummer, **1951**.

King Charles I, **1649**; Frank Doubleday, US publisher and editor, **1934**; Orville Wright, US aviation pioneer, **1948**; Mohandas Karamchand Gandhi, Indian leader, assassinated, **1948**; Francis Poulenc, French composer, **1963**; Stanley Holloway, English actor and singer, **1982**.

31 Feast day of Saints Cyrus and John of Alexandria, St Francis Xavier Bianchi, St Adamnan of Coldingham, St Aidan or Maedoc of Ferns, St Eusebius of St Gall, St Marcella of Rome, St John Bosco, and St Ulphia.

  1606 The executions of Winter, Rockwood, Keys, and Guy Fawkes, the Gunpowder Conspirators, took place in London. **1747** The first clinic specialising in the treatment of venereal diseases was opened at London Dock Hospital. **1858** The Great Eastern, the five-funnelled steamship designed by Brunel, was launched at Millwall. **1876** All Native American Indians were ordered to move into reservations. **1929** The USSR exiled Leon Trotsky; he found asylum in Mexico. **1958** Explorer I, the first US Earth satellite, was launched from Cape Canaveral. **1983** The wearing of seat belts in cars became compulsory in Britain.

Franz Schubert, Austrian composer, **1797**; Zane Grey, US novelist, **1872**; Anna Pavlova, Russian ballerina, **1882**; Freya Stark, English traveller and writer, **1893**; Norman Mailer, US novelist, **1923**; Jean Simmons, English film actress, **1929**.

Charles Edward Stuart, the Young Pretender, **1788**; John Galsworthy, English novelist, **1933**; Jean Giraudoux, French novelist and dramatist, **1944**; C B Cochran, British theatrical producer, **1951**; A A Milne, English author, **1956**; Samuel Goldwyn, US film producer, **1974**.

FEBRUARY

1 Feast day of St John of the Grating, St Henry Morse, St Pionius, St Bride or Brigid of Kildare, St Seiriol, and St Sigebert III of Austria.

  1884 The first edition of the Oxford English Dictionary was published. **1893** Thomas Edison opened the first film studio – to produce films for peepshow machines – in New Jersey, USA. **1896** Puccini's opera *La Bohème* was first staged in Turin. **1930** *The Times* published its first crossword puzzle. **1958** The United Arab Republic was formed by a union of Egypt and Syria (it was broken 1961). **1965** Medical prescriptions on the NHS became free of charge (they remained so until June 1968). **1979** Ayatollah Khomeini returned to Iran after 16 years of exile.

Victor Herbert, US composer, **1859**; John Ford, US film director, **1895**; Clark Gable, US film actor, **1901**; Stanley Matthews, English footballer, **1915**; Renata Tebaldi, Italian operatic soprano, **1922**; Don Everly, US rock singer, **1937**; Princess Stephanie of Monaco, **1966**.

René Descartes, French scientist and philosopher, **1650**; Mary Wollstonecraft Shelley, English novelist, **1851**; Carlos I, King of Portugal, assassinated, **1908**; Aritomo Yamagata, Japanese soldier and politician, **1922**; Piet Mondrian, Swiss painter, **1944**; Buster Keaton, US silent film comedian, **1966**.

2

Candlemas (Wives' Feast Day). Feast day of The Purification, St Joan de Lestonnac, St Adalbald of Ostrevant, and The Martyrs of Ebsdorf.

1801 The first parliament of the United Kingdom of Great Britain and Ireland assembled. **1852** Britain's first men's public flushing toilets opened on Fleet Street, London. **1878** Greece declared war on Turkey. **1943** The German army surrendered to the Soviet army at Stalingrad. **1972** The British Embassy in Dublin was burned down by protesters angered by the 'Bloody Sunday' shootings in Londonderry. **1986** Women in Liechtenstein went to the polls for the first time. **1989** The USSR's military occupation of Afghanistan ended after nine years. **1991** A protest against the Gulf War was held in London's Hyde Park, attended by more than 40,000 people.

Nell Gwyn, English actress and mistress of Charles II, **1650**; Charles Maurice de Talleyrand-Périgord, French statesman and diplomat, **1754**; James Joyce, Irish author, **1882**; Elaine Stritch, US actress, **1927**; Stan Getz, US jazz saxophonist, **1927**; Farrah Fawcett, US TV actress, **1946**.

Pope Clement XIII, **1769**; Dmitri Ivanovich Mendeleyev, Russian chemist, **1907**; Bertrand Russell, English philosopher, **1970**; Sid Vicious, British punk singer, **1979**; Alistair Maclean, Scottish novelist.

3

Feast day of St Laurence of Spoleto, St Anskar, St Ia the Virgin, St Laurence of Canterbury, St Blaise, St Werburga, and St Margaret 'of England'.

1488 The Portuguese navigator Bartholomeu Diaz landed at Mossal Bay in the Cape – the first European known to have landed on the southern extremity of Africa. 1913 The 16th Amendment to the US Constitution, authorising the power to impose and collect income tax, was ratified. 1919 The League of Nations held its first meeting in Paris, with US President Wilson chairing. 1966 The first rocket-assisted controlled landing on the Moon was made by the Soviet space vehicle Luna IX. 1969 At the Palestinian National Congress in Cairo, Yasser Arafat was appointed leader of the PLO. 1989 South African politician P W Botha unwillingly resigned both party leadership and the presidency after suffering a stroke.

Felix Mendelssohn, German composer, 1809; Gertrude Stein, US author, 1874; Alvar Aalto, Finnish architect, 1898; James Michener, US novelist, 1907; Simone Weil, French writer, 1909; Frankie Vaughan, English singer, 1928.

John of Gaunt, Duke of Lancaster, 1399; Richard 'Beau' Nash, British dandy and gambler, 1762; Woodrow Wilson, 28th US president, 1924; Buddy Holly, US singer and guitarist, 1959; Boris Karloff, US film actor, 1969; John Cassavetes, US film actor and director, 1989.

4

The national day of Sri Lanka. Feast day of St Theophilus the Penitent, St Nicholas Studites, St Andrew Corsini, bishop, St Joan of Valois, St Isidore of Pelusium, St John de Britto, St Modan, St Phileas, St Joseph of Leonessa, and St Rembert.

1861 Seven secessionist southern states formed the Confederate States of America, in Montgomery, Alabama. 1904 The Russo-Japanese War began after Japan laid seige to Port Arthur. 1928 Black US entertainer Josephine Baker's provocative performance in Munich drew protests from members of the Nazi party. 1945 Allied leaders Roosevelt, Churchill, and Stalin met at Yalta, in the Crimea. 1968 The world's largest hovercraft was launched at Cowes, Isle of Wight. 1987 The US Stars and Stripes won the America's Cup back from Australia. 1993 Russian scientists unfurled a giant mirror in orbit and flashed a beam of sunlight across Europe during the night; observers saw it only as an instantaneous flash.

B Fernand Léger, French painter, 1881; Jacques Prévert, French poet and novelist, 1900; Charles Lindbergh, US aviator, 1902; Ida Lupino, English actress, 1918; Norman Wisdom, English comedian, 1920; Alice Cooper, US pop singer, 1948.

D Lucius Septimius Severus, Roman emperor, 211; Giambattista della Porta, Italian natural philosopher, 1615; Robert Koldewey, German archaeologist, 1925; Oliver Heaviside, English physicist, 1925; Karen Carpenter, US singer, 1983; Liberace, US entertainer, 1987.

5 Feast day of St Agatha, Saints Indractus and Dominica, St Adelaide of Bellich, St Bertulph or Bertoul of Renty, St Avitus of Vienne, and St Vodalus or Voel.

1782 The Spanish captured Minorca from the British. 1924 The BBC time signals, or 'pips', from Greenwich Observatory were heard for the first time; they are broadcast every hour. 1940 Glenn Miller recorded 'Tuxedo Junction' with his orchestra. 1961 The first issue of the *Sunday Telegraph* was published. 1967 Due to a Musicians' Union ban, the Rolling Stones were not allowed to play their hit 'Let's Spend the Night Together' when they appeared on an ITV show. 1974 Patricia Hearst, granddaughter of US newspaper tycoon William R Hearst, was kidnapped by the Symbionese Liberation Army. 1982 Laker Airways collapsed with debts of $270 million. 1983 Expelled from Bolivia, Nazi war criminal Klaus Barbie flew to France to be tried for crimes against humanity.

B Robert Peel, British politician, 1788; Adlai Stevenson, US politician and ambassador, 1900; John Carradine, US film actor, 1906; William Burroughs, US novelist, 1914; Bob Marley, Jamaican reggae singer, 1945; Charlotte Rampling, British actress, 1946.

D Joost van den Vondel, Dutch poet and dramatist, 1679; Thomas Carlyle, English author and historian, 1881; A B 'Banjo' Paterson, Australian poet and journalist, 1941; George Aliss, English actor, 1946; Marianne Moore, US poet, 1972; Joseph Mankiewicz, US director and author, 1993.

JAN FEB MAR APR MAY JUN JUL AUG SEP OCT NOV DEC

6

The national day of New Zealand. Feast day of St Paul Miki and his Companions, St Vedast or Vaast, St Hidegund, St Amand, Saints Mel and Melchu, and St Guarinus of Palestrina.

1508 Maximilian I assumed the title of Holy Roman Emperor. **1778** Britain declared war on France. **1840** The Treaty of Waitangi was signed by Great Britain and the Maori chiefs of New Zealand, granting British sovereignty. **1918** Women over 30 were granted the right to vote in Britain. **1958** An aeroplane carrying the Manchester United football team crashed on take-off at Munich, killing seven players. **1964** Britain and France reached an agreement on the construction of a Channel Tunnel. **1968** The 10th Winter Olympic games opened in Grenoble, France. **1991** Debris from *Salyut 7*, a Soviet space station abandoned in **1986**, re-entered the Earth's atmosphere; it was believed that most of it landed in the Atlantic Ocean.

B

Christopher Marlowe, English dramatist, **1564**; Queen Anne, **1665**; Ronald Reagan, 40th US president, **1911**; Zsa Zsa Gabor, Hungarian actress, **1920**; François Truffaut, French film director, **1932**; Rick Astley, British pop singer, **1966**.

D

Lancelot 'Capability' Brown, English landscape gardener, **1783**; Carlo Goldoni, Italian dramatist, **1793**; Joseph Priestley, English chemist, **1804**; Gustav Klimt, Austrian painter, **1918**; Marghanita Laski, English author, **1988**; Arthur Ashe, US tennis player, **1993**.

7

Feast day of St Luke the Younger, St Theodore of Heraclea, St Adaucus, St Moses, St Richard, 'King of the English', and St Silvin.

1301 Edward Caernarvon (later King Edward II) became the first Prince of Wales. **1792** Austria and Prussia formed an alliance against France. **1845** The Portland Vase, a Roman cameo glass vase dating to the 1st century BC, was smashed by a drunken visitor to the British Museum. **1863** HMS Orpheus was wrecked off the New Zealand coast, with the loss of 185 lives. **1947** The main group of the Dead Sea Scrolls, dating to about 150 BC–AD 68, was found in caves on the W side of the Jordan River. **1974** Grenada became a fully independent state within the Commonwealth. **1991** British prime minister Major and his senior cabinet ministers escaped an apparent assassination attempt when the IRA fired three mortar shells at 10 Downing Street from a parked van.

B Thomas More, English politician, 1478; Philippe Buache, French cartographer, 1700; Charles Dickens, English novelist, 1812; Alfred Adler, Austrian psychoanalyst, 1870; Sinclair Lewis, US novelist, 1885; Peter Jay, British writer and broadcaster, 1937.

D William Boyce, English organist and composer, 1779; Sheridan Le Fanu, Irish writer, 1873; Adolphe Sax, Belgian inventor of the saxophone, 1894; Daniel Malan, South African statesman, 1959; Igor Vasilevich Kuchatov, Russian nuclear physicist, 1960; Jimmy Van Heusen, US composer, 1990.

8 Feast day of St Jerome Emiliani, St John of Matha, St Cuthman, St Stephen of Muret, St Elfleda, St Nicetius or Nizier of Besançon, and St Meingold.

1725 Catherine I succeeded her husband, Peter the Great, to become Empress of Russia. 1740 The 'Great Frost' of London ended (began 25 Dec 1739). 1920 Odessa was taken by Bolshevik forces. 1924 The gas chamber was used in the USA for the first time, in the Nevada State Prison. 1969 The Boeing 747, the world's largest commercial plane, made its first flight. 1972 A concert by Frank Zappa and the Mothers of Invention was cancelled at the Albert Hall, London, because some of their lyrics were considered obscene. 1974 After 85 days in space, the US Skylab station returned to earth. 1993 All 132 persons aboard an Iran Air passenger jet were killed minutes after take-off when the plane collided with a military aircraft.

B John Ruskin, English writer, artist, and art critic, 1819; William Sherman, US general, 1820; Jules Verne, French novelist, 1828; Lana Turner, US film actress, 1920; Jack Lemmon, US film actor, 1925; James Dean, US film actor, 1931.

D Mary, Queen of Scots, beheaded, 1587; R B Ballantyne, Scottish writer, 1894; Peter Alexeivich Kropotkin, Russian anarchist, 1921; William Bateson, English biologist, 1926; Max Liebermann, German painter and etcher, 1935; Del Shannon, US pop singer, 1990.

9

Feast day of St Apollonia, St Sabinus of Canossa, St Teilo, St Alto, St Ansbert, and St Nicephorus of Antioch.

1801 The Holy Roman Empire came to an end with the signing of the Peace of Luneville between Austria and France. 1830 Explorer Charles Sturt discovered the source of the Murray River in Australia. 1872 Lieutenant Dawson's expedition in search of Dr Livingstone began. 1942 Soap rationing began in Britain. 1949 US film actor Robert Mitchum was sentenced to two months in prison for smoking marijuana. 1972 The British government declared a state of emergency due to the miners' strike, which was in its third month. 1991 The republic of Lithuania held a plebiscite on independence which showed overwhelming support for secession from the USSR.

B

Daniel Bernoulli, Swiss mathematician, 1700; Mrs Patrick Campbell, English actress, 1865; Alban Berg, Austrian composer, 1885; Ronald Colman, English film actor, 1891; Carole King, US singer and songwriter, 1941; Mia Farrow, US film actress, 1945.

D

Nevil Maskelyne, Astronomer Royal, 1811; Fyodor Mikhailovich Dostoevsky, Russian novelist, 1881; Sergei Vladimirovich Ilyushin, Russian aircraft designer, 1977; Bill Haley, US rock musician, 1981; Yuri Andropov, Russian leader, 1984.

10

Feast day of St William of Maleval, St Scholastica, St Trumwin, St Austreberta, and St Soteris.

1354 A street battle between Oxford University students and townspeople resulted in several deaths and many injuries. 1763 Canada was ceded to Britain by the Peace of Paris. 1774 Andrew Becker demonstrated his practical diving suit in the River Thames. 1840 Queen Victoria and Prince Albert, both aged 20, were married in St James' Palace. 1931 New Delhi became the capital of India. 1942 The first gold disc – sprayed with gold by the record company RCA Victor – was presented to Glenn Miller for 'Chattanooga Choo Choo'. 1989 Jamaican-born Tony Robinson became Nottingham's first black sheriff.

B

Harold Macmillan, British politician and publisher, 1894; Bertolt Brecht, German dramatist and poet, 1898; Robert

Wagner, US actor, **1930**; Boris Pasternak, Russian novelist, **1890**; Mark Spitz, US swimmer, **1950**; Greg Norman, Australian golfer, **1955**.

Luca della Robbia, Italian sculptor, **1482**; Alexander Sergeyevich Pushkin, Russian author, **1837**; Wilhelm Konrad von Röntgen, German physicist, **1923**; Edgar Wallace, English thriller writer, **1932**; Billy Rose, US producer and lyricist, **1966**; Sophie Tucker, US singer, **1966**.

11 Feast day of Saints Saturninus and Dativus, St Benedict of Aniane, St Gregory II, pope, St Caedmon, St Pascal, pope, St Lazarus of Milan, St Lucius of Adrianople, and St Severinus of Agaunum.

1818 Independence was proclaimed by Chile. **1858** Bernadette Soubirous, a peasant girl, allegedly had a vision of the Virgin Mary in a grotto in Lourdes. **1878** The first weekly weather report was published by the Meteorological Office. **1945** The Yalta Conference ended, at which the Allied leaders planned the final defeat of Germany and agreed on the establishment of the United Nations. **1975** Margaret Thatcher became the first woman leader of a British political party. **1990** After more than 27 years in prison, ANC president Nelson Mandela walked to freedom from a prison near Cape Town, South Africa.

Henry Fox Talbot, British photographic pioneer, **1800**; Thomas Edison, US inventor, **1847**; Vivian Fuchs, British Antarctic explorer, **1908**; Joseph Mankiewicz, US film writer and director, **1909**; Mary Quant, English fashion designer, **1934**; Burt Reynolds, US film actor, **1936**.

Lazaro Spallanzani, Italian physiologist and chemist, **1799**; Honoré Daumier, French caricaturist, **1879**; John Buchan, Canadian statesman and novelist, **1940**; Sergei Mikhailovich Eisenstein, Russian film director, **1948**; Silvia Plath, US poet, **1963**; Lee J Cobb, US actor, **1976**.

12 Feast day of St Julian the Hospitaller, St Ethelwald of Lindisfarne, St Antony Kauleas, St Marina or Pelagia, St Meletius, and St Ludan.

JAN FEB MAR APR MAY JUN JUL AUG SEP OCT NOV DEC

1554 Lady Jane Grey, queen of England for nine days, was executed on Tower Green for high treason. **1797** Over 1,000 French troops, led by Irish-American General William Tate, made an unsuccessful attempt to invade Britain, on the Welsh coast. **1818** Independence was proclaimed by Chile. **1831** Rubber galoshes first went on sale, in Boston, Massachusetts, USA. **1851** Prospector Edward Hargreaves made a discovery at Summerhill Creek, New South Wales, which set off a gold rush in Australia. **1912** China became a republic following the overthrow of the Manchu Dynasty. **1973** The first group of US prisoners of war were released from North Vietnam. **1993** The South African government and the ANC reached an agreement on a transitional 'government of national unity' in which both parties would be partners for five years.

B Thomas Campion, English composer and poet, **1567**; Abraham Lincoln, 16th US president, **1809**; Charles Darwin, English scientist, **1809**; George Meredith, English novelist, **1828**; Marie Lloyd, English music-hall star, **1870**; Franco Zeffirelli, Italian film director, **1923**.

D Immanuel Kant, German philosopher, **1804**; Hans Guido von Bülow, German pianist and conductor, **1894**; Lillie Langtry, English actress, **1929**; Tom Keating, English painter and art forger, **1984**; Henry Hathaway, US filmmaker, **1985**.

13 Feast day of St Catherine dei Ricci, St Stephen of Rieti, St Ermenilda or Ermengild, St Martinian the Hermit, St Polyeuctes of Melitene, St Licinus or Lesin, and St Modomnoc.

1689 William of Orange and Mary ascended the throne of Great Britain as joint sovereigns. **1692** The massacre of the Macdonalds at Glencoe in Scotland was carried out by their traditional enemies, the Campbells. **1793** Britain, Prussia, Austria, Holland, Spain, and Sardinia formed an alliance against France. **1867** Strauss's waltz *The Blue Danube* was first played publicly, in Vienna. **1886** The James Younger gang made its first 'hit', robbing $60,000 from a bank in Missouri, USA. **1917** Dutch spy Mata Hari was arrested by the French. **1960** The French tested their first atomic bomb in the Sahara. **1974** Russian novelist Alexander Solzhenitsyn was expelled from the USSR.

B John Hunter, Scottish surgeon and anatomist, 1728; Fyodor Chaliapin, Russian operatic bass singer, 1873; Georges Simenon, Belgian novelist, 1901; George Segal, US film actor, 1934; Oliver Reed, British film actor, 1938; Peter Gabriel, British pop musician, 1950.

D Catherine Howard, fifth wife of Henry VIII, executed, 1542; Benvenuto Cellini, Italian sculptor and goldsmith, 1571; Cotton Mather, US colonist and writer, 1728; Richard Wagner, German composer, 1883; Georges Rouault, French painter, 1958; Jean Renoir, French film director, 1979.

14 St Valentine's Day. Feast day of St John the Baptist of the Conception, St Antoninus of Sorrento, St Maro, St Abraham of Carrhae, St Adolf of Osnabrück, St Auxentius, Saints Cyril and Methodius, and St Conran.

 1779 Captain Cook was stabbed to death by natives in the Sandwich Islands (now Hawaii). 1797 The naval Battle of St Vincent took place off SW Portugal, in which Captain Nelson and Admiral Jervis defeated the Spanish fleet. 1852 Great Ormond Street children's hospital, in London, accepted its first patient. 1895 Oscar Wilde's *The Importance of Being Earnest* was first staged in London. 1929 The St Valentine's Day Massacre took place in Chicago, when seven members of Bugsy Moran's gang were gunned down in a warehouse. 1946 The Bank of England was nationalised. 1956 At the 20th Soviet Communist Party Conference, Nikita Khrushchev denounced the policies of Stalin. 1989 The Ayatollah Khomeini issued a fatwa edict calling on Muslims to kill Salman Rushdie for his blasphemous novel *The Satanic Verses*.

B Francesco Cavalli, Italian composer, 1602; Thomas Malthus, English economist, 1766; Christopher Sholes, US inventor of the typewriter, 1819; Jack Benny, US comedian and actor, 1894; Alan Parker, British film director, 1944; Kevin Keegan, British footballer, 1951.

D King Richard II of England, 1400; Fiorenzo di Lorenzo, Italian painter, 1525; William Sherman, US general, 1891; Julian Huxley, English biologist and philosopher, 1975; P G Wodehouse, English novelist, 1975; Frederick Loewe, US composer, 1988.

JAN FEB MAR APR MAY JUN JUL AUG SEP OCT NOV DEC

15 Feast day of St Tanco or Tatto, St Agape of Terni, St Walfrid or Galfrid, and St Sigfrid of Växjö. **1882** The first shipment of frozen meat left New Zealand for England.

1898 The USS *Maine*, sent to Cuba on a goodwill tour, was struck by a mine and sank in Havana harbour, with the loss of 260 lives. **1922** The first session of the Permanent Court of International Justice in' The Hague was held. **1942** Singapore surrendered to Japanese forces. **1971** Britain adopted the decimal currency system. **1974** The battle for the strategic Golan Heights between Israeli and Syrian forces began. **1978** Mohammad Ali lost his world heavyweight boxing title to Leon Spinks in Las Vegas. **1981** For the first time, English Football League matches were played on a Sunday.

Pedro Menendez de Avilés, Spanish navigator, **1519**; Galileo Galilei, Italian astronomer, **1564**; Jeremy Bentham, English philosopher and writer, **1748**; Graham Hill, British racing driver, **1929**; Claire Bloom, English actress, **1931**; Jane Seymour, English actress, **1951**.

Gotthold Ephraim Lessing, German author, **1781**; Mikhail Ivanovich Glinka, Russian composer, **1857**; Herbert Henry Asquith, British statesman, **1928**; Nat King Cole, US singer and musician, **1965**; Ethel Merman, US singer and actress, **1984**.

16 Feast day of St Juliana of Cumae, St Onesimus the Slave, St Gilbert of Sempringham, and Saints Elias, Jeremy, and their Companions.

1659 The first British cheque was written. **1887** 25,000 prisoners in India were released to celebrate Queen Victoria's jubilee. **1932** Irish general election won by Fianna Fál party, led by Éamon de Valera. **1937** US scientist W H Corothers obtained a patent for nylon. **1940** The British navy rescued about 300 British seamen who were held on board the German ship *Altmark*, in a Norwegian fjord. **1959** Fidel Castro became president of Cuba. **1960** The US nuclear submarine Triton set off to circumnavigate the world underwater.

Giambattistsa Bodoni, Italian typographer, **1740**; Francis Galton, English scientist and founder of eugenics, **1822**; Ernst

Haeckel, German naturalist and philosopher, **1834**; Geraint Evans, Welsh operatic baritone, **1922**; John Schlesinger, US film director, **1926**; John McEnroe, US tennis player, **1959**.

Alfonso III, king of Portugal, **1279**; Pierre-Paul Prudhon, French painter, **1823**; Lionel Lukin, English inventor of the lifeboat, **1834**; Henry Walter Bates, English naturalist and explorer, **1892**; Leslie Hore-Belisha, British politician who introduced driving tests and the Highway Code, **1957**.

17 Feast day of Saints Theodulus and Julian, St Evermod, St Loman, St Fintan of Cloneenagh, and St Finan of Lindisfarne.

1461 Lancastrian forces defeated the Yorkists at the Battle of St Albans. **1859** First production of Verdi's opera *Un Ballo in Maschera*, in Rome. **1864** The first successful submarine torpedo attack took place when the USS *Housatonic* was sunk by the Confederate submarine Hunley in Charleston harbour; however, the force of the explosion was so great that the submarine itself was also blown up, killing all on board. **1880** An attempt was made to assassinate the Russian tsar Alexander II with a bomb at the Winter Palace, St Petersburg. **1904** First production of Puccini's *Madame Butterfly*, in Milan. **1958** The Campaign for Nuclear Disarmament (CND) was formed in London. **1968** French skier Jean-Claude Killy won three gold medals at the Winter Olympics in Grenoble. **1972** The House of Commons voted in favour of Britain joining the Common Market.

Arcangelo Corelli, Italian composer, **1653**; Thomas Malthus, English economist, **1766**; Marian Anderson, US operatic contralto, **1902**; Yasser Arafat, Palestinian leader, **1929**; Barry Humphries, Australian actor and creator of 'Dame Edna Everidge', **1934**; Alan Bates, English actor, **1934**.

Tamerlane the Great, Mongol leader, **1405**; Molière, French dramatist, **1673**; Heinrich Heine, German poet, **1856**; Geronimo, Apache leader, **1909**; Graham Sutherland, English painter, **1980**; Lee Strasburg, US actor, **1982**; Thelonious Monk, US jazz pianist, **1982**.

JAN FEB MAR APR MAY JUN JUL AUG SEP OCT NOV DEC

18 National day of Gambia and Nepal. Feast day of St Colman of Lindisfarne, St Flavian of Jerusalem, St Simeon of Jerusalem, St Theotonius, and St Helladius of Toledo.

 1678 Publication of John Bunyan's *Pilgrim's Progress*. **1861** Victor Emmanuel proclaimed king of a united Italy at the first meeting of the Italian parliament. **1876** A direct telegraph link was set up between Britain and New Zealand. **1930** US astronomer Clyde Tombaugh discovered the planet Pluto. **1948** After 16 years in power, the Fianna Fál party was defeated in the Irish general elections. **1965** The Gambia became an independent state within the Commonwealth.

B Mary Tudor, daughter of Henry VIII and Catherine of Aragon, **1517**; Alessandro Volta, Italian scientist and inventor of the electric battery, **1745**; Niccolò Paganini, Italian violinist, **1784**; Andres Segovia, Spanish classical guitarist, **1894**; Helen Gurley Brown, US magazine editor, **1922**; Len Deighton, English novelist, **1929**.

D Martin Luther, German founder of the Reformation, **1546**; Fra Angelico, Florentine painter, **1455**; George, Duke of Clarence, drowned in a butt of Malmsey on the orders of his brother, Richard, Duke of Gloucester, **1478**; Michelangelo Buonarroti, Italian painter and sculptor, **1564**; Richard Wagner, German composer, **1833**; Robert Oppenheimer, US physicist, inventor of the atomic bomb, **1967**.

19 Feast day of St Boniface of Lausanne, St Barbatus, St Conrad of Piacenza, and St Mesrop.

 1800 Napoleon Bonaparte proclaimed himself First Consul of France. **1878** US inventor Thomas Edison patented the phonograph. **1897** The Women's Institute was founded in Ontario, Canada, by Mrs Hoodless. **1906** William Kellogg established the Battle Creek Toasted Cornflake Company, selling breakfast cereals originally developed as a health food for psychiatric patients. **1959** Britain, Greece, and Turkey signed an agreement guaranteeing the independence of Cyprus. **1976** Iceland broke off diplomatic relations with Britain after negotiations failed to produce an agreement over fishing limits in the 'cod war'. **1985** The BBC broadcast the first episode of the soap opera *EastEnders*.

B Nicolaus Copernicus, Polish astronomer, **1473**; David Garrick, English actor and theatre manager, **1717**; Luigi Boccherini, Italian cellist and composer, **1743**; Adelina Patti, Italian soprano, **1843**; Merle Oberon, Tasmanian-born film actress, **1911**; Lee Marvin, US film actor, **1924**; Andrew, Duke of York, **1960**.

D Georg Büchner, German poet and dramatist, **1837**; Charles Blondin, French tightrope walker, **1897**; Ernst Mach, Austrian physicist, **1916**; André Gide, French novelist, **1951**; Luigi Dallapiccola, Italian composer, **1975**; Michael Powell, English documentary filmmaker, **1990**.

20 Feast day of St Eleutherius of Tournai, St Eucherius of Orléans, St Tyranno, St Zenobius, and St Wulfric.

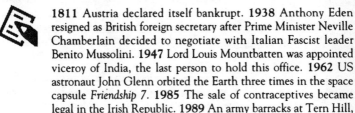

1811 Austria declared itself bankrupt. **1938** Anthony Eden resigned as British foreign secretary after Prime Minister Neville Chamberlain decided to negotiate with Italian Fascist leader Benito Mussolini. **1947** Lord Louis Mountbatten was appointed viceroy of India, the last person to hold this office. **1962** US astronaut John Glenn orbited the Earth three times in the space capsule *Friendship 7*. **1985** The sale of contraceptives became legal in the Irish Republic. **1989** An army barracks at Tern Hill, Shropshire, was destroyed by an IRA bomb.

B Voltaire, French writer and philosopher, **1694**; Honoré Daumier, French painter, **1808**; Marie Rambert, British dancer and founder of the Ballet Rambert, **1888**; Enzo Ferrari, Italian car manufacturer, **1898**; Robert Altman, US film director, **1925**; Sidney Poitier, US film actor, **1927**.

D King James I of Scotland, assassinated **1437**; Benedict Spinoza, Dutch philosopher, **1677**; Aurangzeb, last of the Mogul rulers of India, **1707**; Percy Grainger, Australian-born composer, **1961**; Walter Winchell, US journalist, **1972**; Mikhail Sholokhov, Russian author, **1984**.

21 Feast day of St Robert Southwell, St Peter Damian, St George of Amastris, and St Germanus of Granfel.

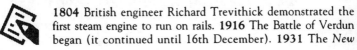

1804 British engineer Richard Trevithick demonstrated the first steam engine to run on rails. **1916** The Battle of Verdun began (it continued until 16th December). **1931** The *New*

JAN FEB MAR APR MAY JUN JUL AUG SEP OCT NOV DEC

Statesman was first published. **1960** All private businesses in Cuba nationalised by Fidel Castro. **1972** US president Richard Nixon arrived in Beijing on a visit intended to improve US–Chinese relations. **1989** Czech writer Vaclav Havel jailed for anti-government demonstrations.

B Antonio Lopez de Santa Anna, Mexican revolutionary and dictator, **1794**; John Henry Newman, English cardinal and theologian, **1801**; W H Auden, English poet, **1907**; Robert Mugabe, first prime minister of Zimbabwe, **1924**; Nina Simone US singer, **1934**; Jilly Cooper, English novelist and journalist, **1937**.

D Robert Southwell, English poet and Jesuit martyr, **1595**; Jethro Tull, English agriculturalist, **1741**; Nikolai Gogol, Russian novelist and dramatist, **1852**; George Ellery Hale, US astronomer, **1938**; Malcolm X, US Black Muslim leader, shot dead at a meeting, **1965**; Howard Walter Florey, Australian pathologist who developed penicillin, **1968**; Margot Fonteyn, English ballet dancer, **1991**.

22 Feast day of St Baradates, St Margaret of Cortona, and Saints Thalassius and Limnaeus.

1797 Over 1,000 French troops landed at Fishguard, in South Wales, but were quickly taken prisoner. **1819** Spain ceded Florida to the USA. **1879** US storekeeper F W Woolworth opened his first 'five-and-ten-cent' store in Utica, New York. **1886** *The Times* newspaper published a classified personal column, the first newspaper to do so. **1940** Five-year-old Tenzin Gyatso was enthroned as the 14th Dalai Lama in Lhasa, Tibet. **1946** Dr Selman Abraham Waksman announced that he had discovered streptomycin, an antibiotic.

B George Washington, first president of the USA, **1732**; Arthur Schopenhauer, German philosopher, **1788**; Robert Baden-Powell, English soldier and founder of the Boy Scout movement, **1857**; Eric Gill, English sculptor and typographer, **1872**; Luis Buñuel, Spanish film director, **1900**; John Mills, English actor, **1908**; Kenneth Williams, English comedy actor, **1926**.

D Amerigo Vespucci, Italian navigator after whom America is named, **1512**; Jean-Baptiste-Camille Corot, French painter,

1875; Charles Lyell, English geologist, 1875; Stefan Zweig, Austrian writer, 1942; Elizabeth Bowen, Irish novelist, 1973; Oskar Kokoschka, Austrian painter, 1980.

23

Feast day of St Polycarp of Smyrna, St Dositheus, St Milburga, St Alexander Akimites, St Boisil, and St Willigis.

1732 First performance of Handel's *Oratorio*, in London. 1820 Discovery of the Cato Street conspiracy; following a tip-off, police arrested revolutionaries who planned to blow up the British Cabinet. 1836 The siege of the Alamo began, under the Mexican general Santa Anna. 1863 Lake Victoria was proclaimed to be the source of the River Nile by British explorers John Speke and J A Grant. 1898 Emile Zola was imprisoned for writing his open letter *J'accuse*, accusing the French government of anti-Semitism and of wrongly imprisoning the army officer Captain Alfred Dreyfus. 1919 Benito Mussolini founded the Italian Fascist Party. 1970 Guyana became an independent republic within the Commonwealth. 1981 Spanish Fascist army officers led by Lt Colonel Antonio Tejero attempted a coup in the Cortes (parliament).

Samuel Pepys, English civil servant and diarist, 1633; George Frederick Handel, German-born British composer, 1685; Victor Fleming, US film director who made *The Wizard of Oz*, 1883; Erich Kästner, German children's author, 1899; Peter Fonda, US film actor, 1940.

Joshua Reynolds, English painter, 1792; John Keats, English poet, 1821; Karl Gauss, German mathematician and astronomer, 1855; Nellie Melba, Australian opera singer, 1931; Edward Elgar, English composer, 1994; Stan Laurel, English-born US film comedian, 1965; Adrian Boult, English conductor, 1983; Andy Warhol, US Pop artist, 1987.

24

Feast day of St Praetextatus and Saints Montanus, Lucius, and their Companions.

AD 303 Galerius Valerius Maximianus issued an edict demanding the persecution of Christians. 1582 The Gregorian Calendar was introduced by Pope Gregory XIII; it replaced the

Julian Calendar, but was not adopted in Britain until 1752. 1905 The Simplon Tunnel through the Alps was completed. 1920 Nancy Astor became the first woman to address the British Parliament. 1932 Malcolm Campbell beat his own land speed record in *Bluebird* at Daytona Beach, USA; he reached a speed of 408.88 kph/253.96 mph. 1938 Nylon toothbrush bristles were first produced in the USA – the first commercial use of nylon. 1946 Juan Perón was elected president of Argentina.

Charles V, Holy Roman Emperor, 1500; Wilhelm Grimm, German philologist and, with his brother Jakob, compiler of fairy tales, 1786; Arnold Dolmetsch, Swiss maker and restorer of musical instruments, 1858; Michel Legrand, French composer of film music, 1932; Alain Prost, French racing driver, 1955; Dennis Waterman, English actor, 1948.

Henry Cavendish, English physicist, 1810; Thomas Bowdler, English editor who produced 'bowdlerised' versions of great literary works such as Shakespeare and the Old Testament, 1825; Nikolai Bulganin, Soviet prime minister, 1975; Memphis Slim, US blues singer, 1987; Bobby Moore, English footballer, 1993.

25 National Day of Kuwait. Feast day of St Ethelbert of Kent, St Walburga, St Gerland, St Louis Versiglia, St Caesarius of Nazianzen, and St Calixto Caravario.

1308 Coronation of King Edward II of England. 1570 Pope Pius V excommunicated Queen Elizabeth I. 1913 English suffragette Emmeline Pankhurst went on trial for a bomb attack on the home of David Lloyd George, chancellor of the Exchequer. 1939 The first Anderson air-raid shelter was built in Islington, N London. 1955 HMS *Ark Royal* was completed, the largest aircraft carrier ever built in Britain. 1988 US televangelist Jimmy Swaggart was suspended after it became known that he had visited a prostitute for three years.

Carlo Goldoni, Italian playwright, 1707; Pierre-Auguste Renoir, French Impressionist painter, 1841; Enrico Caruso, Italian operatic tenor, 1873; Myra Hess, English pianist, 1890; Anthony Burgess, English novelist, 1917; David Puttnam, English film producer, 1941; George Harrison, English pop musician and former member of the Beatles, **1943**.

Robert Devereux, Earl of Essex, executed for high treason, **1601**; Christopher Wren, English architect, **1723**; Paul Julius von Reuter, founder of Reuters international news agency, **1899**; John Tenniel, English artist and illustrator, **1914**; Mark Rothko, US painter, **1970**; Tennessee Williams, US dramatist, **1983**.

26 Feast day of St Alexander of Alexandria, St Porphyry of Gaza, St Nestor of Magydus, and St Victor the Hermit.

1531 An earthquake in Lisbon, Portugal, killed 20,000 people. **1797** The first £ note was issued by the Bank of England. **1815** Napoleon escaped from exile on the island of Elba. **1839** The first Grand National Steeplechase was run at Aintree. **1935** Robert Watson-Watt gave the first demonstration of Radar at Daventry, England. **1936** Adolf Hitler launched the Volkswagen ('people's car'), intended to compete with Ford's Model T and boost the German economy.

Victor Hugo, French novelist and playwright, **1802**; William Cody ('Buffalo Bill'), US showman, **1846**; Frank Bridge, English composer and conductor, **1879**; Fats Domino, US singer, **1928**; Johnny Cash, US country singer, **1932**.

Roger II, king of Sicily, **1154**; John Philip Kemble, English actor, **1823**; Richard Gatling, US inventor of the Gatling gun, **1903**; Harry Lauder, Scottish music-hall comedian, **1950**; Slim Gaillard, US jazz musician, **1991**.

27 Feast day of St Alnoth, St Herefrith of Louth, and St Leander of Seville.

1557 The first Russian Embassy opened in London; exactly one year later, the first trade mission arrived. **1879** US chemists Ira Remsen and Constantine Fahlberg announced their discovery of saccharin. **1881** British troops were defeated by the Boers at Majuba Hill, Transvaal. **1933** The German Reichstag (parliament building) in Berlin was destroyed by fire; it is believed that the Nazis were responsible, though they blamed the Communists. **1948** The Communist Party seized power in Czechoslovakia. **1991** The Gulf War came to an end with the liberation of Kuwait and the retreat of Iraqi forces.

JAN FEB MAR APR MAY JUN JUL AUG SEP OCT NOV DEC

Constantine, Roman emperor, AD 274; Henry Wadsworth Longfellow, US poet, 1807; Rudolf Steiner, Austrian philosopher, 1861; John Steinbeck US novelist, 1902; Lawrence Durrell, English poet and novelist, 1912; Elizabeth Taylor, English-born US film actress, 1932.

John Evelyn, English diarist, 1706; Alexander Borodin, Russian composer and chemist, 1887; Ivan Pavlov, Russian psychologist, 1936; Peter Behrens, German architect, 1940; Henry Cabot Lodge, US politician and diplomat, 1985; Lilian Gish, US film actress, 1993.

28

Feast day of St Oswald of Worcester, St Lupicinus, St Hilarius, pope, St Proterius, and St Romanus.

1784 John Wesley, English founder of the Wesleyan faith, signed its deed of declaration. 1900 Relief forces under General Buller reached British troops besieged for four months at Ladysmith, Natal; Boer troops retreated. 1912 The first parachute jump was made, over Missouri, USA. 1948 The last British troops left India. 1975 A London underground train crashed at Moorgate station, killing 42 people. 1986 Swedish prime minister Olof Palme was shot dead as he walked home from a cinema in Stockholm.

René Antoine de Réaumur, French scientist and inventor of a thermometer scale, 1683; Linus Pauling, US physicist and chemist, 1909; Stephen Spender, English poet and critic, 1909; Vincente Minelli, US film director, 1913; Peter Medawar, English immunologist, 1915; Barry McGuigan, Irish-born boxer, 1951.

Alphonse de Lamartine, French poet, 1869; Henry James, US-born British novelist, 1916; Alfonso XIII, ex-king of Spain, 1941; Rajendra Prasad, first president of India, 1963; Henry Luce, US magazine publisher, 1967.

29

Leap Year Day.

1880 The St Gotthard railway tunnel through the Alps was completed, linking Italy with Switzerland. 1948 The Stern Gang blew up a train carrying British soldiers from Cairo to

Haifa; 27 soldiers were killed. **1956** Pakistan became an Islamic republic. **1960** An earthquake killed about 12,000 people in Agadir, Morocco. **1968** English astronomer Jocelyn Burnell announced the discovery of the first pulsar.

B Ann Lee, English founder of the American Society of Shakers, **1736**; Gioacchino Rossini, Italian composer, **1792**; John Holland, US submarine inventor, **1840**; Shri Morarji Desai, Indian politician, **1896**; Jimmy Dorsey, US bandleader, **1904**; Mario Andretti, Italian racing driver, **1940**.

D St Hilarius, 46th pope, **468**; St Oswald, archbishop of York, **992**; Patrick Hamilton, Scottish Protestant martyr, **1528**; John Whitgift, archbishop of Canterbury, **1604**; John Landseer, English painter, **1852**; Roland Culver, English actor, **1984**.

MARCH

1 National Day of Wales. Feast day of St David, St Swithbert, and St Felix III, pope.

 1780 Pennsylvania became the first US state to abolish slavery. **1845** The USA annexed Texas. **1940** English actress Vivien Leigh won an Oscar for her performance as Scarlett O'Hara in the film *Gone with the Wind*. **1949** US heavyweight boxing champion Joe Louis retired after successfully defending his title 25 times. **1954** The USA conducted its first hydrogen-bomb test at Bikini Atoll, in the Marshall Islands. **1966** The uncrewed Soviet spacecraft *Venus 3* landed on Venus.

B Frédéric Chopin, Polish composer, **1810**; Lytton Strachey, English biographer, **1880**; Glenn Miller, US bandleader, **1904**; David Niven, Scottish-born US film actor, **1910**; Harry Belafonte, US singer, **1927**; Roger Daltrey, English rock musician, singer with The Who, **1945**.

D George Herbert, English poet, **1633**; Girolamo Frescobaldi, Italian composer, **1643**; George Grossmith, English singer and comedian, **1912**; Jackie Coogan, US film actor who in **1921** played the child in Charlie Chaplin's *The Kid*, **1984**.

JAN FEB **MAR** APR MAY JUN JUL AUG SEP OCT NOV DEC

2

Feast day of St Chad and St Joavan.

1717 The first ballet, *The Loves of Mars and Venus* was performed at the Theatre Royal, Drury Lane, London. **1882** An attempt was made to assassinate Queen Victoria at Windsor. **1949** US Airforce Captain James Gallagher returned to Fort Worth, Texas, after flying non-stop around the world in 94 hours with a crew of 13 men; tanker aircraft refuelled their plane four times during the flight. **1955** Severe flooding in N and W Australia killed 200 people. **1969** The French-built supersonic aircraft Concorde made its first test flight from Toulouse. **1970** Rhodesia proclaimed itself a republic.

B

Thomas Bodley, founder of the Bodleian Library, Oxford, **1545**; Bedrich Smetana, Czech composer, **1824**; Kurt Weill, German composer who worked with Bertolt Brecht, **1900**; Basil Hume, archbishop of Westminster, **1923**; Mikhail Gorbachev, Soviet leader, **1931**; J P R Williams, Welsh rugby player, **1949**; Ian Woosnam, Welsh golfer, **1958**.

D

John Wesley, English founder of Methodism, **1791**; Horace Walpole, novelist and historian, **1797**; D H Lawrence, English novelist, **1930**; Howard Carter, English Egyptologist who discovered Tutankhamen's tomb, **1939**; Joan Greenwood, English film actress, **1987**; Randolph Scott, US film actor, **1987**.

3

National Day of Morocco. Feast day of St Ailred of Rievaulx, St Cunegund, empress, St Marinus of Caesarea, St Non, St Winwaloe, St Anselm of Nonantola, St Artelais, St Chef, and St Emeterius.

1802 Beethoven's 'Moonlight Sonata' published. **1875** The first performance of Bizet's opera Carmen was staged at the Opéra Comique, Paris. **1931** 'The Star-Spangled Banner' was adopted as the US national anthem. **1969** US spacecraft *Apollo* 9 was launched. **1985** British miners voted to go back to work after a year of striking over pit closures. **1991** Latvia and Estonia voted to secede from the Soviet Union.

B

George Pullman, US designer of luxury railway carriages, **1831**; Alexander Graham Bell, Scottish-born inventor of the telephone, **1847**; Jean Harlow, US film actress, **1911**; Ronald

Searle, English artist and cartoonist, **1920**; Miranda Richardson, English actress, **1958**; Fatima Whitbread, English javelin champion, **1961**.

Robert Hooke, English physicist, **1703**; Robert Adam, Scottish architect, **1792**; Giandomenico Tiepolo, Italian artist, **1804**; Lou Costello, US comedian, **1959**; Arthur Koestler, Hungarian-born writer and supporter of euthanasia, committed suicide, **1983**; Danny Kaye, US comedian, **1987**.

4

Feast day of St Peter of Cava, St Casimir of Poland, and St Adrian and his Companions.

1681 King Charles II granted a Royal Charter to William Penn, entitling Penn to establish a colony in North America. **1861** Abraham Lincoln was sworn in as the 16th president of the USA. **1877** The Russian Imperial Ballet staged the first performance of the ballet Swan Lake in Moscow. **1882** Britain's first electric trams came into operation in Leytonstone, East London. **1890** The Forth railway bridge, Scotland was officially opened. **1968** Tennis authorities voted to admit professional players to Wimbledon, previously open only to amateur players.

Prince Henry the Navigator, Portuguese patron of explorers, **1394**; Antonio Vivaldi, Italian composer, **1678**; Patrick Moore, English astronomer, **1928**; Bernard Haitink, Dutch conductor, **1929**; Miriam Makeba, South African singer, **1931**; Kenny Dalgleish, Scottish footballer, **1951**.

Saladin, Kurdish-born Muslim leader who defeated the Crusaders, **1193**; Thomas Malory, English writer of the *Morte d'Arthur*, **1470**; Jean-François Champollion, French Egyptologist, **1832**; Nikolai Gogol, Russian novelist and playwright, **1852**; William Carlos Williams, US poet, **1963**.

5

Feast day of St Piran, St Gerasimus, Saints Adrian and Eubulus, St Eusebius, St John Joseph of the Cross, St Kieran of Saighir, St Phocas of Antioch, and St Virgil of Arles.

1461 King Henry VI of England was deposed; he was succeeded by Edward IV. **1770** British troops killed five civilians when they fired into a crowd of demonstrators in Boston; the incident became known as the 'Boston Massacre'. **1933** The Nazi Party won almost half the seats in the elections. **1936** The British fighter plane Spitfire made its first test flight from Eastleigh, Southampton. **1946** The term 'iron curtain' was first used, by Winston Churchill in a speech in Missouri, USA. **1850** English engineer Robert Stephenson's tubular bridge was opened, linking Anglesey with mainland Wales.

B King Henry II of England, **1133**; Gerardus Mercator, Flemish cartographer, **1512**; Augusta Gregory, Irish playwright, **1852**; Heitor Villa-Lobos, Brazilian composer, **1887**; Rex Harrison, English actor, **1908**; Elaine Page, English musical actress, **1952**.

D Antonio Corregio, Italian painter, **1534**; Friedrich Mesmer, Austrian physician and founder of mesmerism, or 'animal magnetism', **1815**; Alessandro Volta, Italian physicist, **1827**; Joseph Stalin, Soviet dictator, **1953**; Sergei Prokofiev, Russian composer, **1953**; Tito Gobbi, Italian operatic baritone, **1984**.

6 National Day of Ghana. Feast day of Saints Baldred and Billfrith, St Chrodegang, St Colette, St Conon, St Cyneburga, St Fridolin, and St Tibba.

1836 The 12-day siege of the Alamo ended, with only six survivors out of the original force of 155. **1899** Aspirin was patented by chemist Felix Hoffman. **1930** Clarence Birdseye's first frozen foods went on sale in Springfield, Massachusetts, USA. **1957** Ghana became independent, the first British colony to do so. **1987** A cross-channel ferry left Zeebrugge, Belgium, with its bow doors open; it capsized suddenly outside the harbour, killing over 180 passengers. **1988** British SAS men shot dead three IRA members in a street in Gibraltar, claiming that they had been about to attack a military parade.

B Cyrano de Bergerac, French novelist and playwright, **1619**; Elizabeth Barrett Browning, English poet, **1806**; Frankie Howerd, English comedian, **1922**; Andrzej Wajda, Polish film director, **1926**; Valentina Tereshkova, Soviet astronaut, **1937**; Kiri Te Kanawa, New Zealand soprano, **1944**.

D Louisa May Alcott, US novelist, **1888**; Gottlieb Daimler, German motor engineer who invented the motorcycle, **1900**; Ivor Novello, Welsh composer and actor, **1951**; George

Formby, English entertainer, **1961**; Pearl Buck, US novelist, **1971**; Donald Maclean, English-born Soviet spy, **1984**.

7

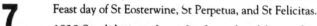

Feast day of St Eosterwine, St Perpetua, and St Felicitas.

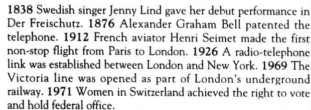

1838 Swedish singer Jenny Lind gave her debut performance in Der Freischutz. **1876** Alexander Graham Bell patented the telephone. **1912** French aviator Henri Seimet made the first non-stop flight from Paris to London. **1926** A radio-telephone link was established between London and New York. **1969** The Victoria line was opened as part of London's underground railway. **1971** Women in Switzerland achieved the right to vote and hold federal office.

Tomas Masaryk, Czech leader, **1850**; Piet Mondrian, Dutch painter, **1872**; Maurice Ravel, French composer, **1875**; Viv Richards, Antiguan cricketer, **1952**; Ivan Lendl, Czech tennis player, **1960**; Rik Mayall, English comedian, **1958**.

Antoninus Pius, Roman emperor, AD **161**; St Thomas Aquinas, Christian philosopher, **1274**; Herman Mankiewicz, US screenwriter, **1953**; Percy Wyndham Lewis, English writer and artist, **1957**; Stevie Smith, English poet and novelist, **1971**.

8

Feast day of St Felix of Dunwich, St Duthac, St Julian of Toledo, St Pontius of Carthage, St Veremund, St Senan, and St John of God.

1702 Anne became queen of Britain after William III died in a riding accident. **1910** The first pilot's licences were issued, to an Englishman, J T C Moore Brabazon, and a Frenchwoman, Elise Deroche. **1917** The February Revolution began in Petrograd (St (Petersburg), Russia. **1930** In India, a campaign of civil disobedience began, led by Mahatma Gandhi. **1965** 3,500 US marines landed in South Vietnam. **1971** US boxer Muhammad Ali was defeated by Joe Frazier.

Kenneth Grahame, Scottish author of *The Wind in the Willows*, **1859**; Otto Hahn, German physicist and chemist, **1879**; Douglas Hurd, British politician, **1930**; James Dean, US film actor, **1931**; Lynn Seymour, Canadian ballet dancer, **1939**; Norman Stone, English historian, **1941**.

JAN FEB MAR APR MAY JUN JUL AUG SEP OCT NOV DEC

Abraham Darby, English ironmaster, the first to use coke for smelting iron, **1717**; Hector Berlioz, French composer, **1869**; John Ericsson, Swedish-born US inventor of the screw propeller, **1889**; William Howard Taft, 27th president of the USA, **1930**; Thomas Beecham, English conductor, **1961**; Harold Lloyd, US comedian and silent-film actor, **1971**.

9

Feast day of the Forty Martyrs of Sebaste, St Frances of Rome, St Bosa, St Constantine, St Gregory of Nyssa, St Pacianus, and St Dominic Savio.

1074 Pope Gregory VII excommunicated all married priests. **1796** French army commander Napoleon Bonaparte married Josephine de Beauharnais. **1831** The French Foreign Legion was founded in Algeria; its headquarters moved to France in **1962**. **1918** The Russian capital was transferred from Petrograd (St Petersburg) to Moscow. **1923** Lenin retired as Soviet leader after suffering a severe stroke; he died the following year. **1956** Archbishop Makarios of Cyprus was deported to the Seychelles to prevent his involvement in terrorist activities. **1961** Russian dog Laika was launched into space aboard the spacecraft *Sputnik 9*.

William Cobbett, author and politician, **1763**; Vita Sackville-West, English novelist, **1892**; Yuri Gagarin, Soviet astronaut, the first man in space, **1934**; Bobby Fischer, US chess champion, **1943**; Vyacheslav Molotov, Soviet politician, **1890**; Bill Beaumont, English rugby player, **1952**.

David Rizzio, secretary to Mary Queen of Scots, murdered **1566**; Jules Mazarin, French cardinal and politician, **1661**; Frank Wedekind, German playwright, **1918**; Wilhelm I of Prussia, **1888**; Bob Crosby, US bandleader, **1993**.

10

Feast day of St Kessog, St John Ogilvie, St Attalas, St Hymelin, St Macarius of Jerusalem, St Simplicius, pope, and St Anastasia Patricia.

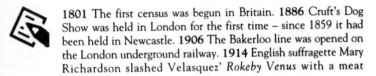

1801 The first census was begun in Britain. **1886** Cruft's Dog Show was held in London for the first time – since 1859 it had been held in Newcastle. **1906** The Bakerloo line was opened on the London underground railway. **1914** English suffragette Mary Richardson slashed Velasquez' *Rokeby Venus* with a meat cleaver. **1969** James Earl Ray was sentenced to 99 years' imprisonment after pleading guilty to the murder of civil-rights leader Martin Luther King. **1974** A Japanese soldier was discovered hiding on Lubang Island in the Philippines. He was unaware that World War II had ended, and was waiting to be picked up by his own forces.

Marcello Malpighi, Italian physiologist, **1628**; Tamara Karsavina, Russian ballet dancer, **1885**; Arthur Honegger, French composer, **1892**; Bix Beiderbecke, US jazz musician and composer, **1903**; Prince Edward, youngest son of Queen Elizabeth II, **1964**.

Giuseppe Mazzini, Italian nationalist, **1832**; Mikhail Bulgakov, Russian novelist and playwright, **1940**; Jan Masaryk, Czech politician, allegedly committed suicide after Communist takeover, **1948**; Konstantin Chernenko, Soviet leader, **1985**; Ray Milland, US film actor, **1986**.

11 Feast day of St Oengus, St Vindician, St Sophronius of Jerusalem, St Constantine of Cornwall, St Eulogius of Cordova, St Aurea, St Benedict of Milan, and St Teresa Margaret Redi.

1682 The Royal Chelsea Hospital for soldiers was founded by Charles II. **1702** The first successful English daily newspaper, the *Daily Courant* was published in London. **1941** US Congress passed the Lend-Lease Bill, authorising huge loans to Britain to finance World War II. **1985** Mikhail Gorbachev became leader of the USSR. **1988** The Bank of England replaced pound notes with pound coins. **1990** US tennis player Jennifer Capriati, aged 13, became the youngest-ever finalist in a professional contest.

Urbain Leverrier, French astronomer, **1811**; Malcolm Campbell, English speed record holder, **1885**; Harold Wilson, British politician, **1916**; Rupert Murdoch, Australian newspaper proprietor, **1931**; Douglas Adams, English author of *The Hitch-Hiker's Guide to the Galaxy*, **1952**; Nigel Lawson, British politician, **1932**.

Rolf Boldrewood, Australian author, **1915**; David Beatty, British admiral, **1936**; Alexander Fleming, Scottish bacteriologist who discovered penicillin, **1955**; Richard Evelyn

Bird, US aviator and explorer, **1957**; Erle Stanley Gardner, US lawyer and crime writer, **1970**.

12

Feast day of St Alphege, St Bernard of Winchester, St Gregory, St Maximilian of Theveste, St Mura, St Paul Aurelian, St Theophanes, and St Pionius.

1609 Bermuda became a British colony. **1881** France made Tunisia a protectorate. **1904** Britain's first mainline electric train ran from Liverpool to Southport. **1912** The Girl Guides movement (later called Scouts) was founded in the USA. **1930** Indian leader Mahatma Gandhi began his walk to the sea, known as the Salt March, in defiance of the British government's tax on salt and monopoly of the salt trade in India. **1938** Germany annexed Austria. **1940** The Russo-Finnish war ended with Finland signing over territory to the USSR.

John Aubrey, English antiquary and author of *Brief Lives*, **1626**; Thomas Arne, English composer who wrote 'Rule Britannia', **1710**; Kemal Ataturk, Turkish leader, **1881**; Vaslav Nijinsky, Russian ballet dancer, **1890**; Max Wall, English actor and comedian, **1908**; Liza Minelli, US film actress and singer, **1946**.

St Gregory, pope, **604**; Cesare Borgia, Italian cardinal and politician, **1507**; Sun Yat-sen, Chinese revolutionary leader, **1925**; Anne Frank, Dutch Jewish diarist, died in a Nazi concentration camp, **1945**; Charlie Parker, US jazz saxophonist, **1955**; Eugene Ormandy, US conductor, **1985**.

13

Feast day of St Gerald of Mayo, St Mochoemoc, St Nicephorus of Constantinople, Saints Roderic and Salomon, St Ansovinus, and St Euphrasia.

1781 German-born British astronomer William Herschel discovered the planet Uranus. **1881** Tsar Alexander II of Russia died after a bomb was thrown at him in St Petersburg. **1894** The first public striptease act was performed in Paris. **1928** 450 people drowned when a dam burst near Los Angeles, USA. **1930** US astronomer Clyde Tombaugh discovered the planet Pluto; its existence had been predicted 14 years earlier by US astronomer Percy Lowell. **1979** A Marxist coup led by Maurice

Bishop took place in Grenada while Prime Minister Edward
Gairy was in New York at a meeting of the United Nations.

B Joseph Priestley, English scientist, 1733; Percy Lowell, US
astronomer, 1855; Hugh Walpole, English novelist, 1884;
Henry Hathaway, US film director, 1898; Neil Sedaka, US
singer and songwriter, 1939; Joe Bugner, Hungarian-born
British boxer, 1950.

D Richard Burbage, English actor who built the Globe Theatre,
1619; Susan Anthony, US feminist, 1906; Stephen Benet, US
poet who wrote 'John Brown's Body', 1943; Angela Brazil,
English writer of stories about girls' schools, 1947; John
Middleton Murry, English writer and critic, 1957.

14   Feast day of St Matilda, St Eutychius, and St Leobinus.

1492 Queen Isabella of Castile ordered the expulsion of
150,000 Jews from Spain, unless they accepted Christian
baptism. **1757** British admiral John Byng was executed by firing
squad at Plymouth, for having failed to relieve Minorca from the
French fleet. **1864** English explorer Samuel Baker was the first
European to see the lake he named Lake Albert. **1885** Gilbert
and Sullivan's *Mikado* was first performed at the Savoy Theatre,
London. **1891** The submarine *Monarch* laid the first underwater
telephone cable.

B Georg Telemann, German composer, 1681; Mrs Isabella
Beeton, English cookery writer, 1836; Maxim Gorky, Russian
playwright and novelist, 1868; Albert Einstein, German-born
Swiss physicist, 1879; Michael Caine, English film actor, 1933;
Jasper Carrott, English comedian, 1946.

D John Jervis, English admiral, 1823; Karl Marx, German
philosopher, 1883; George Eastman, inventor of the Kodak
camera, 1932; Nikolai Bukharin, Russian politician, 1938;
Busby Berkeley, US film choreographer, 1976.

15   Feast day of St Longinus, St Louise de Marillac, St Zacharias,
pope, St Lucretia, St Matrona, and St Clement Mary Hofbauer.

1892 US inventor Jesse Reno patented the first escalator. **1909**
US entrepreneur G S Selfridge opened Britain's first department

JAN FEB **MAR** APR MAY JUN JUL AUG SEP OCT NOV DEC

store in Oxford Street, London. **1917** Tsar Nicholas II of Russia abdicated. **1933** Nazi leader Adolf Hitler proclaimed the Third Reich in Germany; he also banned left-wing newspapers and kosher food. **1949** Clothes rationing in Britain ended. **1964** Actors Elizabeth Taylor and Richard Burton were married in Montreal.

Andrew Jackson, seventh president of the USA, **1767**; William Lamb, Viscount Melbourne, British prime minister, **1779**; John Snow, English physician who pioneered the use of ether as an anaesthetic, **1813**; Emil von Behring, German bacteriologist, **1854**; Mike Love, US pop singer, member of the Beach Boys, **1941**; Ry Cooder, US guitarist, **1947**.

Julius Caesar, Roman emperor, assassinated, **44 BC**; Henry Bessemer, English metallurgist who invented the Bessemer converter, **1898**; Aristotle Onassis, Greek shipping tycoon, **1975**; Rebecca West, English novelist, **1983**; Tommy Cooper, English comedian, **1984**; Farzad Barzoft, Iranian-born journalist working for the *Observer*, hanged as a spy in Iraq, **1990**.

16 Feast day of St Finan Lobur, St Abraham Kidunaia, St Julian of Antioch, St Eusebia of Hamage, St Finian Lobhair, St Heribert of Cologne, and St Gregory Makar.

 1660 The Long Parliament of England was dissolved, after sitting for 20 years. **1802** The US Military Academy was established at West Point, New York State. **1872** The Wanderers beat the Royal Engineers 1–0 in the first FA Cup Final, at Kennington Oval. **1926** The first rocket fuelled by petrol and liquid oxygen was successfully launched by US physicist Robert Goddard. **1973** The new London Bridge was opened.

Matthew Flinders, English navigator who explored the coast of Australia, **1774**; Georg Ohm, German physicist, **1787**; Leo McKern, Australian actor, **1920**; Jerry Lewis, US comedy actor, **1926**; Bernardo Bertolucci, Italian film director, **1941**.

Tiberius Claudius Nero, Roman emperor, **AD 37**; Aubrey Beardsley, English illustrator, **1898**; Miguel Primo de Rivera, Spanish politician and dictator, **1930**; Austen Chamberlain, British politician who negotiated the Locarno Pact, **1937**;

William Henry Beveridge, English economist who wrote the report on which the British welfare state was founded, **1963**.

17 National Day of Ireland. Feast day of St Patrick, St Withburga, St Gertrude of Nivelles, St Joseph of Arimathea, St Paul of Cyprus, and the Martyrs of the Serapaeum.

1897 English-born New Zealand boxer Bob Fitzsimmons won the heavyweight title from US champion Jim Corbett. **1899** The first-ever radio distress call was sent, summoning assistance to a merchant ship aground on the Goodwin Sands, off the Kent coast. **1921** English doctor Marie Stopes opened The Mothers' Clinic in London, to advise women on birth-control. **1969** Golda Meir, aged 70, took office as prime minister of Israel, the first woman to do so. **1978** The oil tanker *Amoco Cadiz* ran aground on the coast of Brittany, spilling over 220,000 tons of crude oil and causing extensive pollution. **1990** The Bastille opera house, Paris, was opened.

Edmund Kean, English actor, **1787**; Kate Greenaway, English children's book illustrator, **1846**; Nat 'King' Cole, US singer, **1919**; Penelope Lively, English children's novelist, **1933**; Rudolf Nureyev, Russian ballet dancer, **1938**; Robin Knox-Johnston, the first person to sail single-handed, non-stop around the world, **1939**.

Marcus Aurelius, Roman emperor, AD **180**; Daniel Bernoulli, Swiss mathematician and physicist **1782**; Christian Doppler, Austrian physicist, **1853**; Lawrence Oates, English Antarctic explorer, a member of Scott's expedition, who walked into a blizzard, saying 'I am just going outside, and may be some time', **1912**; George Wilkins, Australian polar explorer, **1958**; John Glubb (Glubb Pasha), English soldier, founder of the Arab Legion, **1986**.

18 Feast day of St Cyril of Jerusalem, St Alexander of Jerusalem, St Christian, St Edward the Martyr, St Finan of Aberdeen, St Anselm of Lucca, St Frigidian, and St Salvator of Horta.

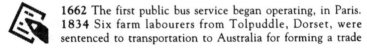

1662 The first public bus service began operating, in Paris. **1834** Six farm labourers from Tolpuddle, Dorset, were sentenced to transportation to Australia for forming a trade union. **1891** The London–Paris telephone link came into operation. **1922** Indian leader Mahatma Gandhi was jailed for six years for sedition. **1931** The first electric razors were manufactured in the USA. **1965** Soviet astronaut Alexei Leonov made the first 'walk' in space.

B Nikolai Rimsky-Korsakov, Russian composer, **1844**; Rudolf Diesel, German engineer who invented the engine named after him, **1858**; Neville Chamberlain, British prime minister who tried unsuccessfully to make peace with Hitler, **1869**; Lavrenti Beria, Soviet chief of secret police, **1889**; Wilfrid Owen, English World War I poet, **1893**; Robert Donat, English film actor, **1905**.

D Edward the Martyr, king of England, murdered at Corfe Castle, **978**; Fra Angelico, Italian monk and painter, **1455**; Ivan IV, 'the Terrible' **1584**; Robert Walpole, first prime minister of Britain, **1745**; Laurence Sterne, Irish novelist, **1768**; Percy Thrower, English gardener and broadcaster, **1988**.

19 Feast day of St Alcmund, St Joseph, St John of Panaca, and St Landoald.

721 BC The first-ever recorded solar eclipse was seen from Babylon. **1628** The New England Company was formed in Massachusetts Bay. **1913** Russian composer Modest Mussorgsky's opera *Boris Godunov* was first performed in full at the Metropolitan Opera, New York. **1932** The Sydney Harbour Bridge, New South Wales, Australia, was opened; it was the world's longest single-span arch bridge, at 503 m/1,650 ft. **1969** British troops landed on the Caribbean island of Anguilla, after the island declared itself a republic; they were well received, and the island remained a UK dependency.

B Georges de la Tour, French painter, **1593**; Tobias Smollett, Scottish physician and author, **1721**; David Livingstone, Scottish missionary and explorer, **1813**; Richard Burton, English explorer and scholar, **1821**; Wyatt Earp, US law officer, **1848**; Sergei Diaghilev, Russian ballet impresario, **1872**.

D Thomas Killigrew, English playwright, **1683**; Mary Anning, English paleontologist who discovered the first ichthyosaurus, **1847**; Arthur James Balfour, British prime minister, **1930**;

Edgar Rice Burroughs, US novelist who wrote the Tarzan stories, 1950; Alan Badel, English actor, 1965.

20 Feast day of St Cuthbert, St Wolfram, St Herbert of Derwentwater, St Martin of Braga, St Photina and her Companions, and the Martyrs of Mar Saba.

1602 The Dutch government founded the Dutch East India Company. 1806 The foundation stone of Dartmoor Prison was laid. 1815 Napoleon returned to Paris from banishment on the island of Elba to begin his last 100 days of power that ended with defeat and exile. 1852 US author Harriet Beecher Stowe's novel *Uncle Tom's Cabin* was published. 1956 Tunisia achieved independence from France. 1980 Pirate radio ship Radio Caroline sank.

Ovid, Roman poet, 43 BC; Henrik Ibsen, Norwegian playwright, 1828; Beniamino Gigli, Italian operatic tenor, 1890; Michael Redgrave, English actor, 1908; Vera Lynn, English singer, 1917; Madan Lal, Indian cricketer, 1951.

King Henry IV of England, 1413; Thomas Seymour, Lord High Admiral of England, executed, 1549; Isaac Newton, English scientist, 1727; Lajos Kossuth, Hungarian revolutionary leader, 1894; Ferdinand Foch, French Army marshal, 1929; Brendan Behan, Irish playwright, 1964.

21 Feast day of St Benedict, St Enda, St Nicholas of Flue, St Fanchea, and St Serapion of Thmuis.

1933 Germany's first Nazi parliament was officially opened in a ceremony at the garrison church in Potsdam. 1946 British minister Aneurin Bevan announced the Labour government's plans for the National Health Service. 1952 Kwame Nkrumah was elected prime minister of the Gold Coast (later Ghana). 1960 The Sharpeville Massacre – in South Africa a peaceful demonstration against the pass laws ended with about 70 deaths when police fired on demonstrators. 1963 Alcatraz, the maximum-security prison in San Francisco Bay, USA, was closed. 1990 A demonstration in London against the poll tax became a riot, in which over 400 people were arrested.

JAN FEB MAR APR MAY JUN JUL AUG SEP OCT NOV DEC

B Johann Sebastian Bach, German composer, **1685**; Paul Tortelier, French cellist, **1914**; Peter Brook, English stage and film director, **1925**; Michael Heseltine, British politician, **1933**; Brian Clough, English footballer and manager, **1935**; Ayrton Senna, Brazilian racing driver, **1960**.

D Thomas Cranmer, archbishop of Canterbury, burned at the stake, **1556**; James Ussher, Irish theologian and archbishop of Armagh, who fixed the date of the Creation at 4004 BC, **1656**; Robert Southey, English poet, **1843**; Alexander Glazunov, Russian composer, **1936**; Philip Wilson Steer, English painter, **1942**; Harry H Corbett, English actor, **1982**.

22 The earliest possible date for Easter. Feast day of St Deogratius, St Basil of Ancyra, St Paul of Narbonne, St Nicholas Owen, and St Benvenuto of Osimo.

1824 The British parliament voted to buy 38 pictures at a cost of £57,000, to establish the national collection which is now housed in the National Gallery, Trafalgar Square, London. **1888** The English Football League was formed. **1895** French cinema pioneers Auguste and Louis Lumière gave the first demonstration of celluloid film, in Paris. **1942** The BBC began broadcasting in morse code to the French Resistance. **1945** The Arab League was founded in Cairo. **1946** Jordan achieved independence from British rule.

B Maximilian I, Holy Roman Emperor, **1459**; Anthony van Dyck, Flemish painter, **1599**; Karl Malden, US film actor, **1913**; Marcel Marceau, French mime, **1923**; Stephen Sondheim, US composer and lyricist, **1930**; Andrew Lloyd Webber, English composer of musicals, **1948**.

D Jean Lully, French composer, **1687**; John Canton, English physicist, **1772**; Johann Wolfgang von Goethe, German poet, novelist, and playwright, **1832**; Thomas Hughes, English author of *Tom Brown's Schooldays*, **1896**; Mike Todd, US film producer, **1958**.

23 National Day of Pakistan. Feast day of St Gwinear, St Turibius, St Benedict the Hermit, St Victorian, St Ethelwald the Hermit, and St Joseph Oriol.

1765 The British parliament passed the Stamp Act, imposing a tax on all publications and official documents in America. 1861 London's first trams began operating, in Bayswater. 1891 Goal nets, invented by Liverpudlian J A Brodie, were used for the first time in an FA Cup Final. 1919 The Italian Fascist Party was formed by Benito Mussolini. 1925 Authorities in the state of Tennessee, USA, forbade the teaching of Darwinian theory in schools. 1956 Pakistan was declared an Islamic republic within the Commonwealth.

Juan Gris, Spanish painter, 1887; Joan Crawford, US film actress, 1904; Akira Kurosawa, Japanese film director, 1910; Wernher von Braun, German-born US rocket engineer, 1912; Jimmy Edwards, English comedian, 1920; Roger Bannister, English neurologist who, as a student, was the first person to run a mile in under four minutes (3 min 59.4 sec), 1929.

Stendhal, French novelist, 1842; Steve Donoghue, English jockey, 1945; Raoul Dufy, French painter, 1953; Peter Lorre, Hungarian-born US film actor, 1964; Claude Auchinleck, British Field Marshal, 1981; Mike Hailwood, English champion motor cyclist, 1981.

24 Feast day of St Dunchad, St Hildelith, St Macartan, St Aldemar, St Simon of Trent, St William of Norwich, St Catherine of Vadstena, and St Irenaeus of Sirmeum.

1401 Tamerlane the Great captured Damascus. 1603 The crowns of England and Scotland were united when King James VI of Scotland succeeded to the English throne. 1877 The Oxford–Cambridge boat race ended in a dead heat, the only time this has happened. 1922 Only three of the 32 horses in the Grand National Steeplechase finished the race. 1942 The national loaf was introduced in Britain. 1976 Isabel Perón, president of Argentina, was deposed.

William Morris, English socialist and craftsman, 1834; Roscoe 'Fatty' Arbuckle, US silent film actor, 1887; Ub Iwerks, US animator who worked with Walt Disney on the creation of Mickey Mouse, 1901; Steve McQueen, US film actor, 1930; Malcolm Muggeridge, English writer and broadcaster, 1903; Archie Gemmill, Scottish footballer, 1947.

JAN FEB MAR APR MAY JUN JUL AUG SEP OCT NOV DEC

Elizabeth I, queen of England, **1603**; Henry Wadsworth Longfellow, US poet, **1882**; Jules Verne, French novelist, **1905**; J M Synge, Irish playwright, **1909**; Orde Charles Wingate, British general, **1944**; Bernard, Viscount Montgomery of Alamein, British Field Marshal, **1976**.

25

National Day of Greece. Feast day of St Barontius, St Alfwold, St Dismus, St Lucy Filippini, St Hermenland, and St Margaret Clitherow.

1306 Robert I 'the Bruce' was crowned king of Scots. **1609** English explorer Henry Hudson set off from Amsterdam, on behalf of the Dutch East India Company, in search of the North West Passage. **1807** The British parliament abolished the slave trade. **1843** A pedestrian tunnel was opened beneath the Thames in London, linking Wapping with Rotherhithe. **1876** In the first football international between Wales and Scotland, played in Glasgow, Scotland won 4–0. **1957** Six European countries (France, Belgium, Luxembourg, West Germany, Italy, and the Netherlands) signed the Treaty of Rome, establishing the European Community.

Henry II, **1133**; Arturo Toscanini, Italian conductor, **1867**; Béla Bartok, Hungarian composer, **1881**; A J P Taylor, English historian, **1906**; David Lean, English film director, **1908**; Aretha Franklin, US singer, **1942**; Elton John, English pop singer and songwriter, **1947**.

Anna Seward, English novelist who wrote *Black Beauty*, **1809**; Nicholas Hawksmoor, English architect, **1836**; Frédéric Mistral, French poet, **1914**; Claude Debussy, French composer, **1918**; King Faisal of Saudi Arabia, assassinated by his nephew, **1975**.

26

Feast day of St William of Norwich, St Liudger, St Felix of Trier, St Castulus of Rome, St Braulio, and St Basil of Rome.

1839 The annual rowing regatta at Henley-on-Thames was established. **1886** The funeral of the first person to be officially cremated in Britain took place in Woking, Surrey. **1920** The British special constables known as the Black and Tans arrived in Ireland. **1934** Driving tests were introduced in Britain. **1973** The first women were allowed on the floor of the London Stock

Exchange. **1979** Israeli prime minister Menachem Begin and Egyptian president Anwar Sadat signed a peace treaty after two years of negotiations.

A E Housman, English poet, **1859**; Robert Frost, US poet, **1874**; Pierre Boulez, French conductor and composer, **1925**; Leonard Nimoy, US actor who played Mr Spock in the TV series *Star Trek*; James Caan, US film actor, **1939**; Diana Ross, US singer, **1944**.

John Vanbrugh, English playwright and architect, **1726**; Ludwig von Beethoven, German composer, **1827**; Walt Whitman, US poet, **1892**; Cecil Rhodes, English-born South African politician, **1902**; Sarah Bernhardt, French actress, **1923**; Raymond Chandler, US novelist who created private eye Philip Marlowe, **1959**; Noel Coward, English playwright and entertainer, **1973**.

27

Feast day of St Rupert, St Athilda, and St John of Egypt.

1794 The United States Navy was formed. **1871** England and Scotland played their first rugby international, in Edinburgh; Scotland won. **1914** The first successful blood transfusion was performed, in a Brussels hospital. **1958** Nikita Khrushchev became leader of the Soviet Union. **1964** The ten Great Train Robbers who were caught were sentenced to a total of 307 years in prison. **1977** Pan Am and KLM jumbo jets collided on the runway at Tenerife airport, in the Canary Islands, killing 574 people.

Henry Royce, English car designer and manufacturer, **1863**; Ludwig Mies van der Rohe, German architect, **1886**; Gloria Swanson, US film actress, **1899**; Cyrus Vance, US secretary of state, **1917**; Sarah Vaughan, US jazz singer, **1924**; Mstislav Rostropovich, Russian cellist and conductor, **1927**; Duncan Goodhew, English Olympic swimmer, **1957**.

King James I of Great Britain, **1625**; Giovanni Battista Tiepolo, Italian painter, **1770**; George Gilbert Scott, English architect, **1878**; James Dewar, Scottish physicist and chemist who invented the thermos flask, **1923**; Arnold Bennett, English novelist, **1931**; Anthony Blunt, English art historian and Soviet spy, **1983**.

JAN FEB MAR APR MAY JUN JUL AUG SEP OCT NOV DEC

28

Feast day of St Alkelda of Middleham, St Gontran, and St Tutilo.

1910 The first seaplane took off near Marseille, S France. **1912** Both the Oxford and the Cambridge boats sank in the University boat race. **1930** The cities of Angora and Constantinople, in Turkey, changed their names to Ankara and Istanbul respectively. **1939** The Spanish Civil War came to an end as Madrid surrendered to General Franco. **1945** Germany dropped its last V2 bomb on Britain. **1979** The nuclear power station at Three Mile Island, Pennsylvania, suffered a meltdown in the core of one of its reactors.

Raphael, Italian painter, **1483**; St Teresa of Avila, Carmelite nun, **1515**; King George I, **1660**; Flora Robson, English actress, **1902**; Dirk Bogarde, English actor and author, **1921**; Neil Kinnock, British politician, **1942**,

James Thomas Brudenell, 7th earl of Cardigan, leader of the disastrous Charge of the Light Brigade at Balaclava, **1868**; Virginia Woolf, English novelist, **1941**; Sergei Rachmaninov, Russian composer, **1943**; Marc Chagall, Russian-born French painter, **1985**; W C Handy, US blues composer, **1958**; Dwight Eisenhower, 34th president of the USA, **1969**.

29

Feast day of Saints Gwynllyw and Gwladys, St Cyril of Heliopolis, St Berthold, St Mark of Arethusa, St Rupert of Salzburg, Saints Jonas, Barachisius and Others, Saints Armogastes, Masculas, Achinimus, and Saturus.

1461 Over 28,000 people are said to have been killed in the Battle of Towton, N Yorkshire; the Lancastrians under Henry VI were defeated. **1871** The Albert Hall, London, was opened by Queen Victoria. **1886** Coca Cola went on sale in the USA; it was marketed as a 'Brain Tonic' and claimed to relieve exhaustion. **1971** In the USA, Lt. William Calley was sentenced to life imprisonment after being found guilty of the murder of civilians in the South Vietnamese village of My Lai in 1969. **1973** The last US troops left Vietnam. **1974** US spacecraft *Mariner 10* took close-up photographs of the planet Mercury.

B   Elihu Thomson, US inventor, **1853**; Edwin Lutyens, English architect, **1869**; William Walton, English composer, **1902**; Pearl Bailey, US singer, **1918**; Norman Tebbit, British politician, **1931**; John Major, British prime minister, **1943**.

D   Charles Wesley, English evangelist and hymn-writer, **1788**; Maria Fitzherbert, mistress of King George IV, **1837**; Georges-Pierre Seurat, French painter, **1891**; Robert Falcon Scott, Antarctic explorer, **1912**; Joyce Cary, Irish novelist, **1957**; Vera Brittain, English socialist writer, **1970**.

---

30   Feast day of St Osburga, St John Climacus, St Zosimus of Syracuse, St Ludolf, St Leonard Murialdo, and St Rieul.

1775 The British parliament passed an Act forbidding its North American colonies to trade with anyone other than Britain. **1842** Ether was first used as an anaesthetic during surgery, by US doctor Crawford Long. **1856** The Crimean War was brought to an end by the signing of the Treaty of Paris. **1867** The USA bought Alaska from Russia for $7.2 million (oil had not yet been discovered). **1893** Thomas Bayard, the USA's first ambassador to Great Britain, arrived in London. **1981** In Washington DC, USA, would-be assassin John Hinckley shot President Reagan in the chest.

B   Francisco de Goya, Spanish painter, **1746**; Paul Verlaine, French poet, **1844**; Vincent Van Gogh, Dutch painter, **1853**; Sean O'Casey, Irish playwright, **1880**; Melanie Klein, Austrian-born British psychologist, **1882**; Eric Clapton, English guitarist, **1945**.

D   William Hunter, Scottish anatomist and obstetrician, **1783**; 'Beau' Brummel, English dandy, **1840**; Rudolf Steiner, Austrian philosopher, **1925**; Friedrich Bergius, German scientist, **1949**; Léon Blum, French politician, **1950**; James Cagney, US film actor, **1986**.

---

31   Feast day of St Benjamin, St Balbina, St Acacius, and St Guy of Pomposa.

1282 The Sicilian Vespers, a massacre of the French in Sicily, begun the previous evening, ended. **1889** In Paris, the Eiffel Tower, built for the Universal Exhibition, was inaugurated.

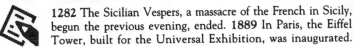

1896 The first zip fastener was patented in the USA by its inventor, Whitcomb Judson. 1959 Tibetan Buddhist leader the Dalai Lama fled from Chinese-occupied Tibet. 1973 Racehorse Red Rum set a record of 9 min 1.9 sec for the Grand National Steeplechase. 1986 Hampton Court Palace, near Richmond, SW London, was severely damaged by a fire which broke out in the south wing.

René Descartes, French philosopher and mathematician, 1596; Andrew Marvell, English poet, 1621; Franz Joseph Haydn, Austrian composer, 1732; Nikolai Gogol, Russian novelist, 1809; Robert Bunsen, German chemist, 1811; John Fowles, English novelist, 1927.

King Francis I of France, 1547; King Philip III of Spain, 1621; John Donne, English poet, 1631; John Constable, English painter, 1837; Charlotte Brontè, English novelist, 1855; Jesse Owens, US athlete, 1980; Enid Bagnold, English novelist, 1981.

APRIL

1 All Fools' Day Feast day of St Agilbert, St Gilbert of Caithness, St Tewdric, St Walaric, St Catharine of Palma, St Melito, St Valery, St Hugh of Bonnevaux, and St Hugh of Grenoble.

1908 The British Territorial Army was founded. 1918 The Royal Air Force was formed when the Royal Naval Air Service and the Royal Flying Corps were merged. 1947 Britain's school-leaving age was raised to 15. 1948 The USSR began its blockade of Berlin. 1960 The USA launched the world's first weather satellite, Tiros I. 1973 In Britain, Value Added Tax (VAT) replaced Purchase Tax and Selective Employment Tax.

William Harvey, English physician who explained the circulation of the blood, 1578; Otto von Bismarck, first chancellor of the German Empire, 1815; Edmond Rostand, French playwright, author of Cyrano de Bergerac, 1868; Lon Chaney, US silent-film actor, 1883; Ali McGraw, US film actress, 1938; David Gower, English cricketer, 1957.

D Eleanor of Aquitaine, queen of England and France, **1204**; King Robert III of Scotland, **1406**; Scott Joplin, US composer, **1917**; Karl Franz Josef, emperor of Austria, **1922**; Max Ernst, German Surrealist painter, **1976**; Marvin Gaye, US singer, **1984**.

2 Feast day of St Francis of Paola, St Mary of Egypt, St John Payne, St Zosimus, St Nicetius of Lyons, and Saints Apphian and Theodosia.

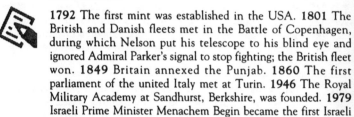

1792 The first mint was established in the USA. **1801** The British and Danish fleets met in the Battle of Copenhagen, during which Nelson put his telescope to his blind eye and ignored Admiral Parker's signal to stop fighting; the British fleet won. **1849** Britain annexed the Punjab. **1860** The first parliament of the united Italy met at Turin. **1946** The Royal Military Academy at Sandhurst, Berkshire, was founded. **1979** Israeli Prime Minister Menachem Begin became the first Israeli leader to visit Cairo when he met Egyptian President Sadat. **1982** Argentina invaded the Falkland Islands.

B Charlemagne, king of the Franks, **742**; Hans Christian Andersen, Danish author, **1805**; Emile Zola, French novelist, **1840**; Alec Guinness, English actor, **1914**; Jack Brabham, Australian racing driver, **1926**; Penelope Keith, English actress, **1939**.

D Honoré Mirabeau, French politician and writer, **1791**; Richard Cobden, British politician, **1865**; Samuel Morse, US inventor, **1872**; C S Forester, English novelist, **1966**; Georges Pompidou, president of France, **1974**.

3 Feast day of Saints Agape, Chionia, and Irene, St Pancras of Taormina, St Richard of Chichester, St Nicetas, St Burgundofara, and St Sixtus I, pope.

1721 Robert Walpole became the first prime minister of Britain. **1860** In the USA, the Pony Express came into operation, with despatch riders regularly making the 3,000-km /2,000-mi trip from St Joseph, Missouri to San Francisco, California. **1922** In the USSR, Stalin was appointed as general secretary of the Communist Party. **1930** Haile Selassie became emperor of Ethiopia. **1987** At an auction in Geneva, jewellery belonging to the late Duchess of Windsor raised over £31 million.

B King Henry IV, first Lancastrian king of England, 1367; Washington Irving, US historian and short-story writer, 1783; Doris Day, US film actress and singer, 1924; Marlon Brando, US actor, 1924; Helmut Kohl, German politician, 1930; Eddie Murphy, US film actor, 1961.

D Bartolomé Murillo, Spanish painter, 1682; James Clark Ross, English explorer, 1862; Johannes Brahms, German composer, 1897; Jesse James, US outlaw, 1882; Graham Greene, English novelist, 1991; Martha Graham, US dancer and choreographer, 1991; Dieter Plage, German wildlife photographer, 1993.

4 National Day of Hungary. Feast day of St Ambrose, St Isidore, St Plato, St Tigernach, St Benedict the Black, and Saints Agathopus and Theodulus.

1541 Spanish Jesuit Ignatius de Loyola became the order's first superior-general. 1581 English navigator Francis Drake returned home after sailing around the world, and was knighted by Queen Elizabeth I. 1933 In the USA, 73 people died when the helium-filled airship *Akron* crashed into the sea off the New Jersey coast. 1934 'Cat's-eye' reflective studs were first used on roads near Bradford, Yorkshire. 1949 The North Atlantic Treaty Organization (NATO) was formed in Washington DC, USA; 11 countries signed the treaty. 1958 Members of the Campaign for Nuclear Disarmament (CND) held the first Aldermaston March, walking from Hyde Park Corner, London, to the Atomic Weapons Research Establishment at Aldermaston, Berkshire.

B Grinling Gibbons, Dutch-born Woodcarver and sculptor, 1648; William Siemens, German-born British metallurgist and inventor, 1823; Marguerite Duras, French author, 1914; Muddy Waters, US blues singer, 1915; Maya Angelou, US author, 1928; Anthony Perkins, US actor, 1932.

D John Napier, Scottish mathematician who invented logarithms, 1617; Oliver Goldsmith, Irish playwright, 1774; Karl Benz, German motor-car engineer, 1929; André Michelin, French tyre manufacturer, 1931; Martin Luther King, US civil-rights leader, assassinated, **1968**; Zulfikar Ali Bhutto, Pakistani prime minister, executed, **1979**.

5 Feast day of St Derfel, St Vincent Ferrer, St Ethelburga of Lyminge, St Albert of Montecorvino, and St Gerald of Sauve-Majeure.

1614 In England, the Addled Parliament began sitting, so called because it passed no Bills. **1874** Johann Strauss's opera *Die Fledermaus* was first performed, in Vienna. **1955** British prime minister Winston Churchill resigned. **1964** Automatic, driverless trains began operating on the London Underground. **1976** Harold Wilson resigned as prime minister of Britain, and was succeeded by James Callaghan.

Thomas Hobbes, English philosopher, **1588**; Elihu Yale, American merchant and founder of the college named after him, **1649**; Spencer Tracey, US film actor, **1900**; Bette Davis, US film actress, **1908**; Herbert von Karajan, Austrian conductor, **1908**; Gregory Peck, US film actor, **1916**.

Georges Danton, French revolutionary leader, guillotined, **1794**; John Wisden, English cricketer who compiled the almanacs named after him, **1884**; Douglas MacArthur, US general, **1964**; Chiang Kai-shek, Chinese soldier and politician, **1975**; Howard Hughes, US industrialist and multi-millionaire, **1976**; George Herbert, earl of Carnarvon, British Egyptologist, **1923**.

6 Feast day of St Elstan, St Irenaeus of Sirmium, St Celestine I, pope, St Marcellinus of Carthage, St Prudentius of Troyes, St Eutychius of Constantinople, and St William of Eskilsoè.

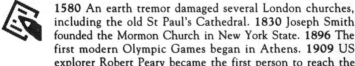

1580 An earth tremor damaged several London churches, including the old St Paul's Cathedral. **1830** Joseph Smith founded the Mormon Church in New York State. **1896** The first modern Olympic Games began in Athens. **1909** US explorer Robert Peary became the first person to reach the North Pole. **1917** The USA declared war on Germany. **1965** Early Bird, the first commercial communications satellite, was launched by the USA.

B
Gustave Moreau, French painter, **1826**; Harry Houdini, US escapologist, **1874**; John Betjeman, English poet, **1906**; James Watson, US biologist, **1928**; André Previn, US conductor, **1929**; Paul Daniels, English magician and entertainer, **1938**.

D
King Richard I, 'the Lion-Heart', **1199**; Albrecht Dürer, German painter, **1528**; Francis Walsingham, English politician, **1590**; Jules Bordet, Belgian bacteriologist, **1961**; Igor Stravinsky, Russian composer, **1971**; Isaac Asimov, US scientist, **1992**.

7
Feast day of St Celsus, St Goran, St Finan Cam, St George the Younger, St Hegesippus, St Aphraates, St Henry Walpole, St Herman Joseph, and St John Baptist de la Salle.

1827 The first matches were sold in Stockton, England, by their inventor, chemist John Walker. **1853** Chloroform was used as an anaesthetic on Queen Victoria, during the birth of her eighth child, Prince Leopold. **1906** A major eruption of the Italian volcano, Vesuvius, took place. **1939** Italy invaded Albania. **1948** The World Health Organization (WHO) was established.

B
St Francis Xavier, Spanish Jesuit missionary, **1506**; William Wordsworth, English poet, **1770**; Billie Holiday, US jazz singer, **1915**; Ravi Shankar, Indian sitar player, **1920**; David Frost, English TV presenter and interviewer, **1939**; Francis Ford Coppola, US film director, **1939**.

D
El Greco, Greek-born Spanish painter, **1614**; Dick Turpin, English highwayman, **1739**; Phineas T Barnum, US showman, **1891**; Henry Ford, US car manufacturer, **1947**; Theda Bara, US silent-film actress, **1955**; Jim Clark, English racing driver, killed in a crash, **1968**.

8
Feast day of St Walter of Pontoise, St Julia Billart, St Perpetuus of Tours, and St Dionysus of Corinth.

1513 Spanish explorer Juan Ponce de Leon arrived in Florida and claimed it for Spain. **1838** Isambard Brunel's steamship *Great Western* set off on its first voyage, from Bristol to New York; the journey took 15 days. **1898** Lord Kitchener defeated Sudanese leader the Mahdi, at the Battle of Atbara. **1908**

Herbert Asquith became prime minister of Britain. **1939** In Albania, King Zog abdicated after Italy occupied the country. **1946** The League of Nations met for the last time. **1953** British colonial authorities in Kenya sentenced Jomo Kenyatta to seven years' imprisonment for allegedly organising the Mau guerrillas.

Adrian Boult, English conductor, **1889**; Mary Pickford, US film actress, **1893**; Ian Smith, Rhodesian prime minister, **1919**; Eric Porter, English actor, **1928**; Dorothy Tutin, English actress, **1931**; Hywel Bennett, Welsh actor, **1944**.

Caracalla, Roman emperor, assassinated, AD **217**; Domenico Donizetti, Italian composer, **1848**; Elisha Graves Otis, US inventor of the safety lift, **1861**; Pablo Picasso, Spanish painter, **1973**; Marian Anderson, US contralto, **1993**.

Feast day of St Madrun, St Uramar, St Hugh of Rouen, St Gaucherius, St Mary Cleophas, and St Waldetrudis.

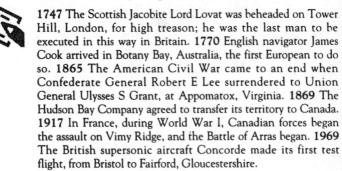

1747 The Scottish Jacobite Lord Lovat was beheaded on Tower Hill, London, for high treason; he was the last man to be executed in this way in Britain. **1770** English navigator James Cook arrived in Botany Bay, Australia, the first European to do so. **1865** The American Civil War came to an end when Confederate General Robert E Lee surrendered to Union General Ulysses S Grant, at Appomatox, Virginia. **1869** The Hudson Bay Company agreed to transfer its territory to Canada. **1917** In France, during World War I, Canadian forces began the assault on Vimy Ridge, and the Battle of Arras began. **1969** The British supersonic aircraft Concorde made its first test flight, from Bristol to Fairford, Gloucestershire.

Isambard Kingdom Brunel, English engineer, **1806**; Charles Baudelaire, French poet, **1821**; Paul Robeson, US actor and singer, **1898**; Hugh Gaitskell, British politician, **1906**; Jean-Paul Belmondo, French film actor, **1933**; Severiano Ballesteros, Spanish golfer, **1957**.

Edward IV of England, **1483**; Lorenzo de'Medici, Florentine ruler, **1492**; Francis Bacon, English philosopher and politician, **1626**; Dante Gabriel Rosetti, English painter and poet, **1882**; Dietrich Bonhoeffer, German theologian, **1945**; Frank Lloyd Wright, US architect, **1959**.

10 Feast day of St Hedda of Peterborough, Saints Beocca and Hethor, St Bademus, St Macarius of Ghent, St Paternus of Abdinghhof, St Michael de Sanctis, St Fulbert of Chartres, and the Martyrs under the Danes.

1633 Bananas, never seen before in England, were on sale in a London shop. 1820 The first British settlers landed at Algoa Bay, South Africa. 1841 The US newspaper *New York Tribune* was first published. 1849 The safety pin was patented in the USA; unaware of this, a British inventor patented his own safety pin later the same year. 1864 Austrian Archduke Maximilian was made Emperor of Mexico. 1972 Earthquakes in Iran killed over 3,000 people.

King James V of Scotland, 1512; William Hazlitt, English essayist and critic, 1778; William Booth, English founder of the Salvation Army, 1829; Joseph Pulitzer, US newspaper proprietor who founded the Pulitzer Prize for literature and journalism, 1847; Max von Sydow, Swedish actor, 1929; Omar Sharif, Egyptian film actor, 1932.

Joseph-Louis Lagrange, French mathematician, 1813; Algernon Charles Swinburne, English poet, 1909; Emiliano Zapata, Mexican revolutionary leader, shot by government troops, 1919; Auguste Lumière, French cinema pioneer, 1954; Evelyn Waugh, English novelist, 1966; Chris Hani, South African ANC leader, asssassinated, 1993.

11 Feast day of St Guthlac, St Stanislas, St Godeberta, St Barsanuphius, St Gemma Galgani, St Isaac of Spoleto, and St Stanislaus of Cracow.

1689 The coronation of William III and Mary II took place in London. 1713 The War of the Spanish Succession was ended by the signing of the Treaty of Utrecht; France ceded Newfoundland and Gibraltar to Britain. 1814 Napoleon abdicated and was exiled to the island of Elba; Louis XVIII became king of France. 1855 Britain's first pillar boxes were put up in London; there were just six of them, and they were painted green. 1945 Allied troops liberated the Nazi concentration camp at Buchenwald. 1951 US General Douglas

MacArthur was relieved of his command in Korea, after a disagreement with President Truman. **1961** Nazi war criminal Adolf Eichmann went on trial in Jerusalem after being kidnapped from Argentina, where he had fled after World War II.

James Parkinson, English physician who discovered Parkinson's disease, **1755**; George Canning, British prime minister, **1770**; Charles Hallé, German-born British pianist and conductor, **1819**; Dean Acheson, US politician, **1893**; Dan Maskell, British tennis player, coach, and commentator, **1908**; Joel Grey, US actor and singer, **1933**.

Donato Bramante, Italian architect who began St Peter's, Rome, **1514**; Thomas Wyatt, English soldier and conspirator, **1554**; Luther Burbank, US botanist, **1926**; Archibald McIndoe, New Zealand-born plastic surgeon, **1960**; John O'Hara, US novelist, **1970**; Erskine Caldwell, US novelist, **1987**.

12 Feast day of St Zeno of Verona, St Julius I, pope, St Sabas the Goth and Others, and St Alferius.

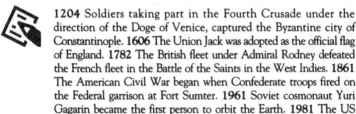

1204 Soldiers taking part in the Fourth Crusade under the direction of the Doge of Venice, captured the Byzantine city of Constantinople. **1606** The Union Jack was adopted as the official flag of England. **1782** The British fleet under Admiral Rodney defeated the French fleet in the Battle of the Saints in the West Indies. **1861** The American Civil War began when Confederate troops fired on the Federal garrison at Fort Sumter. **1961** Soviet cosmonaut Yuri Gagarin became the first person to orbit the Earth. **1981** The US space shuttle Columbia was launched from Cape Canaveral.

Henry Clay, American politician, **1777**; Lionel Hampton, US bandleader, **1913**; Raymond Barre, French politician, **1924**; Alan Ayckbourn, English playwright, **1939**; Bobby Moore, English footballer, **1941**.

William Kent, English architect and landscape gardener, **1748**; Fyodor Chaliapin, Russian operatic bass, **1938**; Franklin Delano Roosevelt, 32nd president of the USA, **1945**; Josephine Baker, US-born French singer and dancer, **1975**; Alan Paton, South African novelist and politician, **1988**.

JAN FEB MAR APR MAY JUN JUL AUG SEP OCT NOV DEC

13 Feast day of St Guinoch, St Martin I, pope, Saints Carpus, Papylus, and Agathonice, St Hermenegild, and St Martius.

1598 Henry IV of France issued the Edict of Nantes, giving religious freedom to the Huguenots. 1668 English poet John Dryden became the first Poet Laureate. 1829 The British Parliament passed the Catholic Emancipation Act, lifting restrictions imposed on Catholics at the time of Henry VIII. 1919 The Amritsar Massacre took place in the Punjab, India; British troops fired into a crowd of 10,000 which had gathered to protest at the arrest of two Indian Congress Party leaders, 379 people were killed and 1,200 wounded. 1936 Luton Town footballer Joe Payne set a goal-scoring record when he scored ten goals in one match against Bristol Rovers. 1980 Spanish golfer Severiano Ballesteros became the youngest-ever winner of the US Masters Tournament.

B Thomas Jefferson, 3rd president of the USA, 1743; Richard Trevithick, English engineer, 1771; F W Woolworth, US founder of chain stores, 1852; John Braine, English novelist, 1922; Seamus Heaney, Irish poet, 1939; Gary Kasparov, Russian chess player, 1963.

D Boris Godunov, Russian tsar, 1605; Jean de La Fontaine, French writer of fables, 1695; William Orchardson, Scottish painter, 1910; Abdul Salam Arif, president of Iraq, 1966; Christmas Humphreys, English judge, 1983.

14 Feast day of St Tiburtius and Companions, St Caradoc, St Lambert of Lyons, St Ardalion, Saints Anthony, John, and Eustace, St Benezet, St John of Vilna, St Bernard of Tiron or Abbeville, and the Martyrs of Lithuania.

1471 The Battle of Barnet took place in the Wars of the Roses, in which Yorkist forces defeated the Lancastrians, leading to the restoration of Edward IV. 1828 US lexicographer Noah Webster published his *American Dictionary of the English Language*. 1929 The first Monaco Grand Prix was held in Monte Carlo. 1931 Spanish King Alfonso XIII fled the country after Republican successes in elections. 1931 The British Ministry of Transport published the first Highway Code. 1983 The first cordless telephone went on sale in Britain.

B Christiaan Huygens, Dutch astronomer and physicist, **1629**; Peter Behrens, German architect and designer, **1868**; John Gielgud, English actor, **1904**; François Duvalier, Haitian dictator, **1907**; Rod Steiger, US film actor, **1925**; John Roberts, English historian, **1928**.

D Richard Neville, 'the Kingmaker', killed at the Battle of Barnet, **1471**; Thomas Otway, English playwright, **1685**; George Frederick Handel, English composer, **1759**; Lazarus Zamenhof, Polish linguist who devised Esperanto, **1917**; Ernest Bevin, British politician and trade-union leader, **1951**; Simone de Beauvoir, French feminist writer, **1986**.

15 Feast day of St Ruadhan, St Paternus of Wales, St Hunna, and Saints Anastasia and Basilissa.

 1755 English lexicographer Dr Samuel Johnson published his *Dictionary*; he had taken eight years to compile it. **1797** Sailors at Spithead, near Portsmouth, mutinied, demanding better conditions; the British government met their demands. **1891** US inventor Thomas Edison gave a public demonstration of his kinetoscope, a moving-picture machine. **1912** Over 1,500 people died when the passenger liner *Titanic* sank after colliding with an iceberg on its first voyage. **1922** Insulin was discovered by Canadian physiologist Frederick Banting and J J R Macleod. **1942** The George Cross was awarded to the island of Malta, for bravery under heavy attack by German and Italian forces during World War II.

B Guru Nanak, founder of Sikhism, **1469**; Henry James, US-born British novelist, **1843**; Joe Davis, English snooker player, **1901**; Neville Marriner, British conductor, **1924**; Jeffrey Archer, English politician and novelist, **1940**; Emma Thompson, English actress, **1959**.

D Mme de Pompadour, mistress of French King Louis XV, **1764**; Abraham Lincoln, 16th president of the USA, assassinated **1865**; Matthew Arnold, English poet and educationalist, **1888**; Father Damien, Belgian missionary, **1889**; Jean-Paul Sartre, French philosopher and writer, **1980**; Arthur Lowe, English actor, **1982**.

JAN FEB MAR APR MAY JUN JUL AUG SEP OCT NOV DEC

16 Feast day of St Bernadette, St Magnus, St Paternus of Avranches, St Encratis, St Fructuosus Braga, St Turibius of Astorga, St Drogo, St Joseph Benedict Labre, and St Optatus and the Martyrs of Saragossa.

 1746 Charles Edward Stuart (Bonnie Prince Charlie) was defeated at the Battle of Culloden. 1883 Paul Kruger became president of South Africa. 1912 US pilot Harriet Quimby became the first woman to fly across the English Channel. 1951 Seventy-five people died when the British submarine Affray sank in the English Channel. 1954 The first stock-car race meeting was held in Britain, at the Old Kent Road stadium, London. 1972 The US spacecraft *Apollo 16* was launched.

John Franklin, English Arctic explorer who discovered the Northwest Passage, 1786; Wilbur Wright, US aviator, 1867; Charlie Chaplin, English-born film actor and director, 1889; Spike Milligan, English comedian and writer, 1918; Peter Ustinov, English actor and novelist, 1921; Kingsley Amis, English novelist, 1922.

Aphra Behn, English playwright, 1689; Francisco de Goya, Spanish painter, 1828; Marie Tussaud, French wax-modeller, 1850; St Bernadette of Lourdes, French saint, 1879; Samuel Smiles, Scottish social reformer and author of *Self-Help*, 1904; David Lean, English film director, 1991.

17 National Day of Syria. Feast day of St Donnan, St Aybert, St Stephen Harding, St Innocent of Tortona, St Mappalicus and Others, and St Robert of Chaise-Dieu.

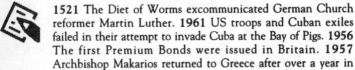 1521 The Diet of Worms excommunicated German Church reformer Martin Luther. 1961 US troops and Cuban exiles failed in their attempt to invade Cuba at the Bay of Pigs. 1956 The first Premium Bonds were issued in Britain. 1957 Archbishop Makarios returned to Greece after over a year in exile in the Seychelles. 1969 The age at which a person is eligible to vote in Britain was lowered from 21 to 18. 1975 The Cambodian communist Khmer Rouge captured the capital, Pnomh Penh. 1980 Southern Rhodesia became Zimbabwe.

John Ford, English playwright, 1586; Leonard Woolley, English archaeologist, 1880; Nikita Khrushchev, Soviet leader, 1894;

Thornton Wilder, US novelist, **1897**; Sirimavo Bandaranaike, first woman prime minister of Sri Lanka, **1916**; Lindsay Anderson, British film and stage director, **1923**.

Mme de Sévigné, French writer, **1696**; Joseph I, Holy Roman Emperor, **1711**; Benjamin Franklin, American scientist and politician, **1790**; Kawabata Yasunari, Japanese novelist, **1972**; Scott Brady, US actor, **1985**; Turgut Ozal, Turkish politician, **1993**.

18

Feast day of St Laserian, St Galdinus, St Idesbald, St Apollonius, and Saints Eleutherius and Anthia.

1775 At the outbreak of the War of American Independence, US patriot Paul Revere rode from Charleston to Lexington, warning people as he went that British troops were on their way. **1881** The Natural History Museum in South Kensington, London, was opened. **1906** An earthquake and the fire that followed it destroyed most of the city of San Francisco, and killed over 450 people. **1934** The first launderette, called a 'washeteria', was opened in Fort Worth, Texas. **1949** Eire proclaimed itself the Republic of Ireland. **1968** The old London Bridge was sold to a US company, who shipped it, stone by stone, to Arizona, where it was re-erected.

Lucrezia Borgia, duchess of Ferrara, **1480**; Leopold Stokowski, US conductor and composer, **1882**; Clarence Darrow, US lawyer, **1857**; Barbara Hayle, US film actress, **1922**; Hayley Mills, English actress, **1946**; Malcolm Marshall, West Indian cricketer, **1958**.

Albert Einstein, German-born US physicist, **1955**; George Jeffreys, the 'hanging judge', **1689**; Erasmus Darwin, English physician and writer, **1802**; Ottorino Respighi, Italian composer, **1936**; Will Hay, English comedian, **1949**; Benny Hill, English comedian, **1992**; Elisabeth Frink, English sculptor, **1993**.

19

Feast day of St Leo IX, pope, St Alphege, St Geroldus, and St Expeditus.

1587 In the incident known as 'singeing the King of Spain's beard', English navigator Francis Drake sank the Spanish fleet

JAN FEB MAR APR MAY JUN JUL AUG SEP OCT NOV DEC

in Cadiz harbour. **1775** The first battle in the War of American Independence took place at Lexington, Massachusetts. **1951** The first 'Miss World' contest was held in London; it was won by a Swedish contestant. **1958** Footballer Bobby Charlton played his first international match for England. **1956** US film actress Grace Kelly married Prince Rainier III of Monaco. **1972** Bangladesh joined the Commonwealth.

B David Ricardo, English economist, **1772**; Richard Hughes, English novelist, **1900**; Jayne Mansfield, US film actress, **1933**; Dudley Moore, English-born comedy film actor, **1935**; Murray Perahia, US pianist and conductor, **1947**; Trevor Francis, English footballer, **1954**.

D Paolo Veronese, Italian painter, **1588**; George Gordon Byron, English poet, died of malaria on his way to fight for Greek independence, **1824**; Benjamin Disraeli, British politician and novelist, **1881**; Charles Darwin, English biologist who developed the theory of evolution, **1882**; Pierre Curie, French chemist and physicist, **1906**; Konrad Adenauer, German politician, **1967**.

20 Feast day of St Caedwalla, St Agnes of Montepulciano, St Marcellinus of Embrun, St Marcian of Auxerre, St Hildegund, and St Peter of Verona.

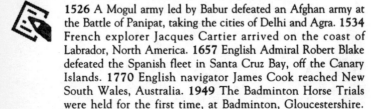

1526 A Mogul army led by Babur defeated an Afghan army at the Battle of Panipat, taking the cities of Delhi and Agra. **1534** French explorer Jacques Cartier arrived on the coast of Labrador, North America. **1657** English Admiral Robert Blake defeated the Spanish fleet in Santa Cruz Bay, off the Canary Islands. **1770** English navigator James Cook reached New South Wales, Australia. **1949** The Badminton Horse Trials were held for the first time, at Badminton, Gloucestershire. **1969** Pierre Trudeau became prime minister of Canada.

B Adolf Hitler, German fascist dictator, **1889**; Joan Miró, Spanish painter, **1893**; Harold Lloyd, US silent-film comedian, **1893**; Donald Wolfit, English actor, **1902**; Ray Brooks, English actor, **1939**; Ryan O'Neal, US film actor, **1941**.

D Jean Louis Petit, French surgeon, **1750**; Canaletto, Italian landscape painter, **1768**; Pontiac, American Indian leader,

1769; Bram Stoker, Irish author of *Dracula*, 1912; Christian X, king of Denmark, 1947.

21 Feast day of St Anselm, St Beuno, St Maelrubba, St Ethilwald, St Anastasius of Antioch, St Conrad of Prazham, and St Simeon Barsabas and Others.

753 BC Traditionally, the date on which the city of Rome was founded. 1509 Henry VIII became king of England. 1960 The new city of Brasilia was declared the capital of Brazil, replacing Rio de Janeiro. 1964 BBC 2 began broadcasting. 1967 King Constantine II of Greece was removed in an army coup, and martial law was imposed. 1983 One-pound coins replaced notes in England and Wales. 1989 Over 100,000 Chinese students gathered in Tiananmen Square, ignoring government warnings of severe punishment.

B Friedrich Froebel, German educationalist, 1782; Henri de Montherlant, French novelist and playwright, 1896; Richard Beeching, British Rail chairman, 1913; Anthony Quinn, US film actor, 1915; John Mortimer, English author and playwright, 1923; Queen Elizabeth II, 1926.

D Henry VII, king of England, 1509; Jean-Baptiste Racine, French playwright, 1699; Mark Twain, US novelist, 1910; Manfred von Richtofen, 'the Red Baron', German fighter pilot, 1918; John Maynard Keynes, English economist, 1946; Richard Stafford Cripps, English lawyer and politician, 1952.

22 Feast day of St Theodore of Sykeon, St Opportuna, St Agipatus I, pope, St Leonides of Alexandria, and Saints Epipodius and Alexander.

1500 Portuguese explorer Pedro Cabral claimed Brazil for Portugal. 1662 King Charles II granted a charter to the Royal Society of London, which became an important centre of scientific activity in England. 1834 The South Atlantic island of St Helena was declared a British Crown Colony. 1838 The first steamship to cross the Atlantic, the British ship *Sirius*, arrived at New York; it made the crossing in 18 days. 1969 Sailor Robin Knox Johnston returned to Falmouth after a 312-day solo voyage around the world. 1972 The first people to row across the Pacific Ocean, Sylvia Cook and John Fairfax, arrived in Australia; they had been at sea for 362 days.

B Henry Fielding, English novelist, 1707; Immanuel Kant, German philosopher, 1724; Mme de Staël, French writer, 1766; Robert Oppenheimer, US physicist who invented the atom bomb, 1904; Kathleen Ferrier, English contralto, 1912; Yehudi Menuhin, US-born British violinist, 1916; George Cole, English actor, 1925; Jack Nicholson, US film actor, 1937.

D John Tradescant, English naturalist, 1662; James Hargreaves, English inventor of the spinning jenny, 1778; John Crome, English landscape painter, 1821; Thomas Rowlandson, English caricaturist, 1827; Henry Campbell-Bannerman, British politician, 1908.

23 National Day of England. Feast day of St George, St Gerard of Toul, St Ibar, St Adalbert of Prague, and Saints Felix, Fortunatus, and Achilleus.

1349 English King Edward III founded the Order of the Garter. 1661 Charles II was crowned king of Great Britain and Ireland. 1662 Connecticut was declared a British colony. 1879 The Shakespeare Memorial Theatre was opened at Stratford-on-Avon. 1924 The British Empire Exhibition opened at Wembley. 1932 The New Shakespeare Memorial Theatre opened at Stratford-on-Avon. 1968 Britain's first decimal coins, the 5p and 10p, were issued in preparation for decimalisation

B William Shakespeare, English playwright and poet, 1564; J M W Turner, English painter, 1775; Max Planck, German physicist, 1858; Ngaio Marsh, New Zealand novelist, 1899; James Donleavy, Irish novelist, 1926; Roy Orbison, US singer, 1936.

D William Shakespeare, 1616; Miguel de Cervantes Saavedra, Spanish author of Don Quixote, 1616; William Wordsworth, English poet, 1850; Rupert Brooke, English poet, 1915; Otto Preminger, US film director, 1986; Satyajit Ray, Indian film director, 1992.

24 Feast day of St Mellitus, St Egbert, St Wilfrid, St Ives, St Fidelis, St Mary Euphrasia Pelletier, and St William Firmatus.

1558 Mary, Queen of Scots married the French Dauphin. 1800 The US Library of Congress was founded in Washington DC. 1895 US sailor Joshua Slocum set off from Boston, USA, to sail single-handed around the world; the voyage took just over three years. 1916 The Easter Rising – a Republican protest against British rule – took place in Dublin. 1949 Sweet-rationing in Britain came to an end. 1970 The Gambia was declared a republic within the Commonwealth.

Anthony Trollope, English novelist, 1815; Henri-Philippe Pétain, French politician and soldier, 1856; William Joyce, 'Lord Haw-Haw', British traitor, 1906; Bridget Riley, English painter, 1931; Shirley MacLaine, US actress, 1934; John Williams, Australian guitarist, 1941; Barbra Streisand, US film actress and singer, 1942.

Daniel Defoe, English author, 1731; Willa Cather, US novelist, 1947; Bud Abbott, US comedian, 1974; the Duchess of Windsor, 1986; Bill Edrich, English cricketer, 1986.

25

Anzac Day in Australia. Feast day of St Mark the Evangelist, St Heribald, and St Anianus of Alexandria.

1792 The guillotine was first used in Paris. 1859 Work began on the Suez Canal, supervised by the French engineer Ferdinand de Lesseps, who designed it. 1915 In World War I, Australian and New Zealand troops landed at Gallipoli. 1925 Paul von Hindenburg was elected President of Germany. 1959 The St Lawrence Seaway was officially opened by Queen Elizabeth II and President Eisenhower, linking the Atlantic with ports on the Great Lakes. 1975 The first free elections for 50 years were held in Portugal, resulting in a precarious Socialist government.

Oliver Cromwell, Puritan leader in the English Civil War, 1599; Mark Isambard Brunel, French-born British engineer, 1769; Walter de la Mare, English poet and novelist, 1873; Guglielmo Marconi, Italian inventor and pioneer in the development of radio, 1874; Ella Fitzgerald, US jazz singer, 1918; Al Pacino, US film actor, 1940; Johann Cruyff, Dutch footballer, 1947.

Torquato Tasso, Italian poet, 1595; Anders Celsius, Swedish astronomer who invented the centigrade thermometer, 1744;

William Cowper, English poet, 1800; Carol Reed, English film director, 1976; Celia Johnson, English actress, 1982.

26

Feast day of St Cletus, St Riquier, St Stephen of Perm, St Peter of Braga, St Franca of Piacenza, and St Paschasius Radbertus.

1923 The Duke of York and Elizabeth Bowes-Lyon, later King George VI and Queen Elizabeth, were married in Westminster Abbey. 1937 The Spanish town of Guernica was almost destroyed by German bombers acting in support of the Nationalists in the Spanish Civil War. 1957 English astronomer Patrick Moore presented the first broadcast of *The Sky at Night*. 1964 Tanganyika and Zanzibar merged to become the Republic of Tanzania. 1968 The largest underground nuclear device ever to be tested in the USA exploded in Nevada. 1986 Radioactive material was leaked from a damaged nuclear reactor at Chernobyl, Ukraine; the effects could be measured thousands of miles away.

Marcus Aurelius, Roman emperor, AD 121; John James Audubon, US naturalist and painter, 1785; Ferdinand Delacroix, French painter, 1798; Michel Fokine, Russian ballet dancer and choreographer, 1880; Ludwig Wittgenstein, Austrian philosopher, 1889; Rudolf Hess, German Nazi leader, 1894.

Karl Bosch, German metallurgist and chemist, 1940; Gypsy Rose Lee, US dancer and striptease artist, 1970; Cicely Courtneidge, British actress, 1980; Count Basie, US bandleader, 1984; Broderick Crawford, US film actor, 1986.

27

Feast day of St Zita, St Machalus, St Floribert of Liège, St Asicus, St Anthimus of Nicomedia, and Saints Castor and Stephen.

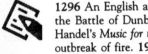

1296 An English army, led by Edward I, defeated the Scots at the Battle of Dunbar. 1749 The first official performance of Handel's *Music for the Royal Fireworks* finished early due to the outbreak of fire. 1937 King George VI performed the official opening of the National Maritime Museum at Greenwich. 1939 Conscription for men aged 20–21 was announced in Britain. 1947 Norwegian anthropologist Thor Heyerdahl set off from

Callao, Peru, heading for Polynesia to prove his theory that the original Polynesian islanders could have come from Peru. **1960** French Togoland became independent as the Republic of Togo. **1961** Sierra Leone became an independent republic within the Commonwealth.

Edward Gibbon, English historian who wrote *The Decline and Fall of the Roman Empire*, **1737**; Mary Wollstonecraft Godwin, English feminist author, **1759**; Samuel Morse, US inventor of Morse Code, **1791**; Ulysses Simpson Grant, US general and 18th president, **1822**; Cecil Day Lewis, English poet, **1904**; Anouk Aimée, French film actress, **1932**; Sandy Dennis, US film actress, **1937**.

Ferdinand Magellan, Portuguese navigator, murdered by islanders in the Philippines, **1521**; Ralph Waldo Emerson, US poet and essayist, **1882**; Alexander Skryabin, Russian composer, **1915**; Harold Hart Crane, US poet, **1932**; Kwame Nkrumah, president of Ghana, **1972**.

28 Feast day of St Louis de Montfort, St Vitalis, St Peter Mary Chanel, St Cyril of Turov, St Valeria, St Pollio, Saints Theodora and Didymus, St Pamphilus of Sulmona, and St Cronan Roscrea.

1603 Queen Elizabeth I's funeral took place at Westminster Abbey. **1770** English navigator Captain James Cook and his crew, including the botanist Joseph Banks, landed in Australia, at the place which was later named Botany Bay. **1789** The crew of the ship *Bounty*, led by Fletcher Christian, mutinied against their captain, William Bligh. **1919** The League of Nations was founded. **1923** The first FA Cup Final was held at Wembley Stadium. **1965** US marines intervened in an attempted communist coup. **1969** French president General de Gaulle resigned.

King Edward IV of England, **1442**; James Monroe, 5th president of the USA, **1758**; Charles Sturt, British explorer of Australia, **1795**; Lionel Barrymore, US actor, **1878**; Kenneth Kaunda, president of Zambia, **1924**; Ann-Margret, Swedish actress, **1941**; Mike Brearley, English cricketer, **1942**.

JAN FEB MAR APR MAY JUN JUL AUG SEP OCT NOV DEC

Gavrilo Princip, Bosnian revolutionary assassin who caused World War I by killing Archduke Franz Ferdinand and his wife, 1918; King Fuad I of Egypt, 1936; Benito Mussolini, 1945; Francis Bacon, Irish-born painter, 1992; Olivier Messiaen, French composer, 1992.

29

National Day of Japan. Feast day of St Catherine of Siena, St Wilfrid the Younger, St Hugh of Cluny, St Endellion, St Joseph Cottolengo, St Robert of Molesme, and St Peter the Martyr.

1429 The Siege of Orléans was lifted by a French army under the leadership of Joan of Arc. 1884 Oxford University agreed to admit female students to examinations. 1913 Swedish-born US inventor Gideon Sundback patented the zip fastener in its modern form – earlier versions had not been successful. 1916 Republican rebels destroyed the Post Office in Dublin. 1945 The German army in Italy surrendered to the Allies under the British General Alexander.

Thomas Beecham, English conductor, 1879; 'Duke' Ellington, US composer and bandleader, 1899; Emperor Hirohito of Japan, 1901; Fred Zinneman, US film director, 1907; Peter de la Bilière, British commander in the Gulf War, 1934; Zubin Mehta, Indian conductor, 1936; Saddam Hussein, president of Iraq, 1937.

George Farquhar, Irish playwright, 1707; Constantinos Cavafy, Greek poet, 1933; Wallace Carothers, US chemist who patented nylon, 1937; Alfred Hitchcock, English film director, 1980; Andrew Cruikshank, English actor, 1988.

30

National Day of the Netherlands. Feast day of St Erkenwald, St Pius V, pope, St Forannan, St Wolfhard, St Maximus of Ephesus, St Eutropius of Saintes, and Saints Marianus, James, and Others.

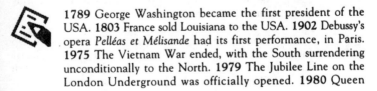

1789 George Washington became the first president of the USA. 1803 France sold Louisiana to the USA. 1902 Debussy's opera *Pelléas et Mélisande* had its first performance, in Paris. 1975 The Vietnam War ended, with the South surrendering unconditionally to the North. 1979 The Jubilee Line on the London Underground was officially opened. 1980 Queen

Juliana of the Netherlands abdicated and was succeeded by her daughter, Beatrix.

David Thompson, English explorer, 1770; Karl Gauss, German mathematician and astronomer, 1777; Franz Lehár, Hungarian composer, 1870; Jaroslav Hasek, Czech novelist, 1883; Queen Juliana of the Netherlands, 1909; Cloris Leachman, US film actress, 1926; King Carl XVI Gustav of Sweden, 1946.

Robert Fitzroy, English admiral and meteorologist, 1865; Edouard Manet, French painter, 1883; Otto Jespersen, Danish philologist, 1943; Adolf Hitler, German fascist dictator, 1945; Eva Braun, German mistress and later wife of Adolf Hitler, 1945; Muddy Waters, US blues singer, 1983; George Balanchine, Russian choreographer, 1983.

MAY

1

May Day. Feast day of St Asaph, St Corentin, St Joseph, St Brioc, St Amator, St Marcoul, Saints Philip and James, St Peregrine Laziosi, St Sigismund of Burgundy, and St Theodard of Narbonne.

1517 In 'Evil May Day' riots in London, apprentices attacked foreign residents. Wolsey suppressed the rioters, of whom 60 were hanged. 1707 The Union of England and Scotland was proclaimed. 1786 The first performance of Mozart's opera *The Marriage of Figaro* was given in Vienna. 1851 Queen Victoria opened the Great Exhibition in Hyde Park, London. 1925 Cyprus became a Crown Colony. 1926 British miners began a strike that continued until 19 November. 1931 The Empire State Building, New York, was completed; it had cost $41 million to build. 1933 A telephone link between Britain and India was established. 1960 A US U-2 aircraft piloted by Gary Powers, was shot down as it flew over the USSR. 1961 Betting shops became legal in Britain.

Arthur Wellesley, Duke of Wellington, 1769; Glenn Ford, US film actor, 1916; Joseph Heller, US novelist, 1923; Sonny Ramadhin, West Indies cricketer, 1929; Una Stubbs, English actress, 1937; Joanna Lumley, English actress, 1946.

JAN FEB MAR APR MAY JUN JUL AUG SEP OCT NOV DEC

D John Dryden, English poet, **1700**; David Livingstone, Scottish missionary, **1873**; Antonín Dvorák, Czech composer, **1904**; Joseph Goebbels, German Nazi propaganda minister, **1945**; William Fox, US film producer, **1952**; Harold Nicolson, English diplomat and author, **1968**.

2 Feast day of St Gennys, St Athanasius, St Mefalda, St Wiborada, St Waldebert, Saints Exuperius and Zoe, and St Ultan of Fosses.

1251 Simon de Montfort suppressed the Gascon rebellion. **1482** Venice, in alliance with the Papacy, declared war on Ferrara, which was supported by Florence, Milan and Naples. **1536** Queen Anne Boleyn was sent to the Tower of London. **1611** The Authorised Version of the Bible (King James Version) was first published. **1670** The Hudson Bay Company was incorporated. **1926** US troops landed to preserve order in Nicaraguan revolt. **1936** Ethiopian Emperor Haile Selassie and his family fled from Addis Ababa, three days before it fell to Italian forces. **1945** Germany surrendered to Allied forces. **1969** The passenger liner *Queen Elizabeth II* set off from Southampton on its first voyage. **1989** Martial law was imposed in China as the government took a firmer stand against pro-democracy demonstrators in Tiananmen Square.

B Catherine II 'the Great' of Russia, **1729**; Jerome K Jerome, English novelist and playwright, **1859**; Theodor Herzl, Hungarian founder of Zionism, **1860**; Benjamin Spock, US childcare specialist, **1903**; Bing Crosby, US singer, **1904**; Peggy Mount, English actress, **1916**; Clive Jenkins, British trade-union leader, **1926**; David Suchet, British actor, **1946**.

D Leonardo da Vinci, Florentine artist and scientist, **1519**; Joseph McCarthy, US politician who investigated suspected communists, **1957**; Nancy Astor, first British woman MP, **1964**; J Edgar Hoover, US director of the FBI, **1972**.

3 Feast day of St Glywys, St Juvenal of Narni, Saints Alexander, Eventius, and Theodulus, and Saints Timothy and Maura.

1381 the weavers of Ghent, led by Philip van Artevelde, take

Bruges; other Flemish towns revolt. **1493** Pope Alexander VI published the first bull *Inter cetera* dividing the New World between Spain and Portugal. **1497** A rising broke out in Cornwall, provoked by taxation; James Tutchet, Lord Audley, led an army of 15,000 from Taunton through the southern counties to attack London. **1747** The Battle of Cape Finisterre took place, at which the British defeated the French. **1808** A duel was fought from two hot-air balloons over Paris, the first of its kind. **1841** New Zealand was declared a British colony. **1898** Bread riots in Milan were put down with heavy loss of life. **1906** The Sinai Peninsula became Egyptian territory after Turkey renounced its claims. **1951** British King George VI opened the Festival of Britain. **1958** US President Eisenhower proposes demilitarisation of Antarctica, subsequently accepted by the countries concerned.

Niccoló Machiavelli, Italian politician, **1469**; John Scott Haldane, Scottish physiologist, **1860**; Golda Meir, Russian-born Israeli prime minister, **1898**; Sugar Ray Robinson, US boxer, **1920**; Norman Thelwell, English cartoonist, **1923**; James Brown, US singer, **1933**; Henry Cooper, English boxer, **1934**.

Eglon van der Neer, Dutch painter, **1703**; Thomas Hood, English poet, **1845**; Henry Cornelius, South African-born film director, **1958**; Karl Freund, Czech-born US film cameraman and photographer, **1969**.

4

Feast day of St Pelagia of Tarsus, St Florian of Lorch, St Robert Lawrence, St Augustine Webster, St Gothard, St John Houghton, St Venerius of Milan, and St Cyriacus.

1471 The Battle of Tewkesbury, the last battle in the Wars of the Roses, took place; the Yorkists defeated the Lancastrians. **1780** The first Derby was run at Epsom; the winner was Diomed. **1896** The first issue of the *Daily Mail* was published in London. **1904** Work began on the Panama Canal. **1926** The General Strike began in Britain, with almost half of the country's 6,000,000 trade-union members participating; it continued until 12 May. **1973** The world's tallest building, Sears Tower, Chicago, was completed. **1979** Margaret Thatcher became prime minister of Britain.

JAN FEB MAR APR MAY JUN JUL AUG SEP OCT NOV DEC

B
Thomas Huxley, English naturalist, **1825**; John Speke, English explorer who discovered the source of the Nile, **1827**; Alice Liddell, the girl for whom Lewis Carroll wrote *Alice in Wonderland*, **1852**; Sylvia Pankhurst, English suffragette, **1882**; Eric Sykes, English comedian, **1923**; Audrey Hepburn, Dutch-born US film actress, **1929**.

D
William Froude, English engineer and mathematician, **1879**; Georges Enesco, Romanian composer, **1955**; Osbert Sacheverell Sitwell, English author, **1969**; Josip Broz Tito, Yugoslavian soldier and president, **1980**; Diana Dors, English film actress, **1984**.

5
Feast day of St Hydroc, St Hilary of Arles, St Hilary of Galeata, St Angelo, St Jutta, St Avertinus, and St Mauruntius.

1525 The Peasants' Revolt in south Germany was suppressed and the Anabaptist preacher Thomas Münzer was hanged a few days later. **1751** Portuguese foreign secretary Sebastiaõ Pombal curbed the power of the Inquisition in Portugal by decreeing that no auto da fé should take place without government approval. **1762** The Treaty of St Petersburg was signed between Russia and Prussia; Russia restored all territory taken and formed an alliance with Prussia. **1816** Carl August of Saxe-Weimar granted the first German constitution. **1863** In the American Civil War, Confederate troops defeated Federal forces at the Battle of Chancellorsville, but 'Stonewall' Jackson died of his wounds five days later. **1864** The indecisive Battle of the Wilderness was fought in Virginia, between Federal troops under Ulysses S Grant and Confederate troops under Robert E Lee. **1865** A revolt in San Domingo forced Spain to renounce sovereignty.

B
Godfrey of Bouillon, Norman crusader, first king of Jerusalem, **1061**; Gerardus Mercator (Gerhard Kremer), German cartographer, **1512**; Leopold III, Holy Roman Emperor, **1747**; George Borrow, English author, **1803**; Sören Kierkegaard, Danish philosopher, **1813**; Karl Marx, German philosopher and author, **1818**; Archibald, Lord Wavell, British soldier, **1883**.

D
Charles, Duke of Bourbon, **1527**; Edward Young, English poet, **1765**; Napoleon Bonaparte, French emperor, **1821**; Francis

Bret Harte, US author, **1902**.

6

Feast day of St Edbert, Saints Marian and James, St Evodius of Antioch, St Petronax, and St John Before the Latin Gate.

1527 The Sack of Rome, when imperialist troops under Charles, Duke of Bourbon (who was killed), mutinied, pillaging the city and killing some 4,000 of the inhabitants. Valuable art treasures were looted. Law was not restored until Feb 1528. **1576** The Fifth War of Religion in France ended; the Huguenots were granted freedom of worship in all places except Paris. **1626** Dutch settler Peter Minuit bought the island of Manhattan from native Americans for goods worth about $25. **1840** The Penny Black, the first postage stamp, was issued in Britain. **1882** Fenians murdered Irish chief secretary, Lord Frederick Cavendish, and T H Burke, Irish under-secretary, in Phoenix Park, Dublin. **1910** George V became king of the United Kingdom on the death of Edward VII. **1937** The German zeppelin *Hindenburg* caught fire in New Jersey, USA, killing 36 passengers.

B

Pope Marcellus II, **1501**; Pope Innocent X, **1574**; Thomas William Coke, Earl of Leicester, **1754**; André Massena, French soldier, **1756**; Maximilien François Robespierre, French revolutionary leader, **1758**; François Guillaume Andrieux **1759**; Sigmund Freud, Austrian psychoanalyst, **1856**; Robert Edwin Peary, US Arctic explorer, **1856**; Rabindranath Tagore, Indian poet and philosopher, **1861**.

D

Juan Luis Vives, Spanish philosopher, **1540**; Francesco Guicciardini, Italian historian, **1540**; Robert Cotton, English antiquary, **1631**; Cornelius Jansen, Dutch theologian, **1638**; Alexander von Humboldt, German explorer, **1859**; Henry David Thoreau, US poet, **1862**; Maurice Maeterlinck, Belgian playwright, **1949**; Marlene Dietrich, German-born singer and actress, **1992**.

7

Feast day of St John of Beverley, St Letard, St Domitian of Maestricht, and Saints Serenicus and Serenus.

1793 The second partition of Poland was effected, with Russia taking Lithuania and W Ukraine, and Prussia taking Danzig,

JAN FEB MAR APR MAY JUN JUL AUG SEP OCT NOV DEC
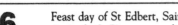

Thorn, Posen, Gnesen, and Kalisch. **1821** The Africa Company was dissolved because of heavy expenses incurred, and Sierra Leone, Gambia, and Gold Coast were taken over by the British government to form British West Africa. **1832** Greece became an independent kingdom. **1848** Polish rebels surrendered after Prussian troops put down an insurrection in Warsaw. **1915** German forces sank the liner Lusitania off the Irish coast, with the loss of 1,198 lives; the USA was brought to the verge of war with Germany. **1928** Women's suffrage in Britain was reduced from the age of 30 to 21. **1954** Dien Bien Phu fell to Communist Vietnamese. **1960** Leonid Brezhnev replaced Marshal Voroshilov as President of the USSR.

B

David Hume, Scottish philosopher and historian, **1711**; Robert Browning, English poet, **1812**; Johannes Brahms, German composer, **1833**; Peter Iljitch Tchaikovsky, Russian composer, **1840**; Archibald Philip Primrose, Lord Rosebery, British politician, **1847**; Gary Cooper, US film actor, **1901**.

D

Jacques de Thou, French historian and politician, **1617**; Mary of Modena, consort of James II, **1718**; Henry, Lord Brougham, British politician, **1868**; Paul Doumer, French president, assassinated, **1932**; George Lansbury, British politician, **1940**; James George Frazer, Scottish anthropologist, **1941**.

8

Feast day of St Indract, St Odger, St Victor, St Wiro, St Peter of Tarentaise, St Benedict II, pope, St Boniface IV, pope, St Gibrian, St Plechelm, St Desideratus of Bourges, and St Acacius.

1559 Queen Elizabeth I of England signed the Act of Uniformity. **1886** The Presidential Succession law was passed in the USA, providing for succession to presidency in the event of the deaths of both the President and the Vice-President. **1892** A ban was imposed on natives of the Congo, prohibiting them from collecting rubber and ivory other than for the state. **1902** On the Caribbean island of Martinique, the volcano Mount Pelée erupted, killing 30,000 people. **1950** Douglas MacArthur appointed commander of UN forces in Korea. **1958** J F Dulles stated in Berlin House of Representatives that an attack on Berlin would be regarded as an attack on the Allies.

B Peter Martyr (Pieto Martire Vermigli), Italian religious reformer, 1500; Phineas Fletcher, English poet, 1582; Francis Quarles, English poet, 1592; Claude de Villars, French soldier, 1653; Alain René Lesage, French novelist and playwright, 1668; Henry Baker, English naturalist, 1698; François Mignet, French historian, 1796; Ruggiero Leoncavallo, Italian composer, 1858; Harry S. Truman, 33rd president of the USA, 1884; David Attenborough, English naturalist and broadcaster, 1926.

D Palla Strozzi, founder of the first public library in Florence, 1462; Antoine Laurent Lavoisier, French chemist, guillotined, 1794; Vittorio Alfieri, Italian poet, 1803; John Stuart Mill, English philosopher, 1873; Gustave Flaubert, French novelist, 1880; Oswald Spengler, German philosopher, 1936; Henry Gordon Selfridge, US-born British store-owner, 1947; Emmanuel Shinwell, British politician, 1986.

9 Feast day of St Beatus of Lungern, St Gerontius of Cervia, St Beatus of Vendôme, and St Pachomius.

1386 The Treaty of Windsor, between kings Richard and John, made a perpetual alliance between England and Portugal. 1695 The Scottish Parliament met and enquired into the massacre of Glencoe. 1828 The British Test and Corporation Acts were repealed so that Catholic and Protestant Nonconformists could hold public office in Britain. 1939 British prime minister Winston Churchill urged military alliance with USSR. 1940 RAF began night bombing of Germany. 1940 Romania placed itself under German protection. 1945 Russian troops took Prague. 1946 Victor Emmanuel III of Italy abdicated and Umberto II proclaimed himself king.

B Giovanni Paisiello, Italian composer, 1741; Jean Sismondi, Swiss historian and economist, 1773; John Brown, US abolitionist, 1800; J M Barrie 1860; Howard Carter, British Egyptologist, 1873; Joan Sims, English actress, 1930; Alan Bennett, English actor and playwright, 1934; Glenda Jackson, English actress, 1936.

D James Lancaster, English navigator, 1618; William Bradford, English-born American colonist, 1657; Dietrich Buxtehude,

JAN FEB MAR APR **MAY** JUN JUL AUG SEP OCT NOV DEC

Danish organist and composer, **1707**; Louis-Joseph Gay-Lussac, French physicist and chemist, **1850**; Helena Blavatsky, Russian founder of the Theosophical Society, **1891**; Ethel Smyth, English composer and suffragette, **1944**.

10 Feast day of St Catald, St Conleth, Saints Gordian and Epimachus, St Antoninus, St Alphius, St Calepodius, St Cataldus, St Solange, and St John of Avila.

994 The Danes devastated Anglesey. **1804** Pitt returned to office. **1857** A revolt of Sepoys at Meerut began the Indian Mutiny against British rule. **1893** Natal was granted self-government. **1910** The British House of Commons resolved that the maximum lifetime of Parliament be reduced from seven to five years. **1916** Ernest Shackleton and companions reached South Georgia after sailing 1,300 km/800 mi in 16 days in an open boat to seek help for the remaining members of their party, marooned on Elephant Island, Antarctica. **1941** The House of Commons was destroyed in London's heaviest air raid.

B Sir John Sinclair, Scottish politician and agriculturalist, **1754**; Augustin Thierry, French historian, **1795**; James Bryce, British politician and diplomat, **1838**; Benito Pérez Galdós, Spanish novelist and playwright, **1845**; Karl Barth, Swiss theologian and author, **1886**; Fred Astaire, US dancer, **1899**; David O Selznick, US film producer, **1902**.

D Leonhard Fuchs, German physician and botanist, **1566**; Jean de la Bruyère, French writer, **1696**; Paul Revere, American hero, **1818**; Katsushuka Hokusai, Japanese artist, **1849**; Henry Morton Stanley, US journalist and explorer, **1904**; Joan Crawford, US film actress, **1977**.

11 Feast day of St Comgall, St Credan, St Maieul, St Tudy, St Ansfrid, St Walter of l'Esterp, St Richard Reynolds, St Francis di Girolamo, St Ignatius of Laconi, St Asaph, St Gengulf, and Mamertus.

973 Edgar crowned at Bath as King of all England; he then went to Chester, where eight Scottish and Welsh kings rowed him on the Dee. **1534** English King Henry VIII made peace with his nephew, James V of Scotland. **1709** The first mass emigration of Germans from the Palatinate to North America began. **1812** British prime minister Spencer Perceval was assassinated in House of Commons. **1824** British forces took Rangoon, Burma. **1949** Siam changed its name to Thailand. **1949** Israel was admitted to United Nations.

Hector Berlioz, French composer, **1803**; Chang and Eng, Chinese Siamese twins, **1811**; Irving Berlin, US composer, **1888**; Paul Nash, English painter, **1889**; Margaret Rutherford, English actress, **1892**; Mikhail Sholokhov, Russian novelist, **1905**.

'Abd-al-Mu'min, Almohad ruler of Muslim Spain and NW Africa, **1163**; Matteo Ricci, Jesuit missionary, **1610**; William Pitt, Earl of Chatham, British politician, **1778**; John Herschel, English astronomer, **1871**; William Dean Howells, US novelist and critic, **1920**; Kim Philby, English-born Soviet spy, **1988**.

12 Feast day of St Dominic of the Causeway, St John Stone, St Ethelhard, St Fremund, Saints Nereus and Achilleus, St Pancras of Rome, St Epiphanius of Salamis, St Germanus of Constantinople, St Modoaldus, and St Rictrudis.

1394 Malik Sarvar founded the Muslim kingdom of Jaunpur, on the middle Ganges. **1536** Sir Francis Weston, Mark Smeaton and other alleged lovers of Anne Boleyn are tried for treason; they were executed on the 17th. **1809** Arthur Wellesley defeats French under Soult at Oporto and forces them to retreat from Portugal. **1881** Tunisia became a French protectorate. **1949** Berlin blockade was officially lifted. **1961** United States of the Congo founded, with Léopoldville the federal capital. **1962** South African General Law Amendment bill imposed the death penalty for sabotage. **1965** West Germany established diplomatic relations with Israel; Arab states broke off relations with Bonn.

Claudio Monteverdi, Italian composer, **1567**; Augustus II of Poland and Elector of Saxony, **1670**; Joseph Nicolas Delisle, French astronomer, **1688**; John Bannister, English comedian, **1760**; Justus von Liebig, German chemist, **1803**; Florence Nightingale, English nursing pioneer, **1820**; Dante Gabriel Rossetti, English painter and poet, **1828**; Jules Massenet,

JAN FEB MAR APR MAY JUN JUL AUG SEP OCT NOV DEC

French composer, **1842**.

D George Chapman, English playwright, **1634**; Thomas Wentworth, Earl of Strafford, English politician, executed, **1641**; Bedřich Smetana, Czech composer, **1884**; Joris Karl Huysmans, French novelist, **1907**; Alfred, Lord Milner, British politician, **1925**; Arthur Quiller-Couch ('Q'), English writer, **1944**; Erich von Stroheim, Austrian-born US silent-film actor and director, **1957**; John Masefield, English poet, **1967**.

13 Feast day of St Andrew Hubert Fournet, St John the Silent, St Servatius, St Mucius, St Peter Regalatus, St Erconwald, St Euthymius the Enlightener, St Glyceria of Heraclia, and St Robert Bellarmine.

1203 Byzantine emperor Alexius Comnenus seized Trebizond and established a new Greek empire there. **1607** Riots took place in Northamptonshire and other Midland counties of England in protest at widespread enclosure of common land. **1643** Oliver Cromwell defeated Royalists at Grantham. **1846** Formal declaration of war by USA against Mexico. **1888** Serfdom was abolished in Brazil. **1915** The names of Emperors of Germany and Austria were struck off the roll of Knights of the Garter. **1927** 'Black Friday' with the collapse of Germany's economic system.

B Dante Alighieri, Italian poet, **1265**; Lazare Nicolas Marguerite Carnot, French revolutionary leader, **1753**; Pope Pius IX, **1792**; Alphonse Daudet, French novelist, **1840**; Arthur Sullivan, English composer, **1842**; Ronald Ross, British bacteriologist, **1857**; Daphne du Maurier, English novelist, **1907**; Joe Louis, US boxer, **1914**; Stevie Wonder, US singer, **1950**.

D Johan van Oldenbarneveldt, Dutch lawyer and politician, **1619**; Georges Cuvier, French zoologist, **1832**; John Nash, English architect, **1835**; Friedrich Henle, German anatomist, **1885**; Fridtjof Nansen, Norwegian Arctic explorer, **1930**; Gary Cooper, US film actor, **1961**.

14 Feast day of St Mary Mazzarello, St Pontius of Cimiez, St Carthage the Younger, St Erembert, St Matthias, St Gemma Galgani, and St Michael Garicoïts.

1080 Walcher, Bishop of Durham and Earl of Northumberland was murdered; William (the Conqueror) consequently ravaged the area; he also invaded Scotland and built the castle at Newcastle-upon-Tyne. **1264** The English barons under Simon de Montfort defeated Henry III at the Battle of Lewes. **1147** Conrad and the German crusaders departed from Regensburg. **1897** By treaty with Ethiopia Britain abandoned certain claims in Somaliland but Emperor Menelek refused to surrender his claims to lands near the Nile. **1921** 29 Fascists returned in Italian elections. **1946** Anti-Jewish pogrom in Kielce, Poland. **1948** As the British mandate in Palestine came to an end, a Jewish provisional government was formed in Israel with Chaim Weizmann as president and David Ben-Gurion as premier.

Marguérite de Valois, queen of Navarre, **1553**; Gabriel Daniel Fahrenheit, German physicist, the first to use mercury in thermometers, **1686**; Robert Owen, Welsh social reformer, **1771**; Squire Bancroft, English actor, **1841**; Hall Caine, English novelist, **1853**; Otto Klemperer, German conductor, **1885**; Hastings Banda, president of Malawi, **1905**.

Jean Grolier, French diplomat and bibliophile, **1565**; Henry IV of France, assassinated, **1610**; Daniel Auber, French composer, **1871**; August Strindberg, Swedish playwright, **1912**; Henry Rider Haggard, English novelist, **1925**; Jean Rhys, British novelist, **1979**.

15 Feast day of St Berchtun, St Dympna, St Pachomius, Saints Bertha and Rupert, St Isidore of Chios, St Gerebernus, St Hallvard, St Isias of Rostov, St Hilary of Galeata, St Peter of Lampsacus, St Isidore the Farmer, and St Torquatus and his Companions.

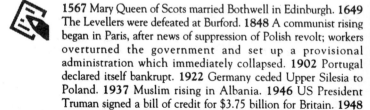

1567 Mary Queen of Scots married Bothwell in Edinburgh. **1649** The Levellers were defeated at Burford. **1848** A communist rising began in Paris, after news of suppression of Polish revolt; workers overturned the government and set up a provisional administration which immediately collapsed. **1902** Portugal declared itself bankrupt. **1922** Germany ceded Upper Silesia to Poland. **1937** Muslim rising in Albania. **1946** US President Truman signed a bill of credit for $3.75 billion for Britain. **1948** Egyptian troops intervened in Palestine on the side of the Arabs.

1957 Britain exploded the first British thermonuclear bomb in megaton range at Christmas Island, in the Central Pacific.

B Clemens Prince Metternich, Austrian politician, **1773**; Pierre Curie, French physicist, **1859**; Arthur Schnitzler, Austrian novelist and playwright, **1862**; James Mason, US film actor, **1909**; Ted Dexter, English cricketer, **1935**; Ralph Steadman, British cartoonist, **1936**.

D Ephraim Chambers, English encyclopedist, **1740**; Richard Wilson, Welsh landscape painter, **1782**; Daniel O'Connell, Irish leader, **1847**; Emily Dickinson, US poet, **1886**; Leslie Ward ('Spy'), English caricaturist, **1922**; Rita Hayworth, US film actress, **1987**.

16 Feast day of St Brendan the Navigator, St Carantoc, St Peregrine of Auxerre, St Simon Stock, St Domnolus of Le Mans, St Honoratus of Amiens, St Germerius, St John Nepomucen, St Possidius, and St Ubaldus of Gubbio.

1152 Henry II married Eleanor of Aquitaine. **1203** Baldwin, Count of Flanders, was crowned Latin Emperor of Constantinople. **1220** Henry II laid the foundation stone of a new Lady Chapel at Westminster Abbey, thus beginning the new abbey-church (1245). **1770** The Dauphin of France (later Louis XVI) married Marie Antoinette, daughter of the Empress Maria Theresa of Austria. **1804** Napoleon was declared Emperor. **1907** The Pact of Cartagena was declared between Britain, France, and Spain to counter German designs on the Balearic and Canary Islands. **1949** Chinese Nationalists organised a Supreme Council under Chiang Kai-shek, which began to remove forces to Formosa.

B Charles IV, Holy Roman Emperor, **1316**; John Sell Cotman, English watercolourist, **1782**; Maria Gaetana Agnesi, Italian scholar, **1718**; Claude Joseph Rouget de Lisle, French soldier who wrote the *Marseillaise*, **1760**; Henry Fonda, US film actor, **1905**; Roy Hudd, English comedian, **1936**.

D Héloise, French nun, **1164**; Peter the Lombard, Bishop of Paris, **1164**; Charles Perrault, French writer of fairy tales, **1703**; Edward Gibbon Wakefield, British colonial politician, **1862**; Edward Augustus Freeman, English historian, **1892**; Bronislaw

Malinowski, Polish anthropologist, 1942.

17 Feast day of St Madron, St Paschal Baylon, and St Bruno of Würzburg.

1215 The English barons in revolt against King John took possession of London. 1527 Archbishop Warham began a secret inquiry at Greenwich into Henry VIII's marriage with Catherine of Aragon, the first step in divorce proceedings. 1536 Archbishop Cranmer declared Henry VIII's marriage to Anne Boleyn invalid; she was executed on the 19th. 1742 Frederick II defeated the Austrians at Chotusitz. 1885 Germany annexed Northern New Guinea and the Bismarck Archipelago. 1900 The Relief of Mafeking by British troops against the besieging Boer forces. 1939 Sweden, Norway and Finland rejected Germany's offer of non-aggression pacts, but Denmark, Estonia and Latvia accepted. 1960 The Kariba Dam, Rhodesia, was opened.

B Maria Theresa, empress, 1717; Edward Jenner, English pioneer of vaccination, 1749; Timothy Healy, Irish nationalist leader, 1855; Erik Satie, French composer, 1866; Dennis Hopper, US film actor, Bhagwat Chandrasekhar, Indian cricketer, 1945; Sugar Ray Leonard, US boxer, 1956.

D Sandro Botticelli, Italian painter, 1510; Matthew Parker, archbishop of Canterbury, 1575; Samuel Clarke, English philosopher, 1729; Charles de Talleyrand-Périgord, French politician, 1838; Cass Gilbert, US architect, 1934.

18 Feast day of St Elgiva, St John I, pope, St Eric, king of Sweden, St Felix of Cantalicio, St Potamon, and Saints Theodotus and Thecusa.

1302 A French garrison was massacred in the 'Matins of Bruges', when the Flemings revolted against the French occupation. 1764 The British Parliament amended the Sugar Act from a commercial to a fiscal measure, to tax American colonists. 1878 Colombia granted a French company a nine-year concession to build the Panama Canal. 1900 Tonga became a British protectorate. 1936 An army revolt under Emilio Mola and Francisco Franco began the Spanish Civil

JAN FEB MAR APR **MAY** JUN JUL AUG SEP OCT NOV DEC

War. **1940** At Japan's request Britain prohibited the passage of war materials for China passing through Burma. **1944** Monte Cassino, Italy, was taken by Allied forces. **1980** Mount St Helens, USA, erupted for the first time since 1857, devastating an area of 600 sq km/230 sq mi.

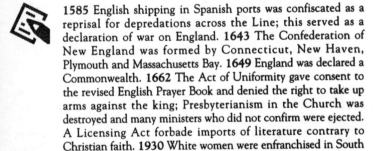

Pieter Breughel, Flemish painter, **1525**; George Gascoigne, English poet and playwright, **1525**; Charles, Cardinal of Lorraine, **1525**; John Stow, English historian, **1525**; Joseph Butler, English philosopher, **1692**; Bertrand Russell, English philosopher, **1872**; Walter Gropius, US architect, **1883**; Pierre Balmain, French fashion designer, **1914**.

Elias Ashmole, English antiquarian, **1692**; Pierre Augustin Caron de Beaumarchais, French playwright, **1799**; Johann Gottfried von Herder, German critic and poet, **1803**; George Meredith, English novelist, **1909**; Gustav Mahler, Austrian composer, **1911**; Paul Dukas, French composer, **1935**; Werner Sombart, German economist, **1941**.

19 Feast day of St Dunstan, St Pudentiana, St Peter Celestine, Saints Calocerus and Parthenius, St Ivo of Kermartin, St Crispin of Viterbo, and St Peter Morrone.

1585 English shipping in Spanish ports was confiscated as a reprisal for depredations across the Line; this served as a declaration of war on England. **1643** The Confederation of New England was formed by Connecticut, New Haven, Plymouth and Massachusetts Bay. **1649** England was declared a Commonwealth. **1662** The Act of Uniformity gave consent to the revised English Prayer Book and denied the right to take up arms against the king; Presbyterianism in the Church was destroyed and many ministers who did not confirm were ejected. A Licensing Act forbade imports of literature contrary to Christian faith. **1930** White women were enfranchised in South Africa. **1964** The USA complained to Moscow about microphones concealed in its Moscow embassy.

Johann Gottlieb Fichte, German philosopher, **1762**; Nellie Melba, Australian singer, **1861**; Ho Chi Minh, Vietnamese leader, **1890**; Max Perutz, Austrian-born British molecular biologist, **1914**; Sandy Wilson, British composer and playwright, 1924; Michael Balcon, English film producer, 1896.

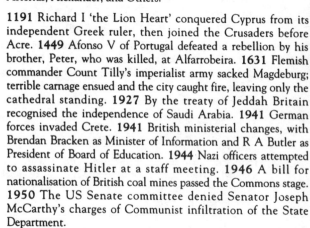

Alcuin of York, English poet, 804; James Boswell, Scottish biographer and diarist, 1795; Nathaniel Hawthorne, US novelist, 1864; William Ewart Gladstone, British politician, 1898; T E Lawrence, English soldier and writer, 1935; Charles Ives, US composer, 1954; Ogden Nash, US poet, 1971; John Betjeman, English poet, 1984.

20 Feast day of St Bernardino of Siena, St Ethelbert of East Anglia, St Basilla, St Austregisilus, St Baudelius, and Saints Thalelaeus, Asterius, Alexander, and Others.

1191 Richard I 'the Lion Heart' conquered Cyprus from its independent Greek ruler, then joined the Crusaders before Acre. 1449 Afonso V of Portugal defeated a rebellion by his brother, Peter, who was killed, at Alfarrobeira. 1631 Flemish commander Count Tilly's imperialist army sacked Magdeburg; terrible carnage ensued and the city caught fire, leaving only the cathedral standing. 1927 By the treaty of Jeddah Britain recognised the independence of Saudi Arabia. 1941 German forces invaded Crete. 1941 British ministerial changes, with Brendan Bracken as Minister of Information and R A Butler as President of Board of Education. 1944 Nazi officers attempted to assassinate Hitler at a staff meeting. 1946 A bill for nationalisation of British coal mines passed the Commons stage. 1950 The US Senate committee denied Senator Joseph McCarthy's charges of Communist infiltration of the State Department.

Donato d'Agnolo Bramante de Urbino, Italian architect, 1444; Sandro Botticelli, Italian painter, 1444; Honoré de Balzac, French novelist, 1799; Thomas Lovell Beddoes, English poet and physiologist, 1803; John Stuart Mill, English philosopher, 1806; James Stewart, US film actor, 1908; Moshe Dayan, Israeli military leader, 1915.

St Bernardino of Siena, 1444; Christopher Columbus, Genoese navigator, 1506; Caterina Sforza, Countess of Forli, 1509; Nicholas Brady, Anglican clergyman, 1726; John Clare, English poet, 1864; Clara Schumann, German pianist, 1896; Max Beerbohm, English writer and caricaturist, 1956; Barbara

Hepworth, English sculptor, **1975**.

21 Feast day of St Godric, St Collen, St Andrew Bobola, and St Theophilus of Corte.

1662 Charles II married Catherine de Braganza, daughter of John IV of Portugal. **1674** John Sobieski was elected King of Poland as John III. **1767** Townshend introduced taxes on imports of tea, glass, paper, and dyestuffs in American colonies to provide revenue for colonial administration. **1840** Britain claimed complete sovereignty over New Zealand. **1851** Gold was first discovered in Australia. **1894** The official opening of the Manchester Ship Canal tool place. **1946** A world wheat shortage led to bread rationing in Britain.

King Philip II of Spain, **1527**; Alexander Pope, English poet and satirist, **1688**; Francis Egerton, Duke of Bridgwater, builder of Britain's first canal, **1736**; Elizabeth Fry, English prison reformer, **1780**; Fats Waller, US jazz pianist and composer, **1904**; Harold Robbins, US novelist, **1916**.

King Henry VI of England, **1471**; Tomaso Campanella, Italian philosopher, **1639**; James, Marquess of Montrose, Scottish general, **1650**; Edward Montagu, Earl of Manchester, Parliamentarian leader in the English Civil War, **1671**; Robert Harley, Earl of Oxford, British politician, **1724**; Karl Wilhelm Scheele, Swedish chemist, **1786**; Geoffrey de Havilland, British aircraft designer, **1965**.

22 Feast day of St Helen of Carnavon, St Rita of Cascia, St Julia of Corsica, St Aigulf of Bourges, St Romanus, Saints Castus and Aemilius, St Humility, St Joachima de Mas, and St Quiteria.

853 A Greek expedition captured Damietta, in Egypt. **853** Olaf the White, son of the King of Norway, received the submission of Vikings and Danes in Ireland and made Dublin his capital. **1455** In the Wars of the Roses, Richard of York and the Nevilles attacked the court at St Albans, capturing Henry VI and killing Edmund Beaufort, Duke of Somerset. **1498** A death sentence was pronounced on Savonarola, former Prior of St Mark's and effective ruler of Florence, who had been excommunicated in June 1497 for attempting to seek the deposition of Pope Alexander VI. **1912** The Reichstag (German parliament) was adjourned following Socialist attacks on German emperor. **1914** Britain acquired control of oil properties in Persian Gulf from Anglo-Persian Oil Company. **1923** Stanley Baldwin formed a Conservative ministry, with Neville Chamberlain as Chancellor of Exchequer. **1972** US President Richard Nixon visited Moscow to discuss arms limitations with Soviet President Leonid Brezhnev.

Richard Wagner, German composer, **1813**; Aston Webb, English architect, **1849**; Arthur Conan Doyle, English novelist, **1859**; Laurence Olivier, English actor, **1907**; Charles Aznavour, French singer, **1924**; George Best, Irish footballer, **1946**.

Thomas Southerne, Irish playwright, **1746**; Augustin Thierry, French historian, **1856**; John French, Earl of Ypres, British soldier, **1925**; Ernst Toller, German poet and playwright, **1939**; Cecil Day Lewis, English poet, **1972**; Rajiv Gandhi, Indian leader, assassinated, **1991**.

23 Feast day of Saints Montanus and Lucius, St William of Rochester, St Aldhelm, St Euphrosyne of Polotsk, St Ivo of Chartres, St Leontius of Rostov, St Desiderius of Vienne, and St John Baptist dei Rossi.

878 The Saxon King Alfred defeated the Danes at Edington; under the peace of Wedmore, their leader, Guthrum, was baptised as a Christian. **1169** 'The First Conquerors' landed in Ireland; they were Normans from Wales enlisted by Dermot MacMurrough to recover his kingdom of Leinster. **1430** Burgundian troops captured Joan of Arc and delivered her to the English. **1568** William of Orange with German mercenaries defeated a Spanish force under Count Aremberg at Heiligerlee; this action marked the beginning proper of the Revolt of the Netherlands. **1618** The Defenestration of Prague, when the Regents, Martinitz and Slawata, were overthrown by the Bohemian rebels, began the Thirty Years' War. **1926** France proclaimed the Lebanon a republic.

Tamerlane the Great, Mongol leader, **1335**; Elias Ashmole, English antiquarian, **1617**; Carl von Linné (Linnaeus), Swedish botanist, **1707**; William Hunter, Scottish anatomist and obstetrician, **1718**; Friedrich Mesmer, Austrian physician, **1733**; Otto Lilienthal, German aviator, **1848**; Edmund Rubbra, English composer, **1901**; Hugh Casson, British architect, **1910**; Joan Collins, English actress, **1933**.

Richard of Wallingford, Abbot of St Albans, **1335**; Girolamo Savonarola, Florentine priest, burned at the stake, **1498**; William Kidd, Scottish pirate, hanged, **1701**; Leopold von Ranke, German historian, **1886**; Henrik Ibsen, Norwegian playwright, **1906**.

24 Feast day of St David of Scotland, St Vincent of Lerins, Saints Donatian and Rogation, and St Nicetas of Pereaslav.

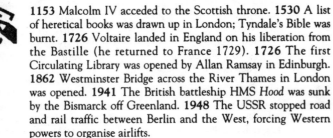

1153 Malcolm IV acceded to the Scottish throne. **1530** A list of heretical books was drawn up in London; Tyndale's Bible was burnt. **1726** Voltaire landed in England on his liberation from the Bastille (he returned to France **1729**). **1726** The first Circulating Library was opened by Allan Ramsay in Edinburgh. **1862** Westminster Bridge across the River Thames in London was opened. **1941** The British battleship HMS *Hood* was sunk by the Bismarck off Greenland. **1948** The USSR stopped road and rail traffic between Berlin and the West, forcing Western powers to organise airlifts.

King Philip III of France, **1245**; William Byrd, English composer, **1543**; William Gilbert, English physician and early researcher into magnetism, **1540**; Jean-Paul Marat, French revolutionary, **1743**; Queen Victoria, **1819**; Joseph Rowntree, social reformer and industrialist, **1836**; Arthur Wing Pinero, English playwright, **1855**; J C Smuts, South African soldier and politician, **1870**; Bob Dylan, US singer and songwriter, **1941**.

Nicolaus Copernicus, Polish astronomer, **1543**; Robert Cecil, Earl of Salisbury, English politician, **1612**; Jonathan Wild, English criminal, hanged, **1725**; John Dulles, US politician, **1959**; 'Duke' Ellington, US jazz composer and musician, **1974**; Hermione Gingold, English actress, **1987**.

25 Feast day of St Madeleine Barat, St Gregory VII, pope, St Mary Magdalen de Pazzi, St Urban, St Zenobius, St Leo of Mantenay,

St Dionysius of Milan, St Gennadius of Astorga, and St Bede.

1234 The Mongols took Kaifeng and destroyed the Chin dynasty. **1524** Henry VIII and Charles V formed a new league to support the Duke of Bourbon in a fresh attack on France. **1657** New Humble Petition and Advice created a new House of Lords, and increased Cromwell's power. **1657** Louis XIV put forward his name as a candidate for the Holy Roman Empire. **1659** Richard Cromwell resigned; the Rump Parliament re-established the Commonwealth. **1694** The ministry in England was remodelled when William III dismissed Tories, except Godolphin and Danby, and introduced Whig Junta of Somers, Russell, Montague, and Wharton. **1911** Porfirio Diaz resigned as president of Mexico. **1914** The British House of Commons passed the Irish Home Rule bill. **1923** The independence of Transjordan under Amir Abdullah was proclaimed. **1953** Denationalisation of road transport in Britain. **1961** US President Kennedy presents an extra-ordinary state of Union message to Congress for increased funds urgently needed for US space, defence, and air programmes.

John Stuart, Earl of Bute, Britain's first Scottish prime minister, 1713; Edward George Bulwer Lytton, Lord Lytton, English novelist, 1803; Ralph Waldo Emerson, US poet and essayist, 1803; Jacob Burckhardt Swiss historian, 1818; Béla Bartók, Hungarian composer, 1881; Josip Broz Tito, Yugoslavian soldier and president, 1892; Miles Davis, US jazz trumpeter, 1926; Ian McKellen, English actor, 1939.

Bede, English monk and historian, 735; Georges D'Amboise, French cardinal and politician, 1510; Gaspard Poussin, French painter, 1675; Pedro Calderón de la Barca, Spanish playwright, 1681; Samuel Pepys, English diarist, 1703; Gustav Holst, English composer, 1934.

26 Feast day of St Priscus, St Augustine of Canterbury, St Philip Neri, St Lambert of Venice, St Quadratus of Athens, and St Mariana of Quito.

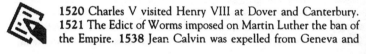

1520 Charles V visited Henry VIII at Dover and Canterbury. **1521** The Edict of Worms imposed on Martin Luther the ban of the Empire. **1538** Jean Calvin was expelled from Geneva and settled in Strasbourg. **1659** Aurangzeb formally becomes Mogul Emperor. **1798** Income tax was introduced in Britain, as a tax of 10% on all incomes over £200. **1805** Napoleon was crowned King of Italy in Milan Cathedral. **1834** Sikhs captured Peshawar. **1846** Robert Peel repealed the Corn Laws (royal assent given 26 June), splitting the Conservative Party. **1865** The surrender of the last Confederate army at Shreveport, near New Orleans, ended the American Civil War. **1924** Calvin Coolidge signed a bill limiting immigration into the USA and entirely excluding the Japanese.

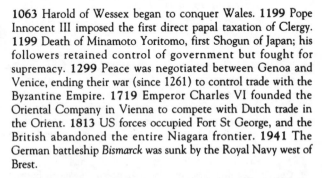

Charles of Orleans, French poet, **1391**; Henry Vane the younger, English politician, **1613**; William Petty, English economist, **1623**; Lady Mary Wortley Montagu, English writer, **1689**; Edmond de Goncourt, French novelist, **1822**; A E Housman, English poet, **1859**; Princess Mary of Teck (Queen Mary, consort of George V), **1867**; Al Jolson, US singer, **1886**; John Wayne, US film actor, **1907**; Peter Cushing, British actor, **1913**.

St Augustine, first archbishop of Canterbury, **604**; Philip Neri, Italian priest, founder of the Oratory, **1595**; Charles Mayo, US surgeon, **1922**; Victor Herbert, US composer and conductor, **1924**; Lincoln Ellsworth, US scientist and polar explorer, **1951**.

27 Feast day of St Julius the Veteran, St Eutropius of Orange, St Restituta of Sora, and St Melangel.

1063 Harold of Wessex began to conquer Wales. **1199** Pope Innocent III imposed the first direct papal taxation of Clergy. **1199** Death of Minamoto Yoritomo, first Shogun of Japan; his followers retained control of government but fought for supremacy. **1299** Peace was negotiated between Genoa and Venice, ending their war (since 1261) to control trade with the Byzantine Empire. **1719** Emperor Charles VI founded the Oriental Company in Vienna to compete with Dutch trade in the Orient. **1813** US forces occupied Fort St George, and the British abandoned the entire Niagara frontier. **1941** The German battleship *Bismarck* was sunk by the Royal Navy west of Brest.

Amelia Bloomer, US feminist and dress reformer, **1818**; Julia

Ward Howe, US writer, **1819**; Vincent D'Indy, French composer, **1851**; Arnold Bennett, English novelist, **1867**; John Cockcroft, English physicist, **1897**; Hubert Humphrey, US politician, **1911**; Vincent Price, US film actor, **1911**; Henry Kissinger, US politician, **1923**.

John Calvin, French religious reformer, **1564**; Archibald Campbell, Marquess of Argyll, Scottish Covenanter, beheaded, **1661**; Marquise de Montespan, mistress of the French King Louis XIV, **1707**; Niccolò Paganini, Italian violinist, **1840**; Robert Koch, German bacteriologist, **1910**; Jawalharlal Nehru, Indian politician, **1964**.

28

Feast day of St Bernard of Aosta, St Ignatius of Rostov, St Senator of Milan, St William of Gellone, St Germanus of Paris, and St Justus of Urgel.

1358 In France the uprising known as the Jacquerie broke out - the peasants were protesting at their impoverished state after the ravages of the Hundred Years' War. **1539** Royal assent was given to an Act (the Six Articles of Religion) 'abolishing diversity of opinions' in England, after Henry VIII personally intervened in the Lords' debate to argue with the Reforming bishops. **1932** The IJselmeer was formed in the Netherlands, by the completion of a dam which enclosed the former Zuider Zee. **1956** France ceded former French settlements in India to the Indian Union. **1959** Britain announced the removal of controls on imports of many consumer goods from the dollar area, with increased import quotas of other goods. **1961** The last journey of the 'Orient Express' train, from Paris to Bucharest; it had been in operation for 78 years.

King George I of Great Britain, **1660**; Joseph Guillotin, French physician and revolutionary, **1738**; William Pitt, British politician, **1759**; Thomas Moore, Irish poet, **1779**; Prosper Mérimée, French novelist, **1803**; F W Maitland, English historian, **1850**; Ian Fleming, English novelist, **1908**; Thora Hird, English actress, **1916**; Dietrich Fischer-Dieskau, German baritone, **1925**.

Lanfranc, Archbishop of Canterbury, **1089**; Edward Montagu, Earl of Sandwich, English admiral, **1672**; Thomas Chippendale,

English cabinet-maker, 1779; Jean Louis Rodolphe Agassiz, Swiss oceanographer and marine zoologist, 1807; Noah Webster, US lexicographer, 1843; Henry Thomas Buckle, English historian, 1862; Lord John Russell, Earl Russell, British politician, 1878; Alfred Adler, Austrian psychiatrist, 1937.

29

Feast day of St Cyril of Caesarea, St Bernard of Montjoux, St Theodosia of Constantinople, St Maximinus of Trier, Saints Sisinnius, Martyrius, and Alexander, and Saints William, Stephen, Raymund, and their Companions.

862 Riurick (of Jutland) founded the first dynasty of Princes of Russia at Novgorod. 1218 The Fifth Crusade landed outside Damietta, N Egypt. 1453 Mohammed II, founder of the Ottoman empire, captured Constantinople; the Byzantine Emperor Constantine XI was killed and the Greek Empire finally extinguished. Constantinople became the Ottoman capital. 1458 Richard Neville, Earl of Warwick, defeated a Castilian fleet in the Channel. 1848 Wisconsin became a US state. 1940 The first British forces were evacuated from Dunkirk. 1947 The Indian constituent assembly outlawed 'untouchability'.

King Charles II of Great Britain, 1630; Louis Jean Marie Daubenton, French naturalist, 1716; Patrick Henry, US politician, 1736; Léon Bourgeois, French politician, 1851; Gilbert Keith Chesterton, English novelist and critic, 1874; Bob Hope, US actor and comedian, 1903; John Fitzgerald Kennedy, 35th president of the USA, 1917.

Bartholomew Diaz de Novaes, Portuguese navigator, 1500; David Beaton, Scottish politician, 1546; Cornelius Van Tromp, Dutch sailor, 1691; Humphry Davy, English scientist who invented a safety lamp for miners, 1829; John Lothrop Motley, US historian and diplomat, 1877; W S Gilbert, English playwright and librettist, 1911.

30

Feast day of St Hubert, St Joan of Arc, St Ferdinand, St Exuperiantius of Ravenna, St Isaac of Constantinople, St Luke Kirby, St Madelgisilus, and St Walstan.

1431 Joan of Arc was burnt as a heretic at Rouen, France. 1536

English King Henry VIII married Jane Seymour, his third wife. 1592 The Spanish defeated an English force under Sir John Norris at Cranon, Brittany. 1913 A peace treaty between Turkey and the Balkan states was signed in London. 1925 The shooting of Chinese students by municipal police in Shanghai and other incidents in Canton provoked a Chinese boycott of British goods. 1929 The British Labour Party won the general election with 287 seats. 1948 The British Citizenship Act conferred the status of British subjects on all Commonwealth citizens.

Peter the Great, tsar of Russia, 1672; Henry Addington, British politician, 1757; Peter Carl Fabergé, Russian goldsmith and jeweller, 1846; Howard Hawks, US film director, 1896; Benny Goodman, US bandleader, 1909.

Christopher Marlowe, English playwright, 1593; Peter Paul Rubens, Flemish painter, 1640; Alexander Pope, English poet and satirist, 1744; François Boucher, French painter, 1770; Voltaire, French author and philosopher, 1778; Boris Pasternak, Russian novelist and poet, 1960; Claude Rains, British-born film actor, 1967.

31 Feast day of St Petronilla, Saints Cantius, Cantianus, Cantianella, and Protus, and St Mechtildi of Edelstetten.

1287 The Genoese defeated the Venetian fleet off Acre and blockaded the coast of Outremer. 1902 The Peace of Vereeniging ended the Boer War, in which British casualties numbered 5,774 killed (and 16,000 deaths from disease) against 4,000 Boers killed in action. 1916 The Battle of Jutland began, in which Royal Navy losses exceeded those of the German fleet. 1942 Czech patriots assassinated Gestapo leader Heydrich. 1952 In the USSR, the Volga–Don Canal was opened. 1961 South Africa became an independent republic outside the Commonwealth, with C R Swart as president.

Margaret Beaufort, consort of Henry VII of England, 1443; Matthias Corvinus, king of Hungary, 1443; Rudolphus Agricola, Dutch humanist, 1443; Guilio Alberoni, Italian cardinal and politician, 1664; Karl August von Hardenberg, Prussian politician, 1750; Walt Whitman, US poet, 1819;

Francis Younghusband, English explorer, **1863**; William Heath Robinson, English illustrator, **1872**; Don Ameche, US film actor, **1908**; Clint Eastwood, US film actor and director, **1930**; Terry Waite, religious adviser to the Archbishop of Canterbury, **1939**.

Jacopo Tintoretto, Italian painter, **1594**; Frederick William I of Prussia, **1740**; Jean Cavalier, French Huguenot preacher and leader, **1740**; Joseph Haydn, Austrian composer, **1809**; Joseph Grimaldi, English clown, **1837**; Walther Funk, German Nazi economist, **1960**; Adolf Eichmann, Nazi leader, hanged as a war criminal, **1962**.

JUNE

1

National Day of Tunisia. Feast day of St Gwen of Brittany, St Justin, St Nicomedes, St Ronan, St Whyte, St Wistan, St Symeon of Syracuse, St Caprasius of Lérins, St Pamphilus of Caesarea, St Inigo, St Proculus the Soldier, St Proculus the Bishop, and St Theobald of Alba.

836 Viking raiders sacked London. **1485** Matthias of Hungary took Vienna in his conquest of Austria (from Frederick III) and made the city his capital. **1666** An English fleet under Lord Albemarle fought an inconclusive battle with the Dutch off the Dunes of Dunkirk. **1679** The Scottish Covenanters defeated Royal troops under Claverhouse at Drumclog. **1792** Kentucky became the 15th US state. **1796** Tennessee became the 16th US state. **1915** The first Zeppelin attack on London took place. **1946** Television licences were issued in Britain for the first time; they cost £2. **1957** ERNIE drew the first premium bond prizes in Britain. **1958** Iceland extended its fishery limits to 12 miles.

Nicolas Carnot, French founder of thermodynamics, **1796**; Brigham Young, US Mormon leader, **1801**; Mikhail Glinka, Russian composer, **1803**; John Drinkwater, English poet, **1882**; Frank Whittle, English inventor who developed the jet engine, **1907**; Marilyn Monroe, **1926**; Morgan Freeman, US film actor, **1937**.

James Gillray, English caricaturist, **1815**; James Buchanan, 15th president of the USA, **1868**; Hugh Walpole, English novelist, **1941**; Leslie Howard, British film actor, **1943**; Ion Antonescu, Romanian dictator, executed, **1946**; Eric Partridge, British lexicographer, **1985**.

2 National Day of Italy. Feast day of St Erasmus, St Oda, St Attalus, Saints Marcellinus and Peter, St Eugenius I, pope, St Nicholas the Pilgrim, St Stephen of Sweden, and St Pothinus and his Companions.

1619 A treaty was signed between England and Holland, regulating the trade in the East between the English and Dutch East India Companies. **1627** Charles I granted a charter of incorporation to the Guiana Company. **1627** The Duke of Buckingham sailed from Portsmouth with a fleet to aid the Huguenots in the defence of La Rochelle. **1780** The Gordon riots began in London, when Lord George Gordon headed a procession for presenting a petition to Parliament for repealing Catholic Relief act of 1778; Roman Catholic chapels were pillaged. **1793** The final overthrow of Girondins and arrest of Jacques Brissot began the Reign of Terror. **1916** The second battle of Ypres took place. **1949** Transjordan was renamed the Hashemite Kingdom of Jordan. **1953** The coronation of Queen Elizabeth II took place in Westminster Abbey.

B John Sobieski, King of Poland, **1624**; Thomas Hardy, English novelist and poet, **1840**; Edward Elgar, English composer, **1857**; Julian Huxley, English biologist, **1887**; Johnny Weissmuller, US swimmer who played Tarzan in films, **1903**; Barry Levinson, US film director, **1942**.

D James Douglas, Earl of Morton, **1581**; Giuseppe Garibaldi, Italian nationalist, **1882**; Alexander Ostrovsky, Russian playwright, **1886**; Alfred Austin, English poet, **1913**; Vita Sackville-West, English writer, **1962**; Andrés Segovia, Spanish classical guitarist, **1987**; Rex Harrison, British actor, **1990**.

3 Feast day of Genesius of Clermont, St Kevin, St Charles Lwanga, St Isaac of Cordova, St Morand, St Cecilius, St Clothilde, St Joseph Mkasa, St Lucillian and his Companions, Saints Liphardus and Urbicius, and Saints Pergentinus and Laurentinus.

1098 The Crusaders took Antioch. 1162 Thomas à Becket was consecrated as Archbishop of Canterbury. 1665 The English fleet defeated the Dutch at the Battle of Lowestoft. 1942 US and Japanese naval forces began the Battle of Midway, in the Pacific. 1946 King Umberto II left Italy and Alcide de Gasperi, the premier, became provisional head of state. 1959 Singapore became self-governing.

William Dampier, English navigator and adventurer, 1652; James Hutton, Scottish geologist, 1726; Sydney Smith, English clergyman and journalist, 1771; Richard Cobden, English economist and political reformer, 1804; William Flinders Petrie, English archaeologist, 1853; George V, 1865; Wilfrid Thesiger, English explorer and writer, 1910.

John Aylmer, bishop of London, 1594; William Harvey, English physician who described the circulation of the blood, 1657; Georges Bizet, French composer, 1875; Johann Strauss, Austrian composer, 1899; Franz Kafka, Austrian novelist, 1924; Mikhail Ivanovich Kalinin, Russian politician, 1946; Arthur Ransome, English children's writer, 1967.

4

Feast day of St Edfrith, St Ninnoc, St Petroc, St Metrophanes, St Francis Caracciolo, St Optatus of Milevis, St Quirinus of Siscia, and St Vincentia Gerosa.

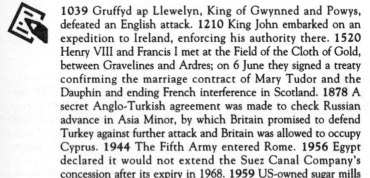

1039 Gruffyd ap Llewelyn, King of Gwynned and Powys, defeated an English attack. 1210 King John embarked on an expedition to Ireland, enforcing his authority there. 1520 Henry VIII and Francis I met at the Field of the Cloth of Gold, between Gravelines and Ardres; on 6 June they signed a treaty confirming the marriage contract of Mary Tudor and the Dauphin and ending French interference in Scotland. 1878 A secret Anglo-Turkish agreement was made to check Russian advance in Asia Minor, by which Britain promised to defend Turkey against further attack and Britain was allowed to occupy Cyprus. 1944 The Fifth Army entered Rome. 1956 Egypt declared it would not extend the Suez Canal Company's concession after its expiry in 1968. 1959 US-owned sugar mills and plantations in Cuba were expropriated.

François Quesnay, French economist and physician, 1694;

George III, 1738; John Scott, later Earl of Eldon, English lawyer and politician, 1751; Harriet Beecher Stowe, US novelist, 1811; Garnet Wolseley, English soldier, 1833; Christopher Cockerell, English engineer who invented the hovercraft, 1910.

William Juxon, archbishop of Canterbury, 1663; Giovanni Casanova, Italian adventurer, 1798; Nassau William Senior, English economist, 1864; Kaiser William II, 1941; Emily Davidson, English suffragette who threw herself in front of the King's horse during the Derby, 1913.

5

National Day of Denmark. Feast Day of St Boniface, St Dorotheus of Tyre, St Tudno, and St Sanctius.

1912 US marines landed in Cuba. 1916 HMS *Hampshire* sank off the Orkneys, with Lord Kitchener aboard. 1945 The Allied Control Commission assumed control throughout Germany, which was divided into four occupation zones. 1947 US Secretary of State George Marshall called for a European Recovery Programme (Marshall Aid). 1967 The Six-Day War broke out between Israel and the Arab states. 1970 Tonga became independent within the Commonwealth. 1975 The Suez Canal was reopened after being closed for eight years.

Nicolas Poussin, French painter, 1594; Adam Smith, Scottish economist, 1723; Pancho Villa, Mexican revolutionary, 1878; John Maynard Keynes, English economist, 1883; Federico García Lorca, Spanish playwright and poet, 1898; Margaret Drabble, English novelist, 1939; David Hare, British playwright, 1947.

Orlando Gibbons, English organist and composer, 1625; Henry Sacheverell, English political preacher, 1724; Carl von Weber, German composer, 1826; Stephen Crane, US poet and novelist, 1900; Horatio, Lord Kitchener, English soldier, 1916; Henri Gaudier-Brzeska, French artist, 1916; Georges Feydeau, French dramatist, 1921.

6

National Day of Sweden. Feast Day of St Jarlath, St Gudwal, St Ceratius, St Norbert, Saints Primus and Felician, St Claude of Besançon, St Eustorgius II of Milan, and St Philip the Deacon.

JAN FEB MAR APR MAY JUN JUL AUG SEP OCT NOV DEC

1457 Polish forces took Marienburg; the Teutonic Knights then made Königsberg their headquarters. 1636 Puritan American colonist Roger Williams, banished from Massachusetts Bay Colony, founded Providence, Rhode Island, a colony with complete religious freedom. 1664 War broke out between England and Holland in the colonies and at sea. 1797 Napoleon Bonaparte founded the Ligurian Republic in Genoa. 1820 Caroline, Princess of Wales, whom George IV wished to divorce, triumphantly entered London, demanding her recognition as Queen. 1844 The Factory Act in Britain restricted female workers to a 12-hour day; children between eight and 13 years were limited to six-and-a-half hours.

B

Diego y Velasquez, Spanish painter, 1599; Pierre Corneille, French playwright, 1606; Henry Newbolt, English poet, 1862; Robert Falcon Scott, English Antarctic explorer, 1868; Thomas Mann, German novelist, 1875; Ninette de Valois, Irish ballet dancer, 1898; Björn Borg, Swedish tennis player, 1956; Mike Gatting, English cricketer, 1958.

D

St. Norbert of Xanten, archbishop of Magdeburg, 1134; George Anson, English sailor and explorer, 1762; Jeremy Bentham, English philosopher and jurist, 1832; James Agate, English critic and essayist, 1947; Carl Gustav Jung, Swiss psychiatrist, 1961; Robert Kennedy, US politician, assassinated, 1968.

7

Feast day of St Meriasek, St Robert of Newminster, St Anthony Gianelli, St Gottschalk, St Vulflagius, St Willibald, St Colman of Dromore, and St Paul I of Constantinople.

1494 By the Treaty of Tordesillas, Spain and Portugal agreed to divide the New World between themselves: Portugal was to have all lands east of a line north and south drawn 370 leagues west of Cape Verde, Spain to have the rest. 1497 English King Henry VII defeats the Cornish rebels under Lord Audley at Blackheath. 1523 Gustavus Vasa was elected Gustavus I of Sweden. 1535 John Fisher, Bishop of Rochester, is tried for treason (he was executed on 22 June). 1672 Dutch Admiral de Ruyter was successful in action against the combined English and French fleets in Southwold Bay. 1832 The Reform Bill became law; over 140 seats were redistributed, and in the boroughs all antiquated forms of franchise were eliminated and the franchise was extended to include leaseholders paying minimum of £10 rent per annum, while in counties the 40-shilling freehold qualification was retained and certain leaseholders acquired the vote.

B John Rennie, Scottish engineer, 1761; Alexander Pushkin, Russian novelist, playwright, and poet, 1799; James Young Simpson, Scottish obstetrician who pioneered the use of anaesthetics, 1811; Pietro Annigoni, Italian painter, 1910; Paul Gauguin, French painter, 1848; James Ivory, US film director, 1928.

D Robert I 'the Bruce', king of Scotland, 1329; David Cox, English painter, 1859; Jean Harlow, US film actress, 1937; Dorothy Parker, US writer, 1967; E M Forster, English novelist, 1970; Henry Miller, US novelist, 1980.

---

8 Feast day of St Medard, St William of York, St Cloud of Metz, and St Maximinius of Aix.

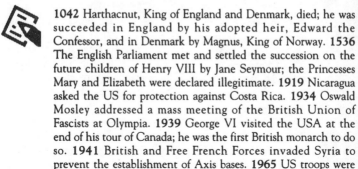 1042 Harthacnut, King of England and Denmark, died; he was succeeded in England by his adopted heir, Edward the Confessor, and in Denmark by Magnus, King of Norway. 1536 The English Parliament met and settled the succession on the future children of Henry VIII by Jane Seymour; the Princesses Mary and Elizabeth were declared illegitimate. 1919 Nicaragua asked the US for protection against Costa Rica. 1934 Oswald Mosley addressed a mass meeting of the British Union of Fascists at Olympia. 1939 George VI visited the USA at the end of his tour of Canada; he was the first British monarch to do so. 1941 British and Free French Forces invaded Syria to prevent the establishment of Axis bases. 1965 US troops were authorised to engage in offensive operations in Vietnam.

B Giovanni Cassini, Italian astronomer, 1625; John Smeaton, English engineer, 1724; Robert Stevenson, English engineer, 1772; Robert Schumann, German composer, 1810; John Everett Millais, English painter, 1829; Frank Lloyd Wright, US architect, 1869.

D Christiaan Huygens, Dutch physicist and astronomer, 1695; Thomas Paine, English author of The Rights of Man, 1809; Sarah Siddons, English actress, 1831; Joseph Paxton, English architect, **1865**; 'George Sand' (Amandine Dudevant, born Dupin), French novelist, **1876**; Gerard Manley Hopkins, English poet, **1889**; Gerhart Hauptmann, German novelist and playwright, **1946**.

9

Feast day of St Columba, St Ephraem, St Richard of Ambria, St Vincent of Agen, and St Pelagia of Antioch.

1572 A new Turkish fleet put to sea against Don John of Austria to complete the capture of Cyprus. **1788** English botanist Joseph Banks founded the Africa Association for arousing interest in exploration and trade. **1885** The Treaty of Tientsin between France and China recognised the French protectorate in Annam. **1934** Cartoon character Donald Duck first appeared. **1959** The USS *George Washington* was launched, the first submarine to be armed with ballistic missiles.

Peter the Great, tsar of Russia, **1672**; George Stephenson, English locomotive engineer, **1781**; Elizabeth Garrett Anderson, English physician, **1836**; Cole Porter, US composer of musicals, **1893**.

William Maitland of Lethingdon, Scottish politician, **1573**; William Lilly, English astrologer, **1681**; Charles Dickens, English novelist, **1870**; Cochise, American Apache leader, **1874**; Maxwell William Aitken, Lord Beaverbrook, Canadian-born politician and newspaper proprietor, **1964**; Sybil Thorndike, English actress, **1976**.

10

Feast day of St Ithamar, St Bogumilus, St Landericus of Paris, and St Getulius and his Companions.

1829 The Oxford team won the first-ever Oxford and Cambridge Boat Race. **1891** L. Starr Jameson became administrator of the South Africa Company's territories. **1893** Alarmed at Belgian advances in the Congo, France sent an occupying force to forestall further annexations. **1899** US Congress appointed a canal commission to report on routes through Panama. **1942** The Czech village of Lidice was destroyed and every man in it killed in reprisal for the assassination of Nazi leader Richard Heydrich. **1943** The ball-point pen was patented in the USA.

James Francis Edward Stuart (the Old Pretender), **1688**; John

Dollond, English optician, **1706**; Gustave Courbet, French painter, **1819**; Henry Morton Stanley, US journalist and explorer, **1840**; G E Buckle, English newspaper editor, **1854**; Saul Bellow, US novelist, **1915**; Prince Philip, Duke of Edinburgh, **1921**; Judy Garland, US film actress and singer, **1922**; Maurice Sendak, US illustrator, **1928**.

Luis Vaz de Camoens, Portuguese poet, **1580**; Alessandro Algardi, Italian sculptor, **1654**; Thomas Hearne, English antiquary and keeper of the Bodleian Library, **1735**; Andrée Ampère, French physicist, **1836**; 'Pierre Loti' (Julien Viaud), French novelist, **1923**; Frederick Delius, English composer, **1934**; Spencer Tracey, US film actor, **1967**.

11 Feast day of St Barnabas, Saints Felix and Fortunatus, and St Parisio.

1509 Henry VIII marries Catherine of Aragon, his first wife. **1727** George I became king of Great Britain. **1891** At an Anglo-Portuguese convention on territories north and south of Zambesi, Portugal assigns Barotseland to Britain; Nyasaland is subsequently proclaimed a British Protectorate. **1895** Britain annexed Togoland to block Transvaal's access to the sea. **1955** US President Eisenhower proposed financial and technical aid to all non-Communist countries to develop atomic energy. **1963** Constantine Karamanlis, the Greek premier, resigned in protest against King Paul's state visit to Britain. **1964** Greece rejected direct talks with Turkey over Cyprus.

Barnabe Googe, English poet, **1540**; Ben Jonson, English playwright, **1572**; John Constable, English painter, **1776**; Millicent Garrett Fawcett, English suffragette, **1847**; Mrs. Humphrey Ward (Mary Augusta Arnold), English novelist, **1851**; Jacques Cousteau, French oceanographer, **1910**; Athol Fugard, South African dramatist and director, **1932**.

Kenelm Digby, English writer and diplomat, **1665**; Louis, Duc de Vendôme, French soldier, **1712**; John Franklin, English Arctic explorer, **1847**; Clemens, Prince Metternich, Austrian politician, **1859**; Frank Brangwyn, British painter, **1956**; Alexander Kerensky, Russian politician, **1970**; John Wayne, US film actor, **1979**.

JAN FEB MAR APR MAY JUN JUL AUG SEP OCT NOV DEC

12 National Day of the Philippines. Feast day of St Basilides, St Eskil, St Leo II, St Odulf, St Onuphrius, St Ternan, St Peter of Mount Athos, St Antonia, St John of Sahagun, and St Paula Frassinetti.

 1088 William II suppressed a revolt in England led by Odo of Bayeux, Bishop of Rochester, who was supporting Robert Curthose. 1667 The Dutch fleet under Admiral de Ruyter burned Sheerness, sailed up the River Medway, raided Chatham dockyard, and escaped with the royal barge, the *Royal Charles*; the nadir of English naval power. 1683 The Rye House Plot, to assassinate King Charles II and his brother James, Duke of York, was discovered. 1901 A Cuban convention making the country virtually a protectorate of the US was incorporated in the Cuban constitution as a condition of the withdrawal of US troops. 1934 Political parties banned in Bulgaria. 1964 Nelson Mandela and seven others were sentenced to life imprisonment for acts of sabotage in the Rivonia trial, Pretoria.

B Harriet Martineau, English writer, 1802; Charles Kingsley, English novelist, 1819; Anthony Eden, Viscount Avon, British politician, 1897; George Bush, 41st president of the USA, 1924; Anne Frank, Jewish Dutch diarist, 1929.

D James, Duke of Berwick, English-born French general, 1734; William Collins, English poet, 1759; Thomas Arnold, English scholar and head of Rugby School, 1842; John Ireland, English composer, 1962; Billy Butlin, English holiday-camp entrepreneur, 1980; Marie Rambert, British ballet dancer and teacher, 1982.

13 Feast day of St Antony of Padua, St Felicula, St Aquilina, and St Triphyllius.

 1849 Communist riots in Paris were easily defeated and led to repressive legislation. 1866 The US 14th Amendment incorporated the Civil Rights Act and gave states the choice of Negro enfranchisement or reduced representation in Congress. 1900 The Boxer Rebellion began in China against Europeans. 1942 British forces lost 230 tanks in desert fighting. 1944 The first flying bomb was dropped on London. 1956 The last British troops left the Suez Canal base. 1961 Austria refused an application by Archduke Otto of Habsburg to return as a private individual.

Richard Barnfield, English poet, 1574; Thomas Arnold, English scholar, head of Rugby school, 1795; James Clerk Maxwell, Scottish physicist, 1831; William Butler Yeats, Irish poet, 1865; Peter Scudamore, British jockey, 1958.

Alexander the Great, 323 BC; St Antonio of Padua, 1231; Arcangelo Corelli, Italian composer, 1713; Henry Seagrave, British racing driver, 1930; Jesse Boot, English pharmacist, drug manufacturer, and philanthropist, 1931; Benny Goodman, US bandleader, 1986.

14 Feast day of St Dogmael, Saints Valerius and Rufinus, and St Methodius I of Constantinople.

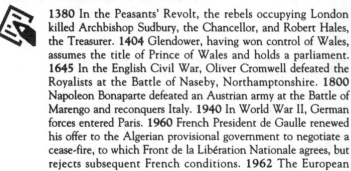

1380 In the Peasants' Revolt, the rebels occupying London killed Archbishop Sudbury, the Chancellor, and Robert Hales, the Treasurer. 1404 Glendower, having won control of Wales, assumes the title of Prince of Wales and holds a parliament. 1645 In the English Civil War, Oliver Cromwell defeated the Royalists at the Battle of Naseby, Northamptonshire. 1800 Napoleon Bonaparte defeated an Austrian army at the Battle of Marengo and reconquers Italy. 1940 In World War II, German forces entered Paris. 1960 French President de Gaulle renewed his offer to the Algerian provisional government to negotiate a cease-fire, to which Front de la Libération Nationale agrees, but rejects subsequent French conditions. 1962 The European Space Research Organisation was established at Paris.

Charles Augustin Coulomb, French physicist, 1736; Henry Keppel, British admiral, 1809; Bernard Bosanquet, English philosopher, 1848; Che Guevara, Argentinian communist revolutionary, 1928; Steffi Graf, German tennis player, 1969.

Henry Vane the younger, English politician, executed after the Restoration for his parliamentarian activities, 1662; Edward Fitzgerald, English poet and translator, 1883; Jerome Klapka Jerome, English novelist, 1927; Gilbert Keith Chesterton, English author, 1936; John Logie Baird, Scottish inventor who developed television, 1946; Jorge Luis Borges, Argentinian author, 1986; Vincent Hamlin, US cartoonist, 1993.

JAN FEB MAR APR MAY JUN JUL AUG SEP OCT NOV DEC

15 Official birthday of Queen Elizabeth II. Feast day of St Trillo, St Vitus and his Companions, St Bardo, St Aleydia, St Germaine Cousin of Pibrac, St Hesychius of Durostorum, St Landelinus, St Edburga of Winchester, St Tatian Dulas, and St Orsiesus.

1520 Pope Leo X excommunicated Martin Luther by the bull Exsurge. **1658** The Mogul emperor Aurangzeb imprisoned his father the Shah, after winning a battle at Samgarh. **1672** The Sluices were opened in Holland to save Amsterdam from the French. **1836** Arkansas became the 25th state of the USA. **1855** Stamp duty on British newspapers was abolished. **1869** Celluloid was patented in the USA. **1954** The Convention People's Party, led by Kwame Nkrumah, won the Gold Coast elections. **1977** Spain had its first general elections since 1936.

B Edward (the Black Prince), **1330**; St Francesco de Paolo, **1416**; Joannes Argyropoulos, Greek scholar, **1416**; Thomas Randolph, English poet and playwright, **1605**; Edvard Grieg, Norwegian composer, **1843**; Richard Baker, English broadcaster, **1925**.

D Wat Tyler, English rebel leader, **1381**; Philip the Good, Duke of Burgundy, **1467**; Marguerite De Launay, Baronne Staal, French writer, **1750**; James Knox Polk, 11th president of the USA, **1849**; Evelyn Underhill, English poet and mystic, **1941**.

16 Feast day of St Cyricus, St Ismael, St Aurelian, St John Francis Regis, Saints Cyr and Julitta, St Benno of Meissen, St Lutgarde, Saints Ferreolus and Ferrutio, and St Tychon of Amathus.

1586 Mary Queen of Scots recognised Philip II of Spain as her heir. **1745** British troops took Cape Breton Island and subsequently Louisburg, at the mouth of the St Lawrence River. **1779** Spain declared war on Britain (after France had undertaken to assist in the recovery of Gibraltar and Florida), and the siege of Gibraltar began. **1836** The formation of the London Working Men's Association began the Chartist Movement. **1871** The University Test Acts allowed students to enter Oxford and Cambridge without religious tests. **1972** Burglars were caught breaking into the Democratic Party headquarters in the Watergate Building, Washington DC, USA. **1977** Leonid Brezhnev became president of the USSR.

B   John Cheke, English classical scholar, **1514**; King Gustav V of Sweden, **1858**; Stan Laurel, English-born US film comedian, **1890**; Enoch Powell, British politician, **1912**; Giacomo Agostini, Italian motorcycle champion, **1942**.

D   Roger van der Weyden, Flemish painter, **1464**; John Churchill, Duke of Marlborough, English general, **1722**; Guilio Alberoni, Italian-born Spanish politician and cardinal, **1752**; Elmer Ambrose Sperry, US inventor, **1930**; Margaret Bondfield, British politician and trade-unionist, **1953**.

17   National day of Iceland. Feast day of St Moling, St Adulf, St Nectan, St Botulf, St Alban, St Avitus, St Bessarion, St Hypatius, St Rainerius of Pisa, St Emily de Vialai, St Hervé, Saints Nicander and Marcian, and Saints Teresa and Sanchia of Portugal.

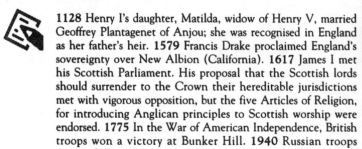

1128 Henry I's daughter, Matilda, widow of Henry V, married Geoffrey Plantagenet of Anjou; she was recognised in England as her father's heir. **1579** Francis Drake proclaimed England's sovereignty over New Albion (California). **1617** James I met his Scottish Parliament. His proposal that the Scottish lords should surrender to the Crown their hereditable jurisdictions met with vigorous opposition, but the five Articles of Religion, for introducing Anglican principles to Scottish worship were endorsed. **1775** In the War of American Independence, British troops won a victory at Bunker Hill. **1940** Russian troops occupied the Baltic states.

B   Edward I, **1239**; Pedro Calderón de la Barca, Spanish playwright, **1600**; Charles XII of Sweden, **1682**; John Wesley, English evangelist, **1703**; Charles François Gounod, French composer, **1818**; William Crookes, English chemist, **1832**; Igor Stravinsky, Russian composer, **1882**.

D   John Sobieski, king of Poland, **1696**; Joseph Addison, English essayist and poet, **1719**; Claude, Duc de Villars, French soldier, **1734**; Prosper Jolyot de Crébillon, French playwright, **1762**; Edward Burne-Jones, English painter, **1898**; Annie S Swan (Mrs Burnett Smith), Scottish novelist, **1943**; Imre Nagy, Hungarian prime minister, executed, **1958**.

JAN FEB MAR APR MAY **JUN** JUL AUG SEP OCT NOV DEC

18 Feast day Saints Mark and Marcellian, St Amandus of Bordeaux, St Eliisabeth of Schönau, and St Gregory Barbarigo.

860 Vikings from Russia were repulsed in an attack on Constantinople. 1429 The French, led by Joan of Arc, defeated the English at the Battle of Patay. 1633 Charles I was crowned King of Scotland at Edinburgh. 1815 The Duke of Wellington and Gebhard von Blücher defeated Napoleon at the Battle of Waterloo. 1928 US aviator Amelia Earhart became the first woman to fly across the Atlantic. 1953 A republic was proclaimed in Egypt, with General M Neguib as president.

Robert Stewart, later Viscount Castlereagh, Irish politician, 1769; Edouard Daladier, French politician, 1884; Nikolaus Horthy de Nagybánya, Hungarian politician, 1868; George Mallory, English mountaineer, 1886; Ian Carmichael, English actor, 1920; Isabella Rosselini, Italian film actress, 1952.

John Hampden, English patriot and politician, 1643; Andrew Jackson, 7th president of the USA, 1845; George Grote, English historian and politician, 1871; Samuel Butler, English novelist, 1902; Roald Amundsen, Norwegian polar explorer, lost this day in the Arctic, 1928; Maxim Gorky, Russian author, 1936.

19 Feast day of Saints Gervase and Protase, St Juliana Falconieri, St Romuald, St Boniface of Querfurt, St Deodatus of Nevers, and St Odo of Cambrai.

1464 An ordinance of Louis XI in France created the poste, organising relays of horses on the main roads for the king's business. 1754 The Anglo-French war broke out in North America when a force under George Washington skirmished with French troops near Fort Duquesne. 1769 Hyder Ali of Mysore compelled the British at Madras to sign a treaty of mutual assistance. 1809 Curwen's Act was passed in Britain, to prevent the sale of Parliamentary seats, thus decreasing the number of seats which the British government can manipulate for its regular supporters. 1829 Robert Peel's Act was passed, to establish a new police force in London and its suburbs. 1867 Emperor Maximilian was executed in Mexico. 1917 The British royal family renounced German names and titles, having

adopted the name of Windsor. **1965** Ben Bella, President of
Algeria, was deposed; Houari Boumédienne headed a
revolutionary council.

James VI of Scotland and I of England, **1566**; Thomas Fuller,
English antiquarian and clergyman, **1608**; Blaise Pascal, French
mathematician, **1623**; Félicité Robert de Lamennais, French
writer, **1783**; Douglas, Earl Haig, British field-marshal, **1861**;
Ernst Chain, German-born British bacteriologist who developed
penicillin, **1906**; Salman Rushdie, British novelist, **1947**.

Alberico Gentili, Italian political writer, **1608**; William
Sherlock, English prelate, **1707**; Ambrose Philips, English poet,
1749; Joseph Banks, English botanist, **1820**; John Dalberg,
Lord Acton, English historian, **1902**; J M Barrie, Scottish
author of Peter Pan, **1937**.

20 Feast day of Edward the Martyr, St Alban, St Govan, St John of
Matera, St Silverius, pope, St Bain, and St Adalbert of
Magdeburg.

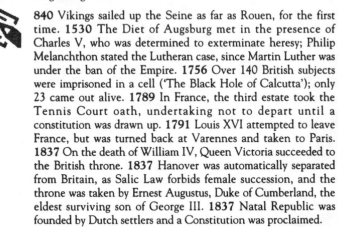

840 Vikings sailed up the Seine as far as Rouen, for the first
time. **1530** The Diet of Augsburg met in the presence of
Charles V, who was determined to exterminate heresy; Philip
Melanchthon stated the Lutheran case, since Martin Luther was
under the ban of the Empire. **1756** Over 140 British subjects
were imprisoned in a cell ('The Black Hole of Calcutta'); only
23 came out alive. **1789** In France, the third estate took the
Tennis Court oath, undertaking not to depart until a
constitution was drawn up. **1791** Louis XVI attempted to leave
France, but was turned back at Varennes and taken to Paris.
1837 On the death of William IV, Queen Victoria succeeded to
the British throne. **1837** Hanover was automatically separated
from Britain, as Salic Law forbids female succession, and the
throne was taken by Ernest Augustus, Duke of Cumberland, the
eldest surviving son of George III. **1837** Natal Republic was
founded by Dutch settlers and a Constitution was proclaimed.

Adam Ferguson, Scottish philosopher and historian, **1723**; John
Costello, Irish politician, **1891**; Jacques Offenbach, German-
born French composer, **1819**; Catherine Cookson, English
novelist, **1906**; Errol Flynn, Australian-born US film actor,

1909; Stephen Frears, English film director, 1941.

Willem Barents, Dutch explorer, 1597; Emmanuel Joseph Sieyès, French revolutionary leader, 1836; William IV, 1837; Nikolai Rimsky-Korsakov, Russian composer, 1908; Pancho Villa, Mexican revolutionary leader, assassinated, 1923; Bernard Baruch, US financier, 1965.

21 Feast day of St Aloysius Gonzaga, St Leufred, St Mewan, St Engelmund, St John Rigby, St Eusebius of Samosata, and St Leutfridus.

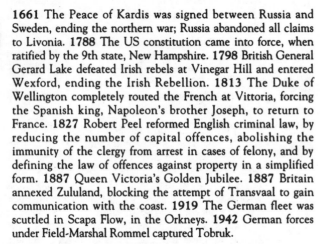

1661 The Peace of Kardis was signed between Russia and Sweden, ending the northern war; Russia abandoned all claims to Livonia. 1788 The US constitution came into force, when ratified by the 9th state, New Hampshire. 1798 British General Gerard Lake defeated Irish rebels at Vinegar Hill and entered Wexford, ending the Irish Rebellion. 1813 The Duke of Wellington completely routed the French at Vittoria, forcing the Spanish king, Napoleon's brother Joseph, to return to France. 1827 Robert Peel reformed English criminal law, by reducing the number of capital offences, abolishing the immunity of the clergy from arrest in cases of felony, and by defining the law of offences against property in a simplified form. 1887 Queen Victoria's Golden Jubilee. 1887 Britain annexed Zululand, blocking the attempt of Transvaal to gain communication with the coast. 1919 The German fleet was scuttled in Scapa Flow, in the Orkneys. 1942 German forces under Field-Marshal Rommel captured Tobruk.

Increase Mather, American clergyman and president of Harvard, 1639; William Stubbs, English historian, 1825; Claude Auchinleck, British field-marshal, 1884; Jean-Paul Sartre, French philosopher, novelist, and playwright, 1905; Jane Russell, US film actress, 1920; Françoise Sagan, French novelist, 1935.

Edward III, 1377; John Skelton, English poet, 1529; Sebastiano del Piombo, Italian painter, 1547; John Smith, Virginian colonist, 1631; Inigo Jones, English architect and stage designer, 1652; Lord William Russell, English politician, 1683; Alexius Petrovich, son of Peter the Great, died in prison, 1718;

Charles, Viscount Townshend, English politician, **1738**;
George Hepplewhite, English cabinet-maker, **1786**; Friedrich
Froebel, German educationalist, **1852**; Jean-Edouard Vuillard,
French painter, **1940**.

22 Feast day of St Acacius, Saints John Fisher and Thomas More,
St Paulinus of Nola, St Nicetas of Remesiana, and St Eberhard
of Salzburg.

1377 Richard II became king of England. **1671** Turkey declared
war on Poland. **1679** The Duke of Monmouth subdued an
insurrection of Scottish Covenanters at Bothwell Bridge. **1826**
The Pan-American Congress met in Panama under the
influence of Simon Bolivar in an unsuccessful effort to unite the
American Republics. **1894** Dahomey was proclaimed a French
Colony. **1907** The Northern Line was opened on the London
Underground.

André-Hercule de Fleury, French cardinal, **1653**; Jean Chardin,
French painter, **1699**; Jacques Delille, French poet, **1738**;
Giuseppe Mazzini, Italian patriot, **1805**; H Rider Haggard,
English novelist, **1856**; John Hunt, English mountaineer, **1910**;
Peter Pears, English tenor, **1910**; Prunella Scales, English
actress, **1932**; Meryl Streep, US film actress, **1949**.

Roger I, king of Sicily, **1101**; Niccolò Machiavelli, Italian
politician and diplomat, **1527**; Jane Shore, mistress of Edward
IV, **1527**; St John Fisher, bishop of Rochester, beheaded, **1535**;
Josiah Child, English merchant, **1699**; Walter de la Mare,
English author, **1956**; Fred Astaire, US dancer and film actor,
1987.

23 National Day of Luxembourg. Feast day of St Cyneburg, St
Etheldreda, St Agrippina, St Lietbertus, St Joseph Cafasso, and
St Thomas Garnet.

1611 English navigator Henry Hudson and eight others were
cast adrift by mutineers; the mutineers returned to England, but
Hudson and his companions were never seen again. **1757**
British troops under Robert Clive captured Plassey, in Bengal,
and recovered Calcutta. **1934** Saudi Arabia and the Yemen
signed a peace agreement after a war of six weeks. **1935** British

JAN FEB MAR APR MAY JUN JUL AUG SEP OCT NOV DEC

Foreign Secretary Anthony Eden offered Benito Mussolini concessions over Abyssinia, which he rejected. **1951** Guy Burgess and Donald Maclean, 'missing diplomats', fled to the USSR. **1952** The US Air Force bombed hydroelectric plants in North Korea.

John Banér, Swedish general, **1596**; Giovanni Battista Vico, Italian philosopher, **1668**; Josephine de Beauharnais, wife of Napoleon, **1763**; Anna Akhmatova, Russian poet, **1889**; Jean Anouilh, French playwright, **1910**; John Habgood, archbishop of York, **1927**.

Vespasian, Roman emperor, AD **79**; Pedro de Mendoza, Spanish explorer, **1537**; John Aubrey, English antiquary, **1697**; Hester Lucy Stanhope, English traveller, **1839**; Cecil Sharp, English collector of folk songs, **1924**.

24 Feast day of St John the Baptist, St Bartholomew of Farne, St Simplicius of Autun, and St Ralph of Bourges.

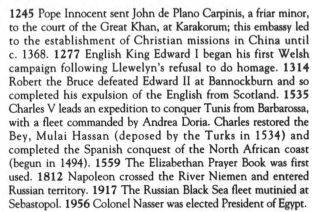

1245 Pope Innocent sent John de Plano Carpinis, a friar minor, to the court of the Great Khan, at Karakorum; this embassy led to the establishment of Christian missions in China until c. 1368. **1277** English King Edward I began his first Welsh campaign following Llewelyn's refusal to do homage. **1314** Robert the Bruce defeated Edward II at Bannockburn and so completed his expulsion of the English from Scotland. **1535** Charles V leads an expedition to conquer Tunis from Barbarossa, with a fleet commanded by Andrea Doria. Charles restored the Bey, Mulai Hassan (deposed by the Turks in 1534) and completed the Spanish conquest of the North African coast (begun in 1494). **1559** The Elizabethan Prayer Book was first used. **1812** Napoleon crossed the River Niemen and entered Russian territory. **1917** The Russian Black Sea fleet mutinied at Sebastopol. **1956** Colonel Nasser was elected President of Egypt.

Theodore Beza, French religious reformer, **1519**; Robert Dudley, Earl of Leicester, English explorer, **1532**; St John of the Cross (Juan de Yepez y Alvarez), **1542**; John Churchill, Duke of Marlborough, **1650**; Horatio, Lord Kitchener, British soldier, **1850**; William Penney. British physicist, **1909**; Juan Fangio, Argentinian racing driver, **1911**; Fred Hoyle, English astronomer, **1915**; Claude Chabrol, French film director, **1930**.

Ferdinand I, king of Castile and Leon, **1065**; Lucrezia Borgia, duchess of Ferrara, **1519**; John Partridge, English astrologer, **1715**; Stephen Grover Cleveland, 22nd and 24th president of the USA, **1908**; Rex Warner, British novelist, **1986**.

25 Feast day of St Adalbert, St Febronia, St Maximus of Turin, St Eurosia, St Gohard, St Gallicanus, St Prosper of Reggio, St Prosper of Aquitaine, St Moloc, St Thea, and St William of Vercelli.

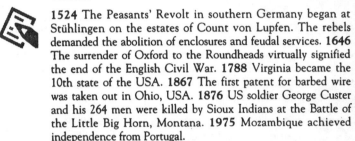

1524 The Peasants' Revolt in southern Germany began at Stühlingen on the estates of Count von Lupfen. The rebels demanded the abolition of enclosures and feudal services. **1646** The surrender of Oxford to the Roundheads virtually signified the end of the English Civil War. **1788** Virginia became the 10th state of the USA. **1867** The first patent for barbed wire was taken out in Ohio, USA. **1876** US soldier George Custer and his 264 men were killed by Sioux Indians at the Battle of the Little Big Horn, Montana. **1975** Mozambique achieved independence from Portugal.

John Horne Tooke, English politician, **1736**; Tsar Nicholas I **1796**; Lord Louis Mountbatten of Burma, **1900**; George Orwell, English essayist and novelist, **1903**; Sidney Lumet, US film director, **1924**.

Anthony Woodville, 2nd Earl Rivers, English politician, executed, **1483**; John Marston, English playwright, **1634**; George Custer, US soldier, **1876**; Margaret Oliphant, English novelist, **1897**; Laurence Alma-Tadema, English painter, **1912**; Tony Hancock, English comedian, **1968**.

26 Feast day of Saints Salvius and Superius, Saints John and Paul, St Anthelmus, bishop, St Maxentius, and St Vigilius of Trent.

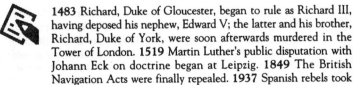

1483 Richard, Duke of Gloucester, began to rule as Richard III, having deposed his nephew, Edward V; the latter and his brother, Richard, Duke of York, were soon afterwards murdered in the Tower of London. **1519** Martin Luther's public disputation with Johann Eck on doctrine began at Leipzig. **1849** The British Navigation Acts were finally repealed. **1937** Spanish rebels took

Santander. **1937** The Duke of Windsor married Mrs Wallis Simpson in France. **1960** Madagascar was proclaimed independent as the Malagasy Republic. **1960** British Somaliland became independent; it joined Somalia on 27. **1962** The Portuguese in Mozambique required Indian nationals to leave within three months of release from internment camps.

Philip Doddridge, English Nonconformist, **1702**; William Thomson, Lord Kelvin, English physicist, **1824**; Pearl S Buck, US novelist, **1892**; Peter Lorre, US film actor, **1904**; Laurie Lee, English poet and author, **1914**; Claudio Abbado, Italian conductor, **1933**.

Francisco Pizarro, Spanish explorer who conquered Peru, assassinated, **1541**; Richard Fanshawe, English scholar and diplomat, **1666**; Ralph Cudworth, English philosopher, **1688**; Gilbert White, English clergyman and naturalist, **1793**; Joseph-Michel Montgolfier, French balloonist, **1810**; Ford Madox Ford, English novelist and poet, **1939**.

27 Feast day of St Cyril of Alexandria, St Zoilus, St Samson of Constantinople, St George Mtasmindeli, the Martyrs of Arras, St John of Chinon, and St Ladislas, King of Hungary.

1771 Russia completed its conquest of the Crimea. **1795** A British force landed at Quiberon to aid the revolt in Brittany. **1795** French forces recaptured St Lucia. **1801** Cairo fell to English forces. **1932** A Constitution was proclaimed in Siam. **1940** The USSR invaded Romania on the refusal of King Carol to cede Bessarabia and Bukovina; Romania appealed for German aid in vain. **1941** Hungary declared war on Russia. **1944** Allied forces took Cherbourg.

Louis XII, king of France, **1462**; Charles Stewart Parnell, Irish nationalist leader, **1846**; John Monash, Australian civil engineer, **1865**; Helen Keller, US author and teacher, **1880**.

Giorgio Vasari, Italian painter and art historian, **1571**; Nathaniel Bailey, English lexicographer, **1742**; Samuel Hood, British admiral, **1816**; James Smithson, English scientist, **1829**; Joseph Smith, founder of the Mormons, **1844**; Malcolm Lowry, British novelist, **1957**; Mohammed Reza Pahlavi, former Shah of Iran, **1980**.

28 Feast day of St Austell, Saints Potamiaena and Basilides, St Irenaeus, St Heimrad, St John Southworth, Saints Sergius and Germanus of Valaam, and St Paul, pope.

1519 Charles I of Spain, Sicily and Sardinia, was elected Holy Roman Emperor as Charles V. **1645** In the English Civil War, the Royalists lost Carlisle. **1895** Union of Nicaragua, Honduras and El Salvador (ended in 1898 by El Salvador's opposition). **1914** Archduke Francis Ferdinand of Austria and his wife were assassinated at Sarajevo by Gavrilo Princip, a Bosnian revolutionary. **1919** Britain and the USA guaranteed France in event of an unprovoked German attack, which the USA later refused to ratify. **1948** Yugoslavia was expelled from Cominform for hostility to the USSR. **1950** North Korean forces captured Seoul. **1956** Sydney Silverman's bill for abolition of death penalty passed the Commons; it was defeated in the Lords, 10 July. **1956** Labour riots at Poznan, Poland, were put down with heavy loss of life.

Sigismund of Luxembourg, Holy Roman Emperor, 1368; Henry VIII, 1491; Jean-Jacques Rousseau, French philosopher and writer, 1712; Étienne-François, Duc de Choiseul, French politician, 1719; Luigi Pirandello, Italian playwright, 1867; Harold Evans, British newspaper editor, 1929.

Paul I, pope, 767; Jean de Rotrou, French playwright, 1650; James Madison, 4th president of the USA, 1836; Robert Burke, Irish explorer of Australia, 1861; Alfred Noyes, English poet, 1958; Lord Raglan, British soldier, 1855; Franz Ferdinand, heir to the Austrian throne, assassinated, 1914; Boris Christoff, Bulgarian operatic bass, 1993.

29 Feast day of St Peter, St Paul, St Elwin, Saints Judith and Salome, and St Cassius of Narni.

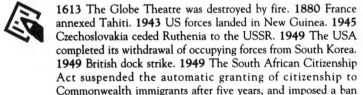

1613 The Globe Theatre was destroyed by fire. **1880** France annexed Tahiti. **1943** US forces landed in New Guinea. **1945** Czechoslovakia ceded Ruthenia to the USSR. **1949** The USA completed its withdrawal of occupying forces from South Korea. **1949** British dock strike. **1949** The South African Citizenship Act suspended the automatic granting of citizenship to Commonwealth immigrants after five years, and imposed a ban

JAN FEB MAR APR MAY **JUN** JUL AUG SEP OCT NOV DEC

on mixed marriages between Europeans and non-Europeans – the beginning of the Apartheid programme. **1954** Following the meeting of President Eisenhower and Winston Churchill in Washington the Potomac Charter, or six-point declaration of western policy, is issued.

Peter Paul Rubens, English painter, 1577; Giacomo Leopardi, Italian poet, 1798; George Ellery Hale, US astronomer, 1868; Antoine de Saint-Exupéry, French author and aviator, 1900; Nelson Eddy, US singer and film actor, 1901; Prince Bernhard of the Netherlands, 1911.

Margaret, Countess of Richmond (The Lady Margaret), 1509; Elizabeth Barrett Browning, English poet, 1861; T H Huxley, English biologist, 1895; Albert Sorel, French historian, 1906; Paul Klee, Swiss painter, 1940; Ignaz Jan Paderewski, Polish pianist, composer, and politician, 1941; Jayne Mansfield, US film actress, 1967.

30 Feast day of St Theobald of Provins, the Martyrs of Rome, St Emma, St Bertrand of Le Mans, St Erentrude, and St Martial of Limoges.

1574 William of Orange persuaded the Estates of Holland to open the dykes to hinder the Spanish siege of Leyden. **1596** English expedition under Lord Howard of Effingham and the Earl of Essex sacked Cadiz, ravaged the Spanish coast, and captured much booty. Philip II was thus prevented from sending an Armada against England. **1782** Spain completed its conquest of Florida. **1797** The Nore mutiny was suppressed. **1846** The Mormons under Brigham Young left Nauvoo City on trail for the Great Salt Lake. **1934** A Nazi purge took place in Germany with summary executions of Kurt von Schleicher, Ernst Roehm and other party leaders for an alleged plot against Hitler. **1965** An India-Pakistan cease-fire was signed.

Philip the Good, Duke of Burgundy, 1396; Charles VIII, king of France, 1469; Paul François Nicolas Barras, French politician, 1755; Georges Duhamel, French novelist and poet, 1884; Stanley Spencer, English painter, 1891; Harold Laski, English politician, 1893.

ⅅ Montezuma II, Aztec ruler, assassinated, **1520**; Johann Reuchlin, German humanist and Hebrew scholar, **1522**; Willem Barents, Dutch explorer, **1597**; William Oughtred, English mathematician, **1660**; Nancy Mitford, English author, **1973**; Lillian Hellman, US playwright, **1984**.

JULY

1

National Day of Canada. Feast day of St Gall of Clermont, Saints Aaron and Julius, St Eparchius or Cybard, St Oliver Plunket, St Carilephus or Calais, St Thierry or Theodoric of Mont d'Or, St Servanus or Serf, St Simeon Salus, and St Shenute.

 1690 At the Battle of the Boyne, William III of England defeated the Jacobites under James II. **1751** The first volume of Diderot's *Encyclopédie* was published in Paris. **1838** Charles Darwin presented a paper to the Linnaean Society in London, on his theory of the evolution of species. **1863** The Battle of Gettysburg, in the American Civil War, began. **1916** The first Battle of the Somme began; more than 21,000 men were killed on the battle's first day. **1937** The telephone emergency service, 999, became operational in Britain. **1940** Guernsey was occupied by German forces. **1990** A state treaty establishing a unified economy and monetary system for East and West Germany went into effect. **1991** The Warsaw Pact, the last vestige of the Cold War-era Soviet bloc, was formally disbanded.

ℬ George Sand, French novelist, **1804**; Louis Blériot, French aviator, **1872**; Charles Laughton, English film actor, **1899**; Olivia de Havilland, US film actress, **1916**; HRH the Princess of Wales, **1961**; Carl Lewis, US athlete, **1961**.

ⅅ Charles Goodyear, US inventor, **1860**; Allan Pinkerton, US founder of the Detective Agency, **1884**; Harriet Beecher Stowe, US author, **1896**; Erik Satie, French composer, **1925**; Juan Perón, Argentinian politician, **1974**.

2

Feast day of Saints Processus and Martinian, St Monegundis, and St Otto of Bamberg.

JAN FEB MAR APR MAY JUN JUL AUG SEP OCT NOV DEC

1644 Oliver Cromwell defeated Prince Rupert at the Battle of Marston Moor, his first victory over the Royalists in the English Civil War. **1865** At a revivalist meeting at Whitechapel, London, William Booth formed the Salvation Army. **1900** The 2nd Olympic Games opened in Paris. **1940** The Vichy Government was set up in France, headed by Henri Pétain. **1956** Elvis Presley recorded 'Hound Dog' and 'Don't Be Cruel' in New York. **1964** President Johnson signed the US Civil Rights Bill prohibiting racial discrimination. **1990** Over a thousand Muslim pilgrims were killed when a stampede occurred in a pedestrian tunnel leading to the holy city of Mecca.

B

Thomas Cranmer, archbishop of Canterbury, **1489**; Christoph Glück, German composer, **1714**; William Henry Bragg, English physicist, **1862**; Hermann Hesse, German poet and novelist, **1877**; David Owen, British politician, **1938**; Kenneth Clarke, British politician, **1940**.

D

Nostradamus, French physician and astrologer, **1566**; Jean Jacques Rousseau, French philosopher and writer, **1778**; Amelia Earhart, US aviator, disappeared over the Pacific, **1937**; Ernest Hemingway, US novelist, **1961**; Betty Grable, US film actress, **1973**; Vladimir Nabokov, Russian novelist, **1977**.

3

Feast day of St Thomas the Apostle, St Anatolius of Constantinople, Saints Irenaeus and Mustiola, St Leo II, pope, St Anatolius of Laodicea, St Rumold or Rombaut, St Bernardino Realino, and St Helidorus of Altino.

1608 French explorer Samuel Champlain founded Québec. **1863** The Union forces, under General Meade, defeated the Confederates at the Battle of Gettysburg. **1905** In Odessa, over 6,000 people were killed by Russian troops to restore order during a general strike. **1954** Nearly nine years after the end of the World War II, food rationing in Britain finally ended. **1962** Following a referendum, France proclaimed Algeria independent. **1976** An Israeli commando force rescued 103 hostages from a hijacked aircraft, who were being held at Entebbe airport, Uganda. **1988** The USS *Vincennes*, patrolling the Gulf during the Iran–Iraq conflict, mistook an Iranian civil airliner for a bomber and shot it down, killing all 290 people on board.

B Robert Adam, Scottish architect and designer, 1728; Leoš Janáček, Czech composer, 1854; Franz Kafka, Czech writer, 1883; Ken Russell, British film director, 1927; Tom Stoppard, British dramatist, 1937; Richard Hadlee, New Zealand cricketer, 1951.

D Marie de' Medici, Queen of France, 1642; Theodor Herzl, Austrian Zionist leader, 1904; Joel Chandler Harris, US author, 1908; Brian Jones, English rock guitarist, 1961; Jim Morrison, US singer, 1971; Rudy Vallee, US singer, 1986; Joe De Rita, US comedian, 1993.

4 Independence Day in the USA. Feast day of The Martyrs of Dorchester, St Andrew of Crete, St Elizabeth of Portugal, St Ulric of Augsburg, St Bertha of Blangy, and St Odo of Canterbury.

1776 The American Declaration of Independence was adopted. 1829 Britain's first regular scheduled bus service began running, between Marylebone Road and the Bank of England, in London. 1848 The Communist Manifesto was published by Karl Marx and Friedrich Engels. 1946 The Philippine Islands were given independence by the USA. 1968 Alec Rose landed at Portsmouth in *Lively Lady*, having sailed single-handed around the world. 1991 Colombia's President Cesar Gaviria Trujillo lifted state of seige that had been in effect since 1984.

B Nathaniel Hawthorne, US author, 1804; Giuseppe Garibaldi, Italian soldier and patriot, 1807; Gertrude Lawrence, English actress, 1898; Louis Armstrong, US jazz trumpeter and singer, 1900; Neil Simon, US dramatist, 1927; Gina Lollobrigida, Italian film actress, 1927.

D Samuel Richardson, English novelist, 1761; Thomas Jefferson, 3rd US president, 1826; John Adams, 2nd US president, 1826; James Monroe, 5th US president, 1831; Marie Curie, Polish scientist, 1934; Suzanne Lenglen, French tennis player, 1939.

5 National Day of Venezuela. Feast day of St Antony-Mary Zaccaria, and St Athanasius the Athonite.

1791 George Hammond was appointed the first British ambassador to the USA. 1946 A swimsuit designed by Louis

Reard, called 'bikini', was first modelled at a Paris fashion show. **1948** Britain's National Health Service came into operation. **1965** Maria Callas, at the age of 41, gave her last stage performance singing Tosca at Covent Garden, London. **1967** Israel annexed Gaza. **1969** The Rolling Stones gave a free concert in Hyde Park two days after the death of guitarist Brian Jones; it was attended by 250,000 people. **1980** Bjorn Borg won the Wimbledon singles championship for a record fifth consecutive time. **1989** Convicted for his involvement in the Iran-Contra affair, US Army Colonel Oliver North was fined $150,000 and given a suspended sentence.

B Sarah Siddons, English actress, **1755**; Cecil Rhodes, South African statesman, **1853**; Dwight Davis, US statesman, **1879**; Jean Cocteau, French poet, novelist, artist, and film director, **1889**; Georges Pompidou, French statesman, **1911**; Elizabeth Emanuel, English dress designer, **1953**.

D Thomas Stamford Raffles, British colonial administrator, **1826**; Austen Henry Layard, British archaeologist, **1894**; Georges Bernanos, French author, **1948**; Thomas Joseph Mboya, Kenyan statesman, **1969**; Walter Adolph Gropius, US architect, **1969**; Georgette Heyer, English novelist, **1974**.

6 National day of Malawi. Feast day of St Romulus of Fiesole, St Dominica, St Mary Goretti, St Goar, St Modwenna, St Godeleva, St Sexburga, and St Sisoes.

 1535 Sir Thomas More was beheaded on London's Tower Hill for treason. **1553** Mary I acceded to the throne, becoming the first queen to rule England in her own right. **1685** James II defeated the Duke of Monmouth, claimant to the throne, at the Battle of Sedgemoor, the last battle to be fought on English soil. **1892** Britain's first non-white MP was elected – Dadabhai Naoraji won the Central Finsbury seat. **1928** The first all-talking feature film, *Lights of New York*, was presented at the Strand Theatre in New York City. **1965** The Beatles' film *A Hard Day's Night* was premiered in London, with royal attendance. **1988** An explosion aboard the North Sea oil rig Piper Alpha resulted in the loss of 166 lives.

B Nicholas I, Tsar of Russia, 1796; Bill Haley, US rock musician, 1925; Janet Leigh, US film actress, 1927; Dalai Lama, Tibetan spiritual leader, 1935; Vladimir Ashkenazy, Russian pianist, 1937; Sylvester Stallone, US film actor, 1946.

D Guy de Maupassant, French writer, 1893; Kenneth Grahame, Scottish children's author, 1932; Aneurin Bevan, British statesman, 1960; William Faulkner, US novelist, 1962; Louis Armstrong, US jazz musician, 1971; Otto Klemperer, German conductor, 1973; John Bolton, English astronomer, 1993.

7 Feast day of St Hedda of Winchester, Saints Ethelburga, Ercongota and Sethrida, St Palladius, Saints Cyril and Methodius, St Pantaenus, and St Felix of Nantes.

1853 US naval officer Commodore Matthew Perry arrived in Japan, and persuaded her to open trade contacts with the West. 1927 Christopher Stone became the first 'disc jockey' on British radio when he presented his 'Record Round-up' from Savoy Hill. 1929 The Vatican City State, with the pope as its sovereign, came into being through the Lateran Treaty. 1982 Queen Elizabeth II was woken by a strange man sitting on her bed in Buckingham Palace; the presence of the intruder, who merely asked her for a cigarette, raised concerns about Palace security. 1985 The unseeded 17-year-old Boris Becker became the youngest ever men's singles champion at Wimbledon. 1990 Martina Navratilova won a record ninth Wimbledon singles title.

B Marc Chagall, Russian painter and designer, 1887; George Cukor, US film director, 1899; Vittorio de Sica, Italian film director, 1901; Pierre Cardin, French fashion designer, 1922; Ringo Starr, English drummer, 1940; Tony Jacklin, English golfer, 1944.

D King Edward I, 1307; Giacomo da Vignola, Italian architect, 1573; R B Sheridan, English dramatist, 1816; Georg Ohm, German physicist, 1854; Arthur Conan Doyle, British author, 1930; Flora Robson, British actress, 1984.

8 Feast day of St Adrian III, pope, St Raymund of Toulouse, Saints Aquila and Prisca or Priscilla, St Kilian and his

Companions, St Sunniva and her Companions, St Withburga, St Grimbald, and St Procopius of Caesarea.

1497 Portuguese navigator Vasco da Gama left Lisbon for a voyage on which he discovered the Cape route to India. **1709** Charles XII of Sweden was defeated by Peter the Great's army at the Battle of Poltava, crushing Sweden's territorial ambitions. **1884** The National Society for Prevention of Cruelty to Children (NSPCC) was founded in London. **1907** Ziegfeld's Follies opened for the first time, on Broadway. **1943** Jean Moulin, the French Resistance leader known as 'Max', was executed by the Gestapo. **1978** Reinhold Messner and Peter Habeler became the first to climb Everest entirely without oxygen. **1991** Iraq admitted to the UN that it had been conducting clandestine programs to produce enriched uranium, a key element in nuclear weapons.

Jean de la Fontaine, French writer, **1621**; Joseph Chamberlain, British statesman, **1836**; John D Rockefeller, US millionaire, **1839**; Arthur Evans, English archaeologist, **1851**; Percy Grainger, Australian composer, **1882**; Billy Eckstine, US singer, **1915**.

Percy Bysshe Shelley, English poet, **1822**; Anthony Hope, British novelist, **1933**; Henry Havelock Ellis, English physician and author, **1939**; Vivien Leigh, English film actress, **1967**; Michael Wilding, English film actor, **1979**; Judith Chrisholm, British aviator, **1988**; Fred Weick, US aeronautical engineer, **1993**.

9 National Day of Argentina. Feast day of St Veronica de Julianis, St Nicholas Pieck and his Companions, St Everild, and the Martyrs of Gorcum.

1810 Napoleon annexed Holland, making his brother, Louis, its king. **1816** Argentina declared independence from Spain at the Congress of Tucuman. **1877** The first Wimbledon Lawn Tennis championship was held at its original site at Worple Road. **1922** Johnny Weissmuller, aged 18, swam the 100m in under a minute (58.6 sec). **1938** In anticipation of World War II, 35 million gas masks were issued to Britain's civilian population. **1979** In Nicaragua, General Somoza was overthrown by the

Sandinista rebels. **1984** Lightning struck York Minster Cathedral and set the roof on fire, destroying the south transept. **1991** The International Olympic Committee lifted a 21-year-old boycott on South Africa.

Elias Howe, US inventor, **1819**; Bruce Bairnsfather, British cartoonist, **1888**; Barbara Cartland, English novelist, **1901**; Edward Heath, British politician, **1916**; Michael Williams, British actor, **1935**; David Hockney, English painter, **1937**.

Jan van Eyck, Flemish painter, **1440**; Edmund Burke, British statesman, **1797**; Zachary Taylor, 12th US president, **1850**; King Camp Gilette, US safety-razor inventor, **1932**; Randall Thompson, US composer, **1984**.

---

10 Feast day of St Felicity, The Seven Brothers, St Amelberga, and Saints Rufina and Secunda.

1460 In the Wars of the Roses, the Yorkists defeated the Lancastrians and captured Henry VI at the Battle of Northampton. **1553** Following the death of Edward VI, Lady Jane Grey was proclaimed Queen of England. **1900** The Paris underground railway, the Metro, was opened. **1958** Britain's first parking meters were installed, in Mayfair, London. **1962** The US communications satellite Telstar was launched, bringing Europe the first live television from the USA. **1976** Seveso, in northern Italy, was covered by a cloud of toxic weedkiller leaked from a chemicals factory; crops and 40,000 animals died. **1985** The Greenpeace campaign ship Rainbow Warrior sank in Auckland, New Zealand, after two explosions tore its hull.

John Calvin, French religious reformer, **1509**; Camille Pissarro, French painter, **1830**; Marcel Proust, French author, **1871**; Carl Orff, German composer, **1895**; Arthur Ashe, US tennis player, **1943**; Arlo Guthrie, US singer, **1947**.

Hadrian, Roman emperor, **138**; El Cid, Spanish hero, **1099**; Louis Jacques Mandé Daguerre, French photographic pioneer, **1851**; Karl Richard Lepsius, German Egyptologist, **1884**; Jelly Roll Morton, US ragtime pianist and composer, **1941**; Giorgio de Chirico, Italian painter, **1978**; Masuji Ibuse, Japanese writer, **1993**.

11 National Day of Mongolia Feast day of St Benedict, St John of Bergamo, St Drostan, St Olga, and St Hidulf.

1708 The Duke of Marlborough's forces defeated the French at the Battle of Oudenarde, in the War of the Spanish Succession. **1776** Captain Cook sailed from Plymouth in the Resolution, accompanied by the Discovery, on his last expedition. **1848** London's Waterloo Station was officially opened. **1950** *Andy Pandy*, the BBC's popular children's television programme, was first transmitted. **1975** Excavations at the tomb of Emperor Qin Shi Huangdi, near the ancient Chinese capital of Xi'an, uncovered an army of 8,000 life-size terracotta warriors dating to about 206 BC **1977** In Britain, *Gay News* was fined £1,000 for publishing a poem which portrayed Jesus as homosexual. **1979** America's Skylab I returned to earth after 34,981 orbits and six years in space.

B Robert the Bruce, King of Scotland, **1274**; Frederick I, King of Prussia, **1657**; John Quincy Adams, 6th US president, **1767**; Yul Brynner, US film actor, **1915**; Peter de Savary, British entrepreneur and yachtsman, **1944**; Leon Spinks, US boxer, **1953**.

D Alfred Dreyfus, French soldier, **1935**; George Gershwin, US composer, **1937**; Arthur John Evans, English archaeologist, **1941**; Paul Nash, English painter, **1946**; Buddy DeSylva, US lyricist and film director, **1950**; Laurence Olivier, English actor and director, **1989**.

12 Orangeman's Day in Northern Ireland. Feast day of St John the Iberian, St Jason, Saints Hermagoras and Fortunatus, St John Gualbert, St John Jones, St Veronica, and St Felix.

1543 Henry VIII married Catherine Parr, his sixth and last wife, at Hampton Court Palace. **1794** British admiral Horatio Nelson lost his right eye at the seige of Calvi, in Corsica. **1878** Cyprus was ceded to British administration by Turkey. **1920** US President Wilson opened the Panama Canal. **1930** Australian batsman Don Bradman scored a record 334 runs – of which a record 309 were scored in one day – against England at Leeds. **1970** Thor Heyerdahl and his crew crossed the Atlantic in 57 days, in a papyrus boat. **1991** Hitoshi Igarashi, the Japanese translator of Salman Rushdie's *Satanic Verses*, was found stabbed to death in Tokyo.

B Gaius Julius Caesar, Roman emperor, 100 BC; Henry Thoreau, US author, 1817; George Eastman, US photographic pioneer, 1854; Amadeo Modigliani, Italian painter and sculptor, 1884; Bill Cosby, US comedian and actor, 1937; Jennifer Saunders, English comedienne and actress, 1958.

D Desiderius Erasmus, Dutch scholar, 1536; Titus Oates, British conspirator, 1705; Charles Stewart Rolls, British engineer and aviator, 1910; Mazo de la Roche, Canadian novelist, 1961; Kenneth More, British actor, 1982.

13 Feast day of Saints Bridget and Maura, St Henry the Emperor, St Silas or Silvanus, St Francis Solano, and St Eugenius of Carthage.

1793 Jean Paul Marat, French revolutionary leader, was stabbed to death in his bath by Charlotte Corday. 1837 Queen Victoria became the first sovereign to move into Buckingham Palace. 1871 The first cat show was held, organised by Harrison Weir, at Crystal Palace, London. 1878 The Treaty of Berlin was signed, granting Bosnia-Herzegovina to Austria-Hungary, and gaining the independence of Romania, Serbia, and Montenegro from Turkey. 1930 The World Football Cup was first held in Uruguay; the hosts beat the 13 other competing countries. 1985 Two simultaneous 'Live Aid' concerts, one in London and one in Philadelphia, raised over £50 million for famine victims in Africa.

B John Dee, English alchemist, astrologer, and mathematician, 1527; George Gilbert Scott, English architect, 1811; Sidney Webb, English social reformer, 1859; David Storey, English novelist and dramatist, 1933; Harrison Ford, US film actor, 1942.

D Richard Cromwell, Lord Protector of England, 1712; James Bradley, English astronomer, 1762; Jean Paul Marat, French revolutionary leader, 1793; John Charles Frémont, US explorer, 1890; Arnold Schoenberg, Austrian composer, 1951; Seretse Khama, Botswanan politician, 1980.

JAN FEB MAR APR MAY JUN JUL AUG SEP OCT NOV DEC

14   National day of France (Bastille Day), and of Iraq. Feast day of St Marcellinus or Marchelm, St Camillus de Lellis, St Ulric of Zell, and St Deusdedit of Canterbury.

1789 The Bastille was stormed by the citizens of Paris and razed to the ground as the French Revolution began. **1823** During a visit to Britain, King Kamehameha II of Hawaii and his queen died of measles. **1867** Alfred Nobel demonstrated dynamite for the first time at a quarry in Redhill, Surrey. **1958** In a military coup led by General Kassem, King Faisal of Iraq was assassinated and a republic proclaimed. **1959** The USS *Long Beach*, the first nuclear warship, was launched. **1967** Abortion was legalized in Britain. **1972** Gary Glitter and the Glittermen (later called the Glitter Band) gave their first concert in Wiltshire. **1989** Over 300,000 Siberian coalminers went on strike, demanding better pay and conditions.

B   Emmeline Pankhurst, English suffragette, **1858**; Isaac Bashevis Singer, Polish author, **1904**; Woody Guthrie, US folk singer, **1912**; Gerald Ford, 38th US president, **1913**; Ingmar Bergman, Swedish film director, **1918**; Bruce Oldfield, British fashion designer, **1950**.

D   Alfred Krupp, German industrialist, **1887**; Paul Kruger, Boer leader, **1904**; William Henry Perkin, English chemist and inventor of aniline dyes, **1907**; Grock, Swiss clown, **1959**; Adlai Stevenson, US statesman, **1965**.

15   Feast day of St Swithin, St Athanasius of Naples, St Bonaventure, St Donald, St Edith of Polesworth, St Barhadbesaba, St David of Munktorp, St Vladimir of Kiev, and St Pompilio Pirrotti.

1099 Jerusalem was captured by the Crusaders with troops led by Godfrey and Robert of Flanders and Tancred of Normandy. **1795** The *Marseillaise*, written by Rouget de Lisle in 1792, was officially adopted as the French national anthem. **1857** During the Indian Mutiny, the second Massacre of Cawnpore (now Kanpur) took place, in which 197 English women and children were killed. **1869** Margarine was patented by Hippolyte Mege Mouries in Paris. **1948** Alcoholics Anonymous, in existence in the USA since 1935, was founded in London. **1965** US *Mariner*

transmitted the first close-up pictures of Mars. **1990** In an ongoing campaign of violence, separatist Tamil Tigers massacred 168 Muslims in Colombo, the Sri Lankan capital.

Inigo Jones, English architect, **1573**; Rembrandt, Dutch painter, **1606**; Hammond Innes, English novelist, **1913**; Iris Murdoch, Irish novelist, **1919**; Julian Bream, English guitarist, **1933**; Harrison Birtwistle, English composer, **1934**; Linda Ronstadt, US singer, **1946**.

General Tom Thumb, circus dwarf, **1883**; Anton Chekhov, Russian dramatist and author, **1904**; Hugo von Hofmannsthal, Austrian dramatist and poet, **1929**; John Pershing, US soldier, **1948**; Paul William Gallico, US writer, **1976**; Margaret Mary Lockwood, English film actress, **1990**.

16 Feast day of St Mary Magdalen Postel, St Fulrad, St Athenogenes, St Helier, St Eustathius of Antioch, and St Reineldis.

622 Traditionally, the beginning of the Islamic Era, when Mohammed began his flight (the Hejira) from Mecca to Medina. **1661** Europe's first banknotes were issued, by the Bank of Stockholm. **1782** Mozart's opera *Die Entführung aus dem Serail* was first performed, in Vienna. **1918** The last tsar of Russia, Nicholas II, along with his entire family, family doctor, servants, and even the pet dog, was murdered by Bolsheviks at Ekaterinburg. **1945** The first atomic bomb developed by Robert Oppenheimer and his team at Los Alamos was exploded in New Mexico. **1965** The Mont Blanc road tunnel, linking France with Italy, was opened. **1990** An earthquake struck the main Philippine island of Luzon, killing over 1,500 people.

Andrea del Sarto, Italian painter, **1486**; Joshua Reynolds, English painter, **1723**; Roald Amundsen, Norwegian polar explorer, **1872**; Barbara Stanwyck, US film actress, **1907**; Ginger Rogers, US film actress and dancer, **1911**; Margaret Court, Australian tennis player, **1942**.

Pope Innocent III, **1216**; Anne of Cleves, 4th wife of Henry VIII, **1557**; Josiah Spode, English potter, **1827**; Hilaire Belloc, British author, **1953**; John Phillips Marquand, US writer, **1960**; Herbert von Karajan, Austrian conductor, **1989**.

17 Feast day of The Seven Apostles of Bulgaria, St Clement of Okhrida and his Companions, St Leo IV, pope, St Ennodius, St Kenelm, St Speratus and his Companions, St Marcellina, and St Nerses Lampronazi.

 1453 With the defeat of the English at the Battle of Castillon, the Hundred Years' War between France and England came to an end. 1841 The first issue of the humorous magazine *Punch* was published in London. 1917 The British royal family changed their name from 'House of Saxe-Coburg-Gotha' to 'House of Windsor'. 1945 The Potsdam Conference of Allied leaders Truman, Stalin, and Churchill (later replaced by Attlee) began. 1975 The US *Apollo* spacecraft and the Russian *Soyuz* craft successfully docked while in orbit. 1981 The Humber Estuary Bridge, the world's longest single-span structure, was officially opened by the Queen. 1990 Iraqi President Saddam Hussein threatened to use force against Kuwait and the United Arab Emirates, to stop them driving oil prices down by overproduction.

B Maxim Litvinov, Soviet leader, 1876; Erle Stanley Gardner, US novelist, 1889; James Cagney, US film actor, 1899; Phyllis Diller, US comedienne, 1917; Donald Sutherland, Canadian film actor, 1935; Wayne Sleep, British dancer and choreographer, 1948.

D Adam Smith, Scottish economist, 1790; Charlotte Corday, murderess of Marat, executed, 1793; James McNeill Whistler, US painter, 1903; Dragolub Mihajlovic, Serbian nationalist, executed, 1946; Billy Holiday, US jazz singer, 1959.

18 National day of Spain. Feast day of St Bruno of Segni, St Pambo, St Arnoul or Arnulf of Metz, and St Frederick of Utrecht.

 64 The great fire began in Rome and lasted for nine days. 1870 The Vatican Council proclaimed the Dogma of Papal Infallibility in matters of faith and morals. 1923 Under the Matrimonial Causes Bill, British women were given equal divorce rights with men. 1925 *Mein Kampf*, Hitler's political testament, was published. 1936 The Spanish Civil War began with an army revolt led by Francisco Franco against the

Republican government. **1955** Disneyland, the 160-acre amusement park, opened near Anaheim, California. **1984** In San Ysidro, California, a security guard walked into a McDonalds and began shooting randomly, killing 20 people and wounding 16.

B   Gilbert White, English naturalist, **1720**; W M Thackeray, English novelist and poet, **1811**; Nelson Mandela, South African politician, **1918**; John Glenn, US astronaut and politician, **1921**; Richard Branson, British entrepreneur, **1950**; Nick Faldo, English golfer, **1957**.

D   Michelangelo Merisi da Caravaggio, Italian painter, **1610**; Antoine Watteau, French painter, **1721**; Peter III, Tsar of Russia, murdered, **1762**; Jane Austen, English novelist, **1817**; Thomas Cook, British pioneer travel agent, **1892**; Jack Hawkins, British film actor, **1973**; Jean Negulesco, Romanian-born US film director, **1993**.

19   Feast day of Saints Justa and Rufina, St Ambrose Autpert, St Macrina the Younger, St Arsenius the Great, St James of Nisibia, St Symmachus, pope, and St John Plesington.

1545 The *Mary Rose*, the pride of Henry VIII's battle fleet, keeled over and sank in the Solent with the loss of 700 lives. (The ship was raised 11 Oct 1982 to be taken to Portsmouth Dockyard.) **1837** Brunel's 70 m/236 ft steamship, the *Great Western*, was launched at Bristol. **1848** At a convention in Seneca Falls, New York, female rights campaigner Amelia Bloomer introduced 'bloomers' to the world. **1903** The first Tour de France cycle race was won by Maurice Garin. **1949** Laos gained independence. **1991** A major political scandal erupted in South Africa after the government admitted that it had made secret payments to the Zulu-based Inkatha Freedom Party.

B   Samuel Colt, US inventor, **1814**; Edgar Degas, French painter, **1834**; Lizzie Borden, alleged US axe murderess, **1860**; Charles Horace Mayo, US physician, **1865**; A J Cronin, Scottish novelist, **1896**; Ilie Nastase, Romanian tennis player, **1946**.

D   Petrarch, Italian poet, **1374**; Matthew Flinders, English navigator and explorer of Australia, **1814**; Tom Hayward, English cricketer, **1939**; Syngman Rhee, Korean politician, **1965**; Clarence White, US pop guitarist, **1973**; Szymon Goldberg, Polish-born violinist and conductor, **1993**.

20 National day of Colombia Feast day of St Margaret of Antioch, St Elias of Jerusalem, St Ansegisus, St Aurelius of Carthage, St Flavian of Antioch, St Wulmar, St Gregory Lopez, St Wilgefortis or Liberata, and St Joseph Barsabas the Just.

1837 London's first railway station, Euston, was opened. **1845** Charles Sturt became the first European to enter Simpson's Desert in central Australia. **1885** Professional football was legalized in Britain. **1940** In the USA, *Billboard* published the first singles-record charts. **1944** German staff officer Colonel von Stauffenburg attempted to assassinate Hitler, in Rastenburg, Germany. **1968** During a BBC radio interview, actress Jane Asher announced that her engagement to Beatle Paul McCartney was off; he was not the first to find out. **1975** After an 11-month journey, the US uncrewed *Viking 1* made a soft landing on Mars.

Petrarch, Italian poet, **1304**; Alberto Santos-Dumont, Brazilian aviator, **1873**; John Reith, Scottish engineer and 1st director general of the BBC, **1889**; Edmund Hillary, New Zealand mountaineer, **1919**; Jacques Delors, French politician, **1925**; Diana Rigg, English actress, **1938**.

Pope Leo XIII, **1903**; Andrew Lang, Scottish historian and folklore scholar, **1912**; Guglielmo Marconi, Italian inventor, **1937**; Ian Macleod, British statesman, **1970**; Bruce Lee, US 'Chinese Western' actor, **1973**; Harry Worth, English comedian, **1989**.

21 National day of Belgium. Feast day of St Laurence of Brindisi, St Victor of Marseilles, St Arbogastes, and St Praxedes.

1798 The Battle of the Pyramids took place, in which Napoleon, soon after his invasion of Egypt, defeated an army of some 60,000 Mamelukes. **1861** The Confederates defeated the Union troops in the first Battle of Bull Run, in the American Civil War. **1897** London's Tate Gallery, built on the site of the

Millbank Prison, was opened. **1944** Guam, in the western Pacific, which had been under Japanese occupation since Dec **1941**, was retaken by US Marines. **1960** Sirimavo Bandaranaika replaced her murdered husband as prime minister of Sri Lanka, becoming the first woman to hold this office. **1969** The lunar module *Apollo 11* landed on the Moon, and US astronauts Armstrong and Aldrin took their first exploratory walk. **1990** More than 150,000 people attended 'The Wall', a large-scale concert staged by rock performers in East Berlin to celebrate the dismantling of the Berlin Wall.

Paul Julius von Reuter, German news agency founder, **1816**; Ernest Hemingway, US novelist, **1899**; Kay Starr, US singer, **1922**; Norman Jewison, canadian film director, **1926**; Jonathan Miller, English TV, film and theatre director, **1934**; Cat Stevens, English rock singer and songwriter, **1948**.

Robert Burns, Scottish poet, **1796**; Ellen Tracy, English actress, **1928**; George Macaulay Trevelyan, British historian, **1962**; Albert Luthuli, South African politician, **1967**; Basil Rathbone, English actor, **1967**.

22 National Day of Poland. Feast day of St Mary Magdalen, St Joseph of Palestine, St Philip Evans, St Vandrille or Wandregesilus, and St John Lloyd.

1812 The Duke of Wellington defeated the French in the Battle of Salamanca, in Spain. **1933** Wiley Post completed the first around the world solo aeroplane flight – the journey took 7 days, 18 hrs and 49.5 min. **1934** US bank robber and 'public enemy no 1', John Dillinger, was gunned down by an FBI squad in Chicago. **1946** Bread rationing started in Britain. **1976** The musical show *A Chorus Line* was staged in London for the first time. **1991** Prime Minister John Major unveiled the government's 'Citizen's Charter' aimed at improving public services.

Philip I, King of Spain, **1478**; Gregor Mendel, Austrian monk and botanist, **1822**; Selman Abraham Waksman, US biochemist, **1888**; Alexander Calder, US sculptor, **1898**; Bryan Forbes, British author, director and producer, **1926**; Terence Stamp, British actor, **1938**.

JAN FEB MAR APR MAY JUN **JUL** AUG SEP OCT NOV DEC

D Marie François Xavier Bichat, French anatomist, **1802**; Florenz Ziegfeld, US theatrical producer, **1932**; Mackenzie King, Canadian statesman, **1950**; Carl Sandburg, US poet, **1967**; Mortimer Wheeler, British archaeologist, **1976**.

23 National Day of Ethiopia and of The United Arab Republic. Feast day of St Anne or Susanna, St John Cassian, St Romula and her Companions, St Apollinaris of Ravenna, The Three Wise Men, St Bridget of Sweden, and St Liborius.

1745 Charles Stuart, the Young Pretender, landed in the Hebrides. **1864** Dr Livingstone returned to England. **1940** The Local Defence Volunteers were renamed the Home Guard by Winston Churchill. **1952** King Farouk of Egypt was deposed by General Neguib. **1967** In the heat of the mountain stage of the Tour de France, British cyclist Tony Simpson, 29, collapsed and died. **1986** Prince Andrew married Lady Sarah Ferguson in Westminster Abbey, and was created Duke of York.

B Arthur Whitten Brown, British aviator, **1886**; Raymond Chandler, US novelist, **1888**; Haile Selassie, Ethiopian emperor, **1892**; Michael Wilding, English actor, **1912**; Richard Rogers, English architect, **1933**; Graham Gooch, English cricketer, **1953**.

D Domenico Scarlatti, Italian composer, **1757**; Isaac Singer, US inventor, **1875**; Ulysses Grant, general and 18th US president, **1885**; D W Griffith, US film director, **1948**; Eddie Rickenbacker, US World War I fighter pilot, **1973**; Jahangir, Pakistani cricketer, **1988**; Raul Gardini, Italian businessman, **1993**.

24 Feast day of St Christina the Astonishing, St Boris or Romanus, St Declan, St Christina of Bolsena, St Lewinna, and St Gleb or David.

1534 Jacques Cartier landed at Gaspé in Canada and claimed the territory for France. **1704** Admiral Sir George Rooke captured Gibraltar from the Spaniards. **1824** The result of the world's first public opinion poll, on voters intentions in the 1824 US Presidential election, was published in the *Harrisburg Pennsylvanian*. **1851** The window tax in Britain was abolished.

1925 A six-year-old girl became the first patient to be successfully treated with insulin, at Guy's Hospital, London. **1990** A Catholic nun and three policemen were killed by an IRA landmine hidden at the side of a road in County Armagh.

Simón Bolívar, South American liberator, **1783**; Alexandre Dumas Pére, French author, **1802**; Frank Wedekind, German dramatist, **1864**; Emelia Earhart, US aviator, **1898**; Peter Yates, British film director, **1919**; Lynda Carter, US actress and singer, **1951**.

Martin van Buren, 8th US president, **1862**; Matthew Webb, English swimmer, **1883**; Sacha Guitry, French actor and dramatist, **1957**; Constance Bennett, US film actress, **1965**; James Chadwick, English physicist, **1974**; Peter Sellers, English actor, **1980**.

25 Feast day of St Christopher, Saints Thea, Valentina and Paul, St James the Greater, and St Magnericus.

1139 Alfonso I of Portugal defeated the Moors at Ourique. **1581** A confederation of the northern provinces of the Netherlands proclaimed their independence from Spain. **1909** French aviator Louis Blériot made the first Channel crossing in an aeroplane, which he had designed. **1917** Magarethe Zelle, the Dutch spy known as Mata Hari, was sentenced to death. **1943** Benito Mussolini was forced to resign as Dictator of Italy, bringing an end to the Fascist regime. **1948** Bread rationing in Britain ended. **1952** The European Coal and Steel Community, established by the treaty of Pari **1951**, was ratified. **1978** The first test-tube baby in Britain was born – Louise Joy Brown, at Oldham General Hospital, Lancashire.

Arthur James Balfour, British statesman, **1848**; Walter Brennan, US film actor, **1894**; Johnny 'Rabbit' Hodges, US jazz saxophonist, **1907**; Annie Ross, British singer, **1930**; Colin Renfrew, British archaeologist, **1937**; Steve Goodman, US songwriter, **1948**.

Flavius Valerius Constantinus, Roman emperor, **306**; Samuel Taylor Coleridge, English poet, **1834**; Charles Macintosh, Scottish chemist and inventor, **1843**; Henry Mayhew, British social investigator and founder of *Punch*, **1887**; Engelbert

Dolfuss, Austrian statesman, **1934**.

26. National Day of Liberia. Feast day of St Anne, St Simeon the Armenian, St Joachim, and St Bartholomea Capitanio.

1745 The first recorded women's cricket match was played near Guildford, Surrey, between teams from Hambledon and Bramley. **1847** Liberia became the first African colony to secure independence. **1908** The US Federal Bureau of Investigation, concerned in particular with internal security, was founded. **1945** The Labour Party won a landslide victory in Britain's General Election. **1956** President Nasser of Egypt nationalized the Suez Canal which led to confrontation with Britain, France, and Israel. **1958** Debutantes were presented at the British Royal Court for the last time. **1987** Cyclist Steve Roche became the first Irishman, and only the second non-continental European, to win the Tour de France.

B George Bernard Shaw, Irish dramatist, **1856**; Carl Jung, Swiss psychologist, **1875**; Aldous Huxley, English novelist, **1894**; Stanley Kubrick, US film director, **1928**; Mick Jagger, British rock singer, **1943**; Vitas Gerulaitis, US tennis player, **1954**.

D Samuel Houston, US general and president of the Republic of Texas, **1863**; George Borrow, English writer, **1881**; Eva Perón, Argentinian populist leader, **1952**; Charles Clore, English financier, **1979**; Averell Harriman, US statesman and diplomat, **1986**.

27 Feast day of The Seven Sleepers of Ephesus, St Theobald of Marly, The Martyrs of Salsette, Saints Aurelia, Natalia and their Companions, and St Pantaleon.

1694 The Bank of England was founded by act of Parliament. **1866** The Great Eastern arrived at Heart's Content in Newfoundland, having successfully laid the transatlantic telegraph cable. **1942** The Battle of El Alamein ended after 17 days, with the British having prevented the German and Italian advance into Egypt. **1953** The Korean armistice was signed at Panmujom, ending three years of war. **1985** Ugandan President Milton Obote was overthrown for a second time, this time by a coup led by Brigadier Tito Okello. **1988** British pole-vault record holder Jeff Gutteridge was banned for life by the British Amateur Athletic Board for taking steroids.

B Alexandre Dumas fils, French dramatist, 1824; Hilaire Belloc, English poet and author, 1870; Anton Dolin, British dancer and choreographer, 1904; Bobbie Gentry, US singer, 1942; Alan Border, Australian cricketer, 1955; Christopher Dean, British ice skater, 1958.

D John Dalton, English physicist and chemist, 1844; William Matthew Flinders Petrie, English Egyptologist, 1942; Gertude Stein, US novelist and poet, 1946; Mohammad Reza Pahlavi, Shah of Iran, 1980; James Mason, English actor, 1984; Osbert Lancaster, British writer and artist, 1986.

28 National Day of Peru. Feast day of Saints Nazarius and Celsus, St Botvid, and St Samson of Dol.

1786 The first potato arrived in Britain, brought from Colombia by Sir Thomas Harriot. 1794 Maximilien Robespierre and 19 other French Revolutionaries went to the guillotine. 1821 San Martin and his forces liberated Peru and proclaimed its independence from Spain. 1858 Fingerprints were first used as a means of identification by William Herschel, who later established a fingerprint register. 1868 The 14th Amendment to the US Constitution, dealing with citizens' rights of all races, was ratified. 1914 Austria-Hungary declared war on Serbia, beginning World War I. 1976 The Tian Shan area of China was struck by an earthquake which caused over 800,000 deaths.

B Gerard Manley Hopkins, English poet, 1844; Beatrix Potter, English author and illustrator, 1866; Marcel Duchamp, French painter, 1887; Rudy Vallee, US singer, 1901; Garfield Sobers, West Indian cricketer, 1936; Riccardo Muti, Italian conductor.

D Thomas Cromwell, Chancellor to King Henry VIII, executed, 1540; Cyrano de Bergerac, French poet and soldier, 1655; Antonio Vivaldi, Italian composer, 1741; Johann Sebastian Bach, German composer, 1750; Nathan Mayer Rothschild, British banker, 1836; Otto Hahn, German nuclear physicist, 1944.

JAN FEB MAR APR MAY JUN **JUL** AUG SEP OCT NOV DEC

29 Feast day of St Martha, Saints Beatrice and Simplicius, Saints Faustinus and Beatrice, St Felix, antipope, St William of Saint-Brieuc, St Lupus of Troyes, and St Olav, King of Norway.

1588 The Spanish Armada was defeated by the English fleet under Howard and Drake, off Plymouth. **1900** King Umberto I of Italy was assassinated by an anarchist and succeeded by Victor Emmanuel. **1948** The 14th Olympic Games opened in London – the first in 12 years, due to World War II. **1949** The first regular televised weather forecast was broadcast by the BBC. **1968** Pope Paul VI reaffirmed the Church's traditional teaching on (and condemnation of) birth control. **1981** The Prince of Wales married Lady Diana Spencer at London's St Paul's Cathedral; the televised ceremony was watched by over 700 million viewers around the world.

Alexis de Tocqueville, French historian and politician **1805**; Booth Tarkington, US author, **1869**; Benito Mussolini, Italian leader, **1883**; Sigmund Romberg, US composer, **1887**; Dag Hammarskjöld, Swedish UN secretary-general, **1905**; Mikis Theodorakis, Greek composer.

Robert Schumann, German composer, **1833**; Vincent van Gogh, Dutch painter, **1890**; John Barbirolli, English conductor, **1970**; Raymond Massey, Canadian actor, **1983**; David Niven, British film actor, **1983**; Luis Buñuel, Spanish film director, **1983**.

30 Feast day of St Julitta of Caesarea, St Tatwin, Archbishop of Canterbury, Saints Abdon and Sennen, and St Peter Chrysologus.

1793 Toronto (known as York until 1834) was founded by General John Simcoe. **1935** 'Penguin' paperback books, founded by Allen Lane, went on sale in Britain. **1948** The world's first radar station was opened, to assist shipping at the port of Liverpool. **1963** Kim Philby, British intelligence officer from **1940** and Soviet agent from 1933, fled to the USSR. **1966** England won the Football World Cup in London, beating West Germany 4–2. **1990** Ian Gow, Conservative MP for Eastbourne, a close friend and personal advisor to Prime Minister Thatcher, was killed by a car bomb at his home.

Giorgio Vasari, Italian painter, architect, and writer, 1511; Emily Brontë, English novelist, 1818; Henry Ford, US car manufacturer, 1863; Henry Moore, English sculptor, 1898; Daley Thompson, British athlete, 1958; Kate Bush, English singer, 1958.

William Penn, English Quaker leader, 1718; Thomas Grey, English poet, 1771; Denis Diderot, French encyclopedist, 1784; Otto von Bismarck, German politician, 1898; Lynn Fontanne, US actress, 1983; Howard Dietz, US lyricist, 1983.

31 Feast day of St Ignatius of Loyola, St Justin de Jacobis, St Neot, and St Helen of Skövde.

1498 Columbus arrrived at Trinidad on his third voyage. 1919 The Weimar Republic was established in post-war Germany. 1910 Dr Crippen was arrested aboard the SS *Montrose* as it was docking at Quebec; charged with the murder of his wife, he was the first criminal to be caught by the use of radio. 1954 Mount Godwin-Austin (K2) in the Himalayas was first climbed by an Italian expedition, led by Ardito Desio. 1965 Cigarette advertising on British television was banned. 1971 US astronauts David Scott and James Irwin entered their Lunar Roving Vehicle and went for a ride on the moon. 1991 At a superpower summit in Moscow, Presidents Bush and Gorbachev signed the Strategic Arms Reduction Treaty (START), and announced that they would be co-sponsoring a Middle East peace conference.

John Ericsson, US naval engineer, 1803; Milton Friedman, US economist, 1912; Peter Nichols, English dramatist, 1927; Lynne Reid Banks, English author, 1929; Geraldine Chaplin, US film actress, 1944; Evonne Cawley, Australian tennis player, 1951.

Ignatius of Loyola, Spanish founder of the Jesuits, 1556; Andrew Jackson, 17th US president, 1875; Franz Liszt, Hungarian composer, 1886; Hedley Verity, English cricketer, 1943; Jim Reeves, US country singer, 1964; Leonard Cheshire, British pilot and philanthropist, 1992; King Baudouin I of the Belgians, 1993.

JAN FEB MAR APR MAY JUN JUL AUG SEP OCT NOV DEC

AUGUST

1

National Day of Switzerland. Feast day of Saints Pistis, Elpis, and Agape (Faith, Hope, and Charity), St Peter Julian Eymard, St Ethelwold of Winchester, St Almedha or Aled, St Alphonse Liguori, and The Holy Macabees.

1498 Christopher Columbus reached the American mainland, and named it Santa Isla, believing it to be an island. **1714** George Louis, Elector of Hanover, was proclaimed King George I of Great Britain. **1774** English chemist Joseph Priestley identified oxygen, which he called 'a new species of air'. **1778** The first savings bank was opened, in Hamburg, Germany. **1793** The kilogram was introduced in France as the first metric weight. **1798** The English under Nelson destroyed the French fleet at the Battle of the Nile, in Aboukir Bay. **1834** Slavery was abolished throughout the British Empire. **1936** The XIth Olympics, the last for 12 years, opened in Berlin. **1975** Thirty-five nations, including the USA and the USSR, signed the Helsinki Agreement on cooperation in human rights and other global issues.

B

Claudius, Roman emperor, **10 BC**; Jean Baptiste de Lamarck, French zoologist, **1744**; Richard Henry Dana, US novelist, **1815**; Herman Melville, US novelist, **1819**; Jack Kramer, US tennis champion, **1921**; Yves Saint-Laurent, French couturier, **1936**.

D

Louis VI, King of France, **1137**; Queen Anne, **1714**; Robert Morrison, English missionary and translator, **1834**; Theodore Roethke, US poet, **1963**; Walter Ulbricht, East German politician, **1973**; John Ogdon, English concert pianist, **1989**; Alfred Manessier, French painter, **1993**.

2

Feast day of St Theodota and her Three Sons, St Eusebius of Vercelli, St Plegmund, St Stephen I, pope, St Syagrius of Autun, and St Sidwell or Sativola.

1718 Britain, France, Austria, and Holland concluded the Quadruple Alliance against Spain, in an attempt to prevent Spain from annexing Sardinia and Sicily. **1858** The rule of the East India Company, which was established throughout India, was transferred to the British government. **1875** Britain's first roller skating rink was opened to the public, in Belgravia, London. **1894** Death duties, now known as inheritance tax, were introduced in Britain. **1945** The Potsdam Conference, establishing the initial post war treatment of Germany and demanding unconditional Japanese surrender, ended. **1980** Right-wing terrorists exploded a bomb in the crowded Bologna Railway Station, northern Italy, killing 84 people. **1990** Iraq invaded and annexed Kuwait, precipitating an international crisis.

John Tyndall, Irish physicist, **1820**; Ethel M Dell, British novelist, **1881**; Arthur Bliss, English composer, **1891**; Myrna Loy, US film actress, **1905**; James Baldwin, US writer, **1924**; Peter O'Toole, Irish actor, **1932**; Sammy McIlroy, Irish footballer, **1954**.

Thomas Gainsborough, English painter, **1788**; Jacques Étienne Montgolfier, French balloonist, **1799**; Enrico Caruso, Italian tenor, **1921**; **1923**; Louis Blériot, French aviator, **1936**; Fritz Lang, Austrian film director, **1976**; Carlos Chavez, Mexican composer, **1978**.

3

Feast day of St Walthen or Waltheof, St Germanus of Auxerre, and St Thomas of Hales or Dover.

1492 Christopher Columbus left Palos de la Frontera in Andalusia, Spain, on his first voyage of discovery. **1778** La Scala opera house opened in Milan, Italy. **1858** Lake Victoria, the source of the Nile, was discovered by the English explorer John Speke. **1904** A British expedition, led by Col Francis E Younghusband, became the first westerners to enter the 'Forbidden City' of Lhasa, Tibet. **1914** Germany declared war on France. **1914** The first ships passed through the completed Panama Canal. **1940** Latvia was incorporated into the USSR as a constituent republic. **1958** The USS *Nautilus*, the first nuclear submarine, passed under the North Pole. **1963** The Beatles played The Cavern in their home town, Liverpool, for the last time.

Joseph Paxton, English architect, **1801**; Stanley Baldwin, British statesman, **1867**; King Haakon VII of Norway, **1872**;

JAN FEB MAR APR MAY JUN JUL AUG SEP OCT NOV DEC

Rupert Brooke, English poet, **1887**; Tony Bennett, US singer, **1926**; Martin Sheen, US actor, **1940**; Osvaldo Ardiles, Argentine footballer, **1953**.

James II, King of Scotland, **1460**; Richard Arkwright, English inventor, **1792**; Roger Casement, Irish nationalist, **1916**; Joseph Conrad, British novelist, **1924**; Colette, French novelist, **1954**; Lenny Bruce, US comedian, **1966**.

4 Feast day of St Molua or Lughaidh, St Ia, St Sezni, and St John Baptist Vianney.

1265 The Battle of Evesham took place, in which Simon de Montfort was defeated by Royalist forces led by the future King Edward I, during the Barons' War. **1578** The Portuguese were defeated by the Berbers at the Battle of Alcazarquivir. **1870** The British Red Cross Society was founded. **1914** Britain declared war on Germany after the Germans had violated the Treaty of London, and World War I began. **1918** The Second Battle of the Marne ended. **1940** Italy invaded Kenya, the Sudan, and British Somaliland. **1966** In a US radio interview, John Lennon claimed that the Beatles were probably more popular than Jesus Christ; Beatles records were consequently banned in many US states and in South Africa.

Percy Bysshe Shelley, English poet, **1792**; William Henry Hudson, British writer and naturalist, **1841**; Knut Hamsun, Norwegian novelist, **1859**; HM Queen Elizabeth, the Queen Mother, **1900**; Osbert Lancaster, English cartoonist and writer, **1908**; Peter Squires, English rugby player, **1951**.

Henry I, King of France, **1060**; Hans Christian Andersen, Danish fairy tale writer, **1875**; James Cruze, US film director, **1942**; Edgar Adrian, British physiologist, **1977**; Pola Negri, German silent-film actress, **1987**.

5 Feast day of St Afra, St Nonna, and Saints Addai and Mari.

1583 English soldier and navigator Humphrey Gilbert claimed Newfoundland for Elizabeth I. **1858** The first transatlantic cable was opened when Queen Victoria exchanged greetings with US President Buchanan. **1891** The first American Express traveller's cheque was cashed. **1914** The first electrical traffic lights were installed, in Cleveland, Ohio. **1924** The Turkish government abolished polygamy. **1960** Upper Volta (now Burkina Faso) achieved full independence from France. **1962** ANC leader Nelson Mandela was arrested and given a life sentence on charges of attempting to overthrow the South African government. **1963** The Test Ban Agreement was signed by the USA, the USSR, and the UK, contracting to test nuclear weapons only underground.

Niels Henrik Abel, Norwegian mathematician, **1802**; Guy de Maupassant, French author, **1850**; John Huston, US film director, **1906**; Joan Hickson, English actress, **1906**; Neil Armstrong, US astronaut, **1930**; Bob Geldof, Irish musician, **1951**.

Thomas Newcomen, English inventor, **1729**; Frederick North, British politician, **1792**; Alexis Benoît Soyer, French chef and writer, **1858**; Friedrich Engels, German political writer, **1895**; Marilyn Monroe, US film actress, **1962**; Richard Burton, Welsh actor, **1984**; Eugen Suchoň, Slovakian composer, **1993**.

6

The national day of Bolivia. Feast of the Transfiguration and Feast day of Saints Justus and Pastor, and St Hormisdas, pope.

939 The Spanish defeated the Moors at the Battle of Salamanca. **1806** The Holy Roman Empire came to an end when Francis II renounced the crown, becoming Francis I, Emperor of Austria. **1889** The Savoy Hotel, in London, opened. **1890** William Kemmler, a murderer, became the first to executed in the electric chair, in Auburn Prison, New York. **1926** US swimmer Gertrude Ederle became the first woman to swim the English Channel, in 14 hr 34 min. **1945** An atomic bomb was dropped on the Japanese city of Hiroshima from a US Boeing B29 bomber. **1962** Jamaica became independent after being a British colony for 300 years. **1988** Russian ballerina Natalia Makarova danced again with the Kirov Ballet in London, 18 years after she defected to the West.

Daniel O'Connell, Irish politician, **1775**; Alfred Tennyson, English poet, **1809**; Paul Claudel, French poet, **1868**; Alexander Fleming, Scottish bacteriologist, **1881**; Robert Mitchum, US film actor, **1917**; Chris Bonington, British mountaineer, **1934**.

JAN FEB MAR APR MAY JUN JUL AUG SEP OCT NOV DEC

Anne Hathaway, wife of William Shakespeare, 1623; Ben Jonson, English playwright, 1637; Diego Velázquez, Spanish painter, 1660; Fulgencio Batista y Zaldivar, Cuban dictator, 1973; Pope Paul VI, 1978.

7 Feast day of St Donatus of Arezzo, St Victricius, Saints Agapitus, Sixtus II and Felicissimus, St Dogmetius the Persian, St Albert of Trapani, St Claudia, and St Cajetan or Gaetano.

1711 The first race meeting was held at Ascot, established by Queen Anne. 1830 Louis Philippe was proclaimed 'Citizen King' (Philippe Egalité), for his support of the 1792 Revolution. 1840 The employment of climbing boys as chimney sweeps was prohibited by an Act of Parliament. 1858 Queen Victoria chose Ottawa as the capital of the Dominion of Canada. 1913 In Britain's first aviation tragedy, US airman 'Colonel' Samuel Cody was killed when his aircraft crashed at Farnborough. 1926 Britain's first motor racing Grand Prix was held at Brooklands; the winning car averaged 71.61 mph. 1942 Guadalcanal, in the southern Solomon Islands, was assaulted by the US Marines in one of the most costly campaigns of World War II. 1960 The Ivory Coast (Côte d'Ivoire) achieved independence from France.

Mata Hari (Margaretha Geertruide Zelle), Dutch courtesan, dancer, and probable spy, 1876; Louis Leakey, British archaeologist, 1903; Ralph Bunche, US diplomat, 1904; Greg Chappell, Australian cricketer, 1948; Alexei Sayle, British comedian, 1952.

Robert Blake, British admiral, 1657; Bix Beiderbecke, US jazz musician and composer, 1931; Konstantin Stanislavsky, Russian theatre director, 1938; Rabindranath Tagore, Indian writer, 1941; Oliver Hardy, US film comedian, 1957.

8 Feast day of St Dominic, Saints Cyriacus, Largus, and Smaragdus, St Hormidas the Martyr, and The Fourteen Holy Helpers.

117 Hadrian became emperor of Rome following the death of his father Trajan. 1786 Mont Blanc, Europe's tallest peak, was climbed for the first time; Swiss scientist Horace Saussure had

offered a prize for the accomplishment of this feat. **1940** The Battle of Britain, which would continue into the following Oct, began. **1945** The USSR declared war on Germany. **1963** The Great Train Robbery, in which over £2.5 million was stolen, took place near Bletchley, Buckinghamshire. **1974** Richard Nixon became the first US president to resign from office in face of threats to impeach him for his implication in the Watergate scandal. **1988** The luckiest day of the decade, according to the Chinese, because the date – 8.8.88 – is a palindrome. **1991** Islamic Jihad released John McCarthy, a British journalist who had been held hostage since April **1986**.

Godfrey Kneller, German-born painter, **1646**; Ernest O Lawrence, US physicist, **1901**; Dino De Laurentis, Italian film producer, **1919**; Esther Williams, US swimmer and film actress, **1923**; Dustin Hoffman, US film actor, **1937**; Nigel Mansell, British racing driver, **1953**.

Girolamo Fracastoro, Italian physician and writer, **1553**; James Tissot, French painter, **1902**; Frank Winfield Woolworth, US chainstore founder, **1919**; James Gould Cozzens, US novelist, **1978**; Louise Brooks, US actress, **1985**.

Feast day of St Oswald of Northumbria, Saints Nathy and Felim, St Romanus, and St Emygius.

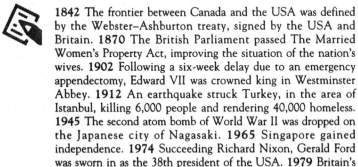

1842 The frontier between Canada and the USA was defined by the Webster–Ashburton treaty, signed by the USA and Britain. **1870** The British Parliament passed The Married Women's Property Act, improving the situation of the nation's wives. **1902** Following a six-week delay due to an emergency appendectomy, Edward VII was crowned king in Westminster Abbey. **1912** An earthquake struck Turkey, in the area of Istanbul, killing 6,000 people and rendering 40,000 homeless. **1945** The second atom bomb of World War II was dropped on the Japanese city of Nagasaki. **1965** Singapore gained independence. **1974** Succeeding Richard Nixon, Gerald Ford was sworn in as the 38th president of the USA. **1979** Britain's first nudist beach was established in Brighton.

Izaak Walton, English author, **1593**; Thomas Telford, Scottish

JAN FEB MAR APR MAY JUN JUL **AUG** SEP OCT NOV DEC

civil engineer, **1757**; Leonid Nikolayevich Andreyev, Russian author, **1871**; Léonide Massine, Russian dancer and choreographer, **1869**; Philip Larkin, English poet, **1922**; Rod Laver, Australian tennis player, **1938**.

Maarten Harpertszoon Tromp, Dutch admiral, **1653**; Ruggiero Leoncavallo, Italian composer, **1919**; Hermann Hesse, German author, **1962**; Joe Orton, English playwright, **1967**; Dmitri Shostakovich, Russian composer, **1975**.

10

National Day of Ecuador. Feast day of St Laurence of Rome.

1675 King Charles II laid the foundation stone of the Royal Observatory, Greenwich. **1787** Wolfgang Amadeus Mozart completed his popular *Eine Kleine Nachtmusik* (A Little Night Music). **1846** The Smithsonian Institution was established in Washington, DC, to foster scientific research. **1889** The screw bottle top was patented by Dan Rylands of Hope Glass Works, Yorkshire. **1895** The first Promenade Concert was held at the Queen's Hall, London, conducted by Henry Wood. **1904** In the Russo-Japanese War, Japan inflicted heavy losses on the Russian fleet at the Battle of the Yellow Sea, off Port Arthur. **1911** British MPs voted to receive salaries for the first time. **1966** Orbiter I, the first US lunar satellite, was launched.

Charles James Napier, British general, **1782**; Camillo Benso, Count Cavour, Italian nationalist politician, **1810**; Herbert Hoover, 31st US president, **1874**; Eddie Fisher, US singer, **1928**; Anita Lonsborough Porter, English swimmer, **1941**.

Allan Ramsay, Scottish portrait painter, **1784**; Edward William Lane, English traveller and translator, **1876**; Otto Lillienthal, German aviator, **1896**.

11

Feast day of St Attracta or Araght, St Clare of Assisi, St Tiburtius, St Susanna, St Equitius, St Alexander of Comana, St Lelia, St Blane, St Gerard of Gallinaro, and St Gery or Gaugericus.

1576 English navigator Martin Frobisher, on his search for the Northwest Passage, entered the bay in Canada now named after him. **1810** Severe earthquakes struck the Azores, causing the village of São Miguel to sink. **1877** Phobos and Deimos, the satellites or 'moons' of Mars, were discovered by US astronomer Asaph Hall. **1941** President Roosevelt and Winston Churchill signed the Atlantic Charter, largely to demonstrate public solidarity between the Allies. **1952** King Talal of Jordan was deposed because of mental illness, and his son, Crown Prince Hussein, succeeded to the throne. **1960** Chad gained its independence from France. **1963** Canton was entered by Chinese General Chiang Kai-shek and his supporters.

Jean Victor Marie Moreau, French General, **1772**; Charlotte Mary Yonge, English novelist, **1823**; Hugh MacDiarmid, Scottish poet, **1892**; Enid Blyton, English author, **1897**; Alun Hoddinott, Welsh composer, **1929**; Anna Massey, English actress, **1937**.

Hans Memling, Flemish painter, **1495**; John Henry Newman, English Roman Catholic theologian, **1890**; Andrew Carnegie, US industrialist and philanthropist, **1919**; Jackson Pollock, US painter, **1956**.

12 Feast day of St Porcarius and his Companions, St Jambert, Archbishop of Canterbury, St Euplus, and St Murtagh or Muredach.

1687 The Austro-Hungarians defeated the Turks at the Battle of Mohács, in Hungary, effectively ending Turkish expansion into Europe. **1812** In the Peninsular War, the Duke of Wellington's troops entered Madrid. **1851** The US schooner *America* won a race around the Isle of Wight, giving rise to the later America's Cup trophy. **1883** The quagga in Amsterdam Zoo died, the last of this species in the world. **1898** Spain and the USA concluded an armistice over Cuba and other possessions. **1944** PLUTO ('pipe line under the ocean') began operating beneath the English Channel, supplying petrol to Allied forces in France. **1969** The world's first communications satellite was launched – America's Echo. **1991** England defeated the West Indies in the fifth Test Match at the Oval, to draw the summer series 2 – 2.

Thomas Bewick, British wood engraver, **1753**; King George IV, **1762**; Robert Southey, English poet, **1774**; Cecil B De Mille, US film director and producer, **1881**; George Hamilton, US film actor, **1939**; Mark Knopfler, rock guitarist, **1949**.

) Giovanni Gabrieli, Italian composer, **1612**; William Blake, English poet, **1827**; George Stephenson, English engineer, **1848**; Thomas Mann, German novelist, **1955**; Ian Fleming, English novelist, **1964**; Henry Fonda, US film actor, **1982**.

13 Feast day of St Simplician of Milan, St Radegund, St Wigbert, St Pontian, pope, St Benildus, St Hippolytus of Rome, St Narses Klaietus, St Cassian of Imola, and St Maximus the Confessor.

1521 Spanish conquistador Hernándo Cortés recaptured Tenochtitlán (Mexico City), and overthrew the Aztec empire. **1705** The Battle of Blenheim took place in southern Germany, in which the Anglo-Austrian army inflicted a decisive defeat on the French armies. **1814** The Cape of Good Hope Province became a British colony when it was ceded by the Dutch (sold for £6 million). **1868** Earthquakes killed over 25,000 people and destroyed four cities in Peru and Ecuador. **1923** Kemal Atatürk was elected the first president of Turkey. **1961** The border between East and West Berlin was sealed off by East Germany with the closure of the Brandenburg Gate to stop the exodus to the West. **1964** The last hangings in Britain took place; two murderers were executed at Liverpool and Manchester. **1972** The last US troops left Vietnam. **1991** Prosecutors announced the discovery of one of the largest bank frauds in Japan's history, involving $2.5 billion in fraudulently obtained loans.

B Queen Adelaide, consort of William IV, **1756**; John Baird, Scottish television pioneer, **1888**; Alfred Hitchcock, English film director, **1899**; Basil Spence, British architect, **1907**; Ben Hogan, US golfer, **1912**; Fidel Castro, Cuban leader, **1927**.

) René Laënnec, French physician, **1826**; Eugéne Delacroix, French painter, **1863**; John Everett Millais, British painter, **1896**; Florence Nightingale, English nurse, **1910**; H G Wells, English writer, **1946**; Henry Williamson, English author, **1977**.

14 Feast day of St Marcellus of Apamea, St Fachanan, St Athanasia of Aegina, St Eusebius of Rome, and St Maximilian Kolbe.

1678 The French repulsed William of Orange at the Battle of

Mons, in Belgium. **1880** Cologne Cathedral was completed; it had been started in the 13th century. **1882** Cetewayo, King of Zululand, South Africa, was received by Queen Victoria. **1893** France became the first country to introduce vehicle registration plates. **1900** The Boxer Uprising was ended and Beijing captured by an international punitive force. **1947** Pakistan became an independent dominion. **1969** The first British troops were deployed in Northern Ireland to restore order. **1986** Pakistani politician Benazir Bhutto was arrested by President Zia and detained in prison for 30 days.

Samuel Wesley, English organist and composer, **1810**; John Galsworthy, English novelist and playwright, **1867**; Fred Davis, English snooker player, **1913**; Frederic Raphael, English novelist, **1931**; Sarah Brightman, English soprano and actress, **1961**.

Augustus Toplady, British priest and hymn-writer, **1778**; Alfred Harmsworth, British newspaper proprietor, **1922**; William Randolph Hearst, US newspaper proprietor, **1951**; Bertolt Brecht, German writer, **1956**; J B Priestley, English novelist and playwright, **1984**.

15

Feast day of The Assumption of the Virgin Mary, St Tarsicius, and St Arnulf of Soissons.

1543 The Jesuit order (Society of Jesus) was founded by Ignatius de Loyola in Paris, with the aims of protecting Catholicism against the Reformation and carrying out missionary work. **1843** The Tivoli Pleasure Gardens were opened in Copenhagen. **1947** India gained independence. **1948** The republic of South Korea was proclaimed. **1965** The National Guard was called in to quell race riots in Watts, Los Angeles, which left 28 dead and 676 injured. **1969** The Woodstock Music and Arts Fair began on a dairy farm in upstate New York. In the three days it lasted, 400,000 attended, two children were born, and three people died. **1987** Caning was officially banned in British schools (excluding independent schools).

Napoleon Bonaparte, French emperor, **1769**; Sir Walter Scott, Scottish novelist, **1771**; Thomas De Quincey, English writer,

JAN FEB MAR APR MAY JUN JUL AUG SEP OCT NOV DEC

1785; T E Lawrence, English soldier and writer, 1888; Robert Bolt, British dramatist, 1924; Princess Anne, the Princess Royal, 1950.

Macbeth, King of Scotland, 1057; Joseph Joachim, Hungarian violinist and composer, 1907; Will Rogers, US humorist, 1935; Wiley Post, US aviator, 1935; Paul Signac, French painter, 1935; René Magritte, Belgian painter, 1967.

16

Feast day of St Stephen of Hungary, St Armel, and St Arsacius.

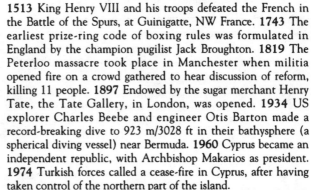

1513 King Henry VIII and his troops defeated the French in the Battle of the Spurs, at Guinigatte, NW France. 1743 The earliest prize-ring code of boxing rules was formulated in England by the champion pugilist Jack Broughton. 1819 The Peterloo massacre took place in Manchester when militia opened fire on a crowd gathered to hear discussion of reform, killing 11 people. 1897 Endowed by the sugar merchant Henry Tate, the Tate Gallery, in London, was opened. 1934 US explorer Charles Beebe and engineer Otis Barton made a record-breaking dive to 923 m/3028 ft in their bathysphere (a spherical diving vessel) near Bermuda. 1960 Cyprus became an independent republic, with Archbishop Makarios as president. 1974 Turkish forces called a cease-fire in Cyprus, after having taken control of the northern part of the island.

Arthur Cayley, British mathematician, 1821; Johan Siegwald Dahl, Norwegian painter, 1827; Menachem Begin, Israeli statesman, 1913; Ted Hughes, English poet, 1930; Jeff Thomson, Australian cricketer, 1950; Madonna, US rock singer, 1958.

Joe Miller, English comedian, 1738; Robert Wilhelm Bunsen, German chemist and inventor, 1899; Umberto Boccioni, Italian sculptor, 1916; Margaret Mitchell, US novelist, 1949; Bela Lugosi, US film actor, 1956; Elvis Presley, US rock singer, 1977; Irene Sharaff, US film-set and costume designer, 1993; Alison Smithson, English architect, 1993; Stewart Granger, English-born US actor, 1993.

17

National day of Indonesia. Feast day of St Joan Delanoue, St Mamas, St Liberatus of Capua, St Rock or Roch, St Clare of Montefalco, St Hyacinth, and St Eusebius, pope.

1833 The Canadian *Royal William*, the first steamship to cross the Atlantic entirely under power, set off from Nova Scotia. 1836 Under the Registration Act, the registration of births, deaths, and marriages was introduced in Britain. 1876 The first performance of Wagner's opera *Götterdämmerung* was given in Bayreuth, Germany. 1896 Gold was discovered at Bonanza Creek in Canada's Yukon Territory, leading to the great gold rush of 1898. 1976 Earthquakes and tidal waves in the Philippines resulted in the deaths of over 6,000 people. 1989 Electronic tagging was used for the first time in Britain, on Richard Hart, accused of theft.

Davy Crockett, US frontiersman, 1786; Mae West, US film actress, 1892; George Melly, English jazz singer, 1926; V S Naipaul, English novelist, 1932; Robert De Niro, US film actor, 1943; Alan Minter, middleweight boxer, 1951; Robin Cousins, ice skater, 1957.

Frederick II (the Great), King of Prussia, 1786; Honoré de Balzac, French novelist, 1850; Fernand Léger, French painter, 1955; Ludwig Mies van der Rohe, US architect, 1973; Ira Gershwin, US lyricist, 1983; Mohammad Zia ul-Haq, Pakistani general, 1988.

18 Feast day of St Helena, Saints Florus and Laurus, St Agapitus, St Alipius, and St Beatrice or Brites da Silva.

1759 The British, under Admiral ('Old Dreadnought') Boscawen, defeated the French fleet at the Battle of Lagos Bay. 1812 Napoleon's forces defeated the Russians at the Battle of Smolensk. 1866 The Treaty of Alliance forming the North German Confederation, under the leadership of Prussia, was signed. 1941 Britain's National Fire Service was established. 1960 The first oral contraceptive was marketed by the Searle Drug Company in the USA. 1964 South Africa was banned from participating in the Olympics because of its racial policies. 1967 The town of Long Beach, in California, purchased the liner *Queen Mary*.

Antonio Salieri, Italian composer, 1750; Franz Josef I, Austro-Hungarian emperor, 1830; Moura Lympany, English concert pianist, 1916; Shelley Winters, US film actress, 1922; Roman

Polanski, Polish film director, **1933**; Robert Redford, US film actor, **1937**.

Genghis Khan, **1227**; Guido Reni, Italian painter, **1642**; André Jacques Garnerin, French balloonist, **1823**; William Henry Hudson, US writer, **1922**; Anita Loos, US writer, **1981**; Nikolaus Pevsner, architectural historian, **1983**.

19 Feast day of St Mocha, Saints Agapius and Timothy, St Sebald, St Thecla, St Andrew the Tribune, St Sixtus III, St Berulf of Bobbio, St Louis of Anjou, St John Eudes, and St Credan of Evesham.

1274 The coronation of Edward I took place. **1796** France and Spain formed an alliance against Britain. **1897** Electric-powered cabs appeared in London; they proved to be uneconomical and were withdrawn in 1900. **1934** A plebiscite was held in Germany giving sole power to Adolf Hitler, the Führer. **1942** British and Canadian troops raided the port of Dieppe, resulting in heavy casualties for the attacking force. **1989** Poland became the first eastern European country to end one-party rule, when a coalition government was formed with Tadeuz Mazowiecki as prime minister.

John Dryden, English poet, **1631**; John Flamsteed, first Astronomer Royal, **1646**; James Nasmyth, Scottish inventor, **1808**; Gabrielle (Coco) Chanel, French couturier, **1883**; Ogden Nash, US humorist, **1902**; Bill Clinton, 42nd US president, **1945**.

Augustus, 1st Roman emperor, **14**; Blaise Pascal, French philosopher and mathematician, **1662**; Sergei Pavlovich Diaghilev, Russian chorographer, **1929**; Federico García Lorca, Spanish poet and playwright, **1936**; 'Groucho' Marx, US comedian, **1977**; Frederick Ashton, British choreographer, **1988**.

20 Feast day of St Rognwald or Ronald, St Bernard of Clairvaux, St Amator or Amadour, St Philibert, and St Oswin. **1710** The French were defeated by the Austrians at the Battle of Saragossa. **1914** German forces occupied Brussels. **1924** Although considered the likely winner, British sprinter Eric

Liddel refused to run in the 100m heats at the Paris Olympics because it fell on a Sunday. **1956** Calder Hall nuclear power plant, Britain's first nuclear power station, began operating. **1960** Senegal gained independence from France. **1968** Russian troops invaded Czechoslovakia. **1977** The US *Voyager I* spacecraft was launched on its journey via Jupiter and Saturn to become the first artificial object to leave the solar system.

B

Thomas Corneille, French playwright, **1625**; Benjamin Harrison, 23rd US president, **1833**; Raymond Poincaré, French statesman, **1860**; H P Lovecraft, US writer, **1890**; Jack Teagarden, US jazz trombonist, **1905**; Jim Reeves, US country singer, **1924**.

D

Friedrich Wilhelm Joseph von Schelling, German philosopher, **1854**; Adolphe William Bouguereau, French painter, **1905**; William Booth, founder of the Salvation Army, **1912**; Paul Ehrlich, German biochemist, **1915**; Leon Trotsky, Russian politician, **1940**.

21

Feast day of St Pius X, pope, St Abraham of Smolensk, St Sidonius Apollinaris, Saints Bonosus and Maximian, and Saints Cisellus and Camerinus.

1808 The French forces, under General Junot, were defeated by Wellington at the Battle of Vimiero. **1901** The Cadillac Motor Company was formed in Detroit, Michigan, USA, named after the French explorer, Antoine Cadillac. **1911** Leonardo da Vinci's painting, the *Mona Lisa*, was stolen from the Louvre in Paris – it was recovered two years later. **1939** Civil Defence, to mitigate the effects of enemy attack, was started in Britain. **1959** Hawaii became the 50th of the United States. **1991** An attempted coup d'état in the USSR failed; faced with international condemnation and popular protests led by Boris Yeltsin, the junta stepped down and Gorbachev was reinstated.

B

William Murdock, Scottish inventor, **1754**; King William IV, **1765**; Aubrey Beardsley, English illustrator, **1872**; Count Basie, US jazz pianist and bandleader, **1904**; HRH Princess Margaret, **1930**; Janet Baker, English mezzo-soprano, **1933**.

D

Richard Crashaw, English poet, **1649**; Aston Webb, English architect, **1930**; Leonard Constant Lambert, English composer,

JAN FEB MAR APR MAY JUN JUL AUG SEP OCT NOV DEC

1951; Jacob Epstein, British sculptor, **1959**; Benigno Aquino, Philippine politician, **1983**; Tatiana Troyanos, US operatic mezzo-soprano, **1993**.

22 Feast day of St Timothy, St Andrew of Fiesole, St Sigfrid of Wearmouth, and St John Kemble.

1642 The English Civil War began, between the supporters of Charles I and of Parliament, when the king raised his standard at Nottingham. **1788** The British settlement in Sierra Leone was founded, the purpose of which was to secure a home in Africa for freed slaves from England. **1846** New Mexico was annexed by the USA. **1864** The International Red Cross was founded by the Geneva Convention to assist the wounded and prisoners of war. **1910** Korea was annexed by Japan. **1985** Following an aborted take-off, a British Airtours Boeing 737 burst into flames on the runway at Manchester Airport; 55 persons were killed.

Claude Debussy, French composer, **1862**; Jacques Lipchitz, US sculptor and painter, **1891**; Dorothy Parker, US humorist and writer, **1893**; Henri Cartier-Bresson, French photographer, **1908**; Ray Bradbury, US writer, **1920**; Karlheinz Stockhausen, German composer, **1928**.

Jean Honoré Fragonard, French painter, **1806**; Michael Collins, Irish nationalist, **1922**; Oliver Lodge, English physicist, **1940**; Michael Fokine, Russian dancer and choreographer, **1942**; William Richard Morris, British car manufacturer, **1963**.

23 The national day of Romania. Feast day of St Rose of Lima, Saints Asterius and Claudius, St Tydfil, St Philip Benizi, and St Eugene or Eoghan of Ardstraw.

1813 The French were driven back by the Prussians under General von Bülow at the Battle of Grossbeeren. **1839** Hong Kong was taken by the British. **1914** The British Expeditionary Force fought its first battle at Mons, in the First World War. **1921** Faisal I was crowned as King of Iraq. **1927** Nicola Sacco and Bartolomeo Vanzetti, two Italo-American anarchists, were falsely accused of robbery and murder, and were sent to the electric chair. **1939** The USSR and Germany signed a non-

aggression pact which, although short-lived, eased the way for
Hitler's invasion of Poland. **1940** The Blitz began as German
bombers began an all-night raid on London. **1948** The World
Council of Churches was founded.

Louis XVI, King of France, **1754**; Edgar Lee Masters, US poet
and novelist, **1869**; Gene Kelly, US dancer and singer, **1912**;
Peter Thomson, Australian golfer, **1929**; Willy Russell, English
playwright, **1947**; Keith Moon, British rock drummer, **1947**.

William Wallace, Scottish patriot, **1305**; Charles Auguste de
Coulomb, French physicist, **1806**; Rudolph Valentino, Italian-
born film actor, **1926**; Oscar Hammerstein II, US lyricist, **1960**;
Didier Peroni, French racing driver, **1987**.

24 Feast day of St Bartholomew, The Martyrs of Utica, and St
Audenoeus or Ouen.

AD 79 Mount Vesuvius erupted and buried the cities of Pompeii
and Herculaneum in hot volcanic ash. **410** The Visigoths, led
by Alaric, sacked Rome. **1572** Charles IX ordered the massacre
of the Huguenots throughout France; in Paris thousands were
killed in what became known as the Massacre of St
Bartholomew. **1704** The French were defeated by the English
and Dutch fleets at the Battle of Malaga. **1814** British forces
captured Washington, DC and set the White House on fire.
1921 The Turkish army, led by Mustafa Kemal, drove back the
Greeks at the Battle of the Sakkaria River. **1959** The
Manchester Guardian was renamed the *Guardian*.

George Stubbs, English painter, **1724**; William Wilberforce,
English philanthropist, **1759**; Max Beerbohm, English writer
and caricaturist, **1872**; Graham Sutherland, English painter,
1903; Charles Causley, English poet, **1917**; Stephen Fry,
English actor and writer, **1957**.

Pliny the Elder, Roman naturalist and writer, **79**; Alaric I, King
of the Visigoths, **410**; Thomas Blood, Irish adventurer, **1680**;
Thomas Chatterton, English poet, **1770**; Nicolas Léonard Sadi
Carnot, French physicist, **1832**; Ronald Knox, British
theologian, **1957**.

JAN FEB MAR APR MAY JUN JUL AUG SEP OCT NOV DEC

25 National Day of Uruguay. Feast Day of St Ebba, St Genesius the Comedian, St Gregory of Utrecht, St Louis IX, King of France, St Mennas of Constantinople, and St Patricia.

325 The Council of Nicaea set the rules for the computation of Easter. 1830 A revolution against the Netherlands union erupted in Brussels. 1914 Louvain was sacked by the Germans. 1919 The first daily scheduled flights started between London and Paris. 1931 Ramsay MacDonald formed a National Government. 1940 The RAF made the first air raid on Berlin. 1944 The Allies liberated Paris. 1960 The XVIIth Olympic Games opened in Rome. 1989 The US space probe *Voyager* reached Neptune; pictures of Triton, its moon, revealed the existence of two additional moons.

B Ivan IV ('The Terrible'), Tsar of Russia, 1530; Allan Pinkerton, founder of the US detective agency, 1819; Leonard Bernstein, US conductor and composer, 1918; Sean Connery, Scottish actor, 1930; Martin Amis, English novelist, 1949.

D Jan Vermeer, Dutch painter, 1691; David Hume, Scottish philosopher, 1776; William Herschel, English astronomer, 1822; Michael Faraday, English chemist and physicist, 1867; Friedrich Wilhelm Nietzsche, German philosopher, 1900; Truman Capote, US author, 1984.

26 Feast Day of St Bergwine, archbishop of Canterbury, St John Wall, St Mary Desmaisieres, St Pandonia, and St Teresa Jornet Ihars.

55 BC Julius Caesar landed in Britain. 1346 King Edward III, aided by the Black Prince, his son, defeated the French at the Battle of Crécy. 1789 The French Assembly adopted the Declaration of the Rights of Man. 1846 Mendelssohn's oratorio *Elijah* was first performed, Birmingham Festival. 1883 Krakatoa, the island volcano, began erupting, killing thousands. 1920 Women in the USA were granted the right to vote. 1936 The Anglo-Egyptian alliance was signed. 1952 The USSR announced that it had successfully tested the ICBM (Intercontinental Ballistic Missile). 1972 The XXth Olympic Games opened in Munich. 1978 Cardinal Albino Luciani was elected Pope John Paul I.

B Sir Robert Walpole, English statesman, **1676**; Prince Albert, Consort to Queen Victoria, **1819**; Lee De Forest, US physicist, **1873**; Jules Romains, French novelist, playwright and poet, **1885**; Christopher Isherwood, English novelist, **1904**.

D Frans Hals, Dutch painter, **1666**; Anton van Leeuwenhoek, Dutch naturalist and microscopist, Louis Philippe, 'Citizen King' of France, **1850**; Charles Lindbergh, US pioneer aviator, **1974**; Charles Boyer, French actor, **1978**.

27 Feast Day of St Caesarius of Arles, St David Lewis, Little St Hugh, St Monica, St Margaret the Barefooted, St Marcellus of Tomi, and St Poemen.

1784 The first balloon ascent was made in Britain by James Tytler at Edinburgh. **1813** Napoleon defeated the Austrians at the Battle of Dresden. **1816** Algiers, then a refuge for Barbary pirates, was bombarded by Lord Exmouth. **1859** Edwin Drake was the first in the USA to strike oil – at Titusville, Pennsylvania. **1913** A Russian pilot, Lieutenant Peter Nesterov, became the first to perform the loop-the-loop. **1928** The anti-war Kellogg-Briand Pact was signed by 15 nations. **1939** The first jet-propelled aircraft, the Heinkel 178, made its first flight. **1958** The USSR launched *Sputnik 3*, carrying two dogs. **1987** At about 30,000 feet above the USA, the amorous behaviour of a just-married couple caused the pilot of a jet-liner on a coast-to-coast flight to land in Houston; the couple faced a maximum of one year in prison.

B Confucius, Chinese philosopher, **551 BC**; Georg Wilhelm Friedrich Hegel, German philosopher, **1770**; Samuel Goldwyn, US film magnate, **1882**; Lyndon B Johnson, 36th US President, **1908**; Donald Bradman, Australian cricketer, **1908**; Lester Young, US jazz saxophonist, **1909**; Mother Teresa, Albanian-born Indian missionary, **1910**.

D Titian, Italian painter, **1576**; James Thomson, Scottish poet, **1748**; Louis Botha, South African statesman, **1919**; Le Corbusier, Swiss architect, **1965**; Haile Selassie, deposed Emperor of Ethiopia, **1975**; Earl Mountbatten of Burma, murdered by the IRA, **1979**.

28

Feast Day of St Augustine of Hippo, St Alexander of Constantinople, St Edmund Arrowsmith, St Julian of Brioude, and St Moses of Abyssinia.

1640 The Indian War in New England ended with the surrender of the Indians. **1849** Venice was taken by the Austrians after a seige. **1850** The Channel telegraph cable was laid between Dover and Cap Gris Nez. **1914** The Battle of Heligoland Bight, the first major naval battle of World War I, was fought. **1933** For the first time, a BBC-broadcasted appeal was used by the police in tracking down a wanted man. **1945** US forces under General George Marshall landed in Japan. **1963** The massive (200,000 people) civil rights march from the South ended in Washington, DC where Martin Luther King delivered his famous 'I have a dream' speech. **1988** The Yan Hee Polyclinic in Bangkok, Thailand, reported on a new slimming technique – overweight Thais were suppressing their appetites by sticking lettuce seeds in their ears and pressing them in ten times before meals.

B

Johann Wolfgang Goethe, German poet, novelist and dramatist, **1749**; Edward Burne-Jones, British painter, **1833**; Liam O'Flaherty, Irish novelist, **1896**; Godfrey Hounsfield, British inventor of the EMI-scanner, **1919**; Ben Gazzara, US film actor, **1930**.

D

Hugo Grotius, Dutch jurist and politician, **1645**; William Smith, British geologist, **1839**; Leigh Hunt, critic and poet, **1859**; Ernest Orlando Lawrence, US physicist, **1958**; Prince William of Gloucester, killed in an air crash, **1972,** John Huston, US film director, **1988**.

29

Feast Day of St Sabina of Rome, St Edwold of Cerne, and St Medericus or Merry.

1526 The Hungarians were defeated by the Turks at the Battle of Mohacs. **1831** Michael Faraday successfully demonstrated the first electrical transformer at the Royal Institute, London. **1835** The city of Melbourne, Australia, was founded. **1842** The Treaty of Nanking was signed between the British and the Chinese, ending the Opium War, and leasing the Hong Kong territories to Britain. **1848** The Boers were defeated by the

British army at Boomplatz. **1882** Australia defeated England at cricket for the first time; the *Sporting Times* published an 'obituary' for English cricket. **1895** The Rugby League (called the 'Northern Union' until 1922) was formed from 21 clubs in the North of England. **1904** The third Olympic Games opened at St Louis, Missouri. **1953** The USSR exploded a hydrogen bomb. **1966** At Candlestick Park, San Francisco, the Beatles played their last live concert. **1991** The Supreme Soviet voted to suspend formally all activities of the Communist Party.

B John Locke, English philosopher, **1632**; Jean Auguste Dominique Ingres, French painter, **1780**; Ingrid Bergman, Swedish actress, **1915**; Charlie Parker, US jazz saxophonist, **1920**; Richard Attenborough, English actor and director, **1923**; Richard Gere, US actor, **1949**; Michael Jackson, US pop singer, **1958**.

D Brigham Young, US Mormon leader, **1877**; Cesare Pavese, Italian novelist, **1950**; Éamon de Valera, Irish nationalist politician, **1975**; Ingrid Bergman, Swedish actress, **1982**; Lee Marvin, US actor, **1987**.

30 Feast Day of Saints Felix and Audauctus, St Fantinus, St Pammachius, St Margaret Ward, and St Ruan or Rumon.

1762 The French defeated Frederick II, King of Prussia, at Johannesburg. **1860** The first British tramway, operated by the Birkenhead Street Railway, was inaugurated by an American, George Francis Train. **1862** 'Stonewall' Jackson led the Confederates to victory at the second Battle of Bull Run, in Virginia, during the American Civil War. **1881** The first stereo system, for a telephonic broadcasting service, was patented in Germany by Clement Adler. **1901** Hubert Cecil Booth patented the vacuum cleaner. **1916** Paul von Hindenburg became Chief of the General Staff of Germany. **1939** In anticipation of German bombing, the great evacuation of children from British cities began, four days before the outbreak of World War II. **1941** The seige of Leningrad by German forces began (ended in Jan 1943). **1963** To reduce the risk of accidental nuclear war, the 'Hotline' between the US President and the Soviet Premier was established.

B Jacques Louis David, French painter, **1748**; Mary Wollstonecraft Shelley, English writer, **1797**; Ernest Rutherford, New Zealand physicist, **1871**; Raymond Massey, Canadian film actor, **1896**; Fred MacMurray, US film actor, **1908**; Denis Healey, British politician, **1917**; Jean Claude Killy, French ski champion, **1943**.

D Cleopatra, queen of Egypt, **30 BC**; Louis XI, King of France, **1483**; John Ross, Scottish explorer, **1856**; Georges Sorel, French socialist philosopher, **1922**; J(oseph) J(ohn) Thomson, English physicist, **1940**.

31 National Day of Malaysia, and of Trinidad and Tobago. Feast Day of St Paulinus of Trier, St Aidan of Lindisfarne, St Raymond Nonnatus, and The Servite Martyrs of Prague.

1422 Henry VI, aged nine months, acceded as King. **1888** The body of Mary Ann 'Polly' Nichols, the first victim of Jack the Ripper, was found mutilated in Buck's Row. **1900** Coca Cola first went on sale in Britain. **1928** The Brecht–Weill musical *The Threepenny Opera* was first performed, in Berlin. **1942** The German offensive was halted by the British at the Battle of Alam al-Halfa, marking the turning-point in the North African Campaign. **1957** Malaya, later Malaysia, became independent. **1972** US swimmer Mark Spitz won five of the seven gold medals he achieved in total at the Munich Olympics. **1983** The USSR shot down a South Korean airliner, killing 269 people aboard. **1984** A tropical storm hit the Philippines, killing over 1,000 people. **1989** Buckingham Palace issued a brief statement stating that the Princess Royal, Princess Anne, was separating from her husband, Captain Mark Phillips.

B Caligula, Roman emperor, **12**; Jahangir, Mogul emperor, **1569**; Maria Montessori, Italian educationalist, **1870**; Fredric March, US actor, **1897**; Bernard Lovell, British astronomer, **1913**; James Coburn, US film actor, **1928**; Van Morrison, Irish rock vocalist, **1945**; Edwin Moses, US athlete, **1955**.

D King Henry V, **1422**; John Bunyan, English author, **1688**; Charles Pierre Baudelaire, French poet, **1867**; Georges Braque, French painter, **1963**; Rocky Marciano, US heavyweight boxer, **1969**; John Ford, US film director, **1973**; Henry Moore, British sculptor, **1986**.

SEPTEMBER ████████

1

National Day of Libya. Feast Day of St Fiacre, St Giles or Aegidiu, St Drithelm, St Lupus or Leu of Sens, St Sebe, St Priscus of Capua, and St Verena.

AD 70 The destruction of Jerusalem under Titus took place. 1853 The world's first triangular postage stamps were issued by the Cape of Good Hope. 1870 The seige of Metz (Franco-German War) started. 1886 The Severn Tunnel was opened for goods traffic. 1920 The state of Lebanon was created by the French. 1923 Nearly 200,000 people were killed in earthquakes in Tokyo and Yokohama. 1928 Albania was declared a kingdom, with Zog I as king. 1933 *The Shape of Things to Come*, the classic science fiction novel by H G Wells, was published. 1939 Germany invaded Poland, starting World War II. 1969 Colonel Khaddhafi seized power in Libya, after overthrowing King Idris I. 1972 Bobby Fischer beat Boris Spassky at Reykjavik, becoming the first US world chess champion.

B

Engelbert Humperdinck, German composer, 1854; Roger David Casement, Irish nationalist, 1864; Edgar Rice Burroughs, US novelist, 1875; Francis Aston, English physicist, 1877; Rocky Marciano, US heavyweight boxer, 1923; Lily Tomlin, US comedienne, 1939; Leonard Slatkin, US conductor, 1954.

D

Pope Adrian IV, the only English pope, 1159; Jacques Cartier, French explorer, 1557; Louis XIV, the 'Sun King' of France, 1715; Richard Westmacott, British sculptor, 1856; Siegfried Sassoon, English writer, 1967; François Mauriac, French novelist, 1970.

2

Feast day of St William of Roskilde, The Martyrs of September 1792, St Agricolus, St Antoninus of Pamiers, St Brocard, and St Castor of Apt.

31 BC Emperor Augustus (Octavian) defeated Antony at the Battle of Actium. 1666 The Great Fire of London started; it destroyed 13,000 buildings in four days. 1752 The Julian calendar was used in Britain and the Colonies 'officially' for the

last time; as in the rest of Europe, the following day became 14 Sept in the Gregorian calendar. **1898** The British, led by Lord Kitchener, defeated the Sudanese at the Battle of Omdurman and re-occupied Khartoum, the capital. **1906** Roald Amundsen completed his sailing round Canada's Northwest Passage. **1923** The Irish Free State held its first elections. **1939** Under the National Service Bill, men aged 19–41 were conscripted in Britain. **1958** China's first television station opened in Peking. **1987** The CD-video, combining digital sound with high-definition video, was launched by Philips.

B   John Howard, English philanthropist, **1726**; Giovanni Verga, Italian novelist and dramatist, **1840**; Wilhelm Ostwald, German chemist, **1853**; Frederick Soddy, English physical chemist, **1877**; Michael Hastings, English dramatist, **1938**; Jimmy Connors, US tennis player, **1952**.

D   José Ribera ('Lo Spagnoletto'), Spanish painter, **1652**; Thomas Telford, Scottish civil engineer, **1834**; Henri Rousseau, French painter, **1910**; Pierre de Coubertin, founder of the modern Olympics, **1937**; J R R Tolkein, English writer, **1973**.

---

3   Feast Day of St Simeon Stylites the Younger, St Phoebe, St Remaclus, St Aigulf or Ayoul of Lerins, St Gregory the Great, St Cuthburga, St Hildelitha, and St Macanisius.

1650 Cromwell defeated the Scots at the second Battle of Dunbar. **1651** The Royalist troops under Charles II were defeated by Oliver Cromwell at the second Battle of Worcester. **1783** Britain recognised US independence with the signing of a treaty in Paris. **1916** The first Zeppelin was shot down over England. **1930** Santo Domingo, in the Dominican Republic, was destroyed by a hurricane which killed 5,000 people. **1935** Malcolm Campbell reached a new world land speed record of 301.13 mph in *Bluebird* on Bonneville Salt Flats, Utah. **1939** Britain, New Zealand, Australia, and France declared war on Germany. **1943** The Allies landed at Salerno, on mainland Italy, and the Italian government surrendered. **1967** Sweden changed from driving on the left to the right. **1976** The US spacecraft *Viking 2* landed on Mars and began sending pictures of the red planet to earth.

B Joseph Wright, British painter, 1734; Louis Henry Sullivan, US architect, 1856; Jean-Léon Jaurès, French socialist politician, 1859; Macfarlane Burnet, Australian immunologist, 1899; Alan Ladd, US actor, 1913; Brian Lochore, New Zealand rugby player, 1940.

D Oliver Cromwell, Lord Protector, 1658; Ivan Sergeyevich Turgenev, Russian dramatist, 1883; e e cummings, poet, US 1962; Frederick Louis MacNiece, British poet, 1963; Ho Chi Minh, president of North Vietnam, 1969; Frank Capra, US film director, 1991; David Brown, English engineer and industrialist, 1993.

4 Feast Day of St Rosalio, St Rose of Viterbo, Saints Marcellus and Valerian, St Marinus of San Marino, St Boniface I, pope, St Ultan of Ardbraccan, and St Ida of Herzfeld.

1260 The Battle of Montaperti, between the rival Guelphs and Ghibellines, was fought in Central Italy. 1870 Emperor Napoleon III, Bonaparte's nephew, was deposed and the Third Republic was proclaimed. 1886 Geronimo, the Apache chief, surrendered to the US army. 1909 The first Boy Scout rally was held at Crystal Palace, near London. 1940 The US Columbia Broadcasting System gave a demonstration of colour TV on station W2XAB. 1944 The Allies liberated Antwerp, Belgium. 1970 Natalia Makarova, of the Kirov Ballet, defected to the West. 1985 The wreck of the *Titanic* on the Atlantic seaboard was photographed by remote control. 1988 British Customs officials thwarted the first known attempt by persons to smuggle drugs into Britain from Holland using a helicopter.

B Vicomte François René de Chateaubriand, French author, 1768; Anton Bruckner, Austrian composer, 1824; Antonin Artaud, French dramatist and director, 1896; Mary Renault, English novelist, 1905; Dawn Fraser, Australian swimmer, 1937; Tom Watson, US golfer, 1949.

D Charles Townshend, British politician, 1767; James Wyatt, English architect, 1813; Robert Schuman, French statesman, 1963; Albert Schweitzer, French organist and missionary surgeon, 1965; Georges Simenon, Belgian crime writer, 1989.

JAN FEB MAR APR MAY JUN JUL AUG **SEP** OCT NOV DEC

5 Feast Day of Saints Urban and Theodore and their Companions, St Laurence Giustiniani, St Bertinus, and St Genebald of Laon.

1774 The first Continental Congress in America opened at Philadelphia. 1800 French troops surrendered Malta to the British, following Nelson's naval blockade. 1914 The first Battle of the Marne, during World War I, began. 1922 US aviator James Doolittle made the first US coast-to-coast flight in 21 hrs, 19 min. 1963 Christine Keeler, one of the women involved in the Profumo scandal, was arrested and charged with perjury. 1972 At the Olympic Games in Munich, terrorists of the Black September group seized Israeli athletes as hostages; nine of the Israelis, four of the terrorists, and one German policeman were killed. 1980 The world's longest road tunnel, the St Gotthard, was opened running 16km/10mi from Goschenen to Airolo, Switzerland. 1988 *No Sex Please – We're British*, the longest running comedy, closed (after 6,671 performances over 16 years).

Louis VIII, King of France, 1187; Louis XIV, the 'Sun King' of France, 1638; Giacomo Meyerbeer, German composer, 1791; Victorien Sardou, French dramatist, 1831; Arthur Koestler, Hungarian author, 1905; Raquel Welch, US actress, 1940; Freddy Mercury, British pop singer, 1946.

Pieter Breughel the Elder, Flemish painter, 1569; Auguste Comte, French philosopher, 1857; Charles Péguy, French poet, 1914; Josh White, US blues singer, 1969; Douglas Bader, British fighter pilot, 1962.

6 Feast Day of St Eleutherius of Spoleto, St Cagnoald or Chainoaldus, and Saints Donatian, Laetus, and Others.

1522 Ferdinand Magellan's 17 surviving crew members reached the Spanish coast aboard the *Vittoria*, having completed the first circumnavigation of the world. 1852 Britain's first free lending library opened in Manchester. 1880 The first cricket test match in England was played between England and Australia at the Oval, London. 1901 US President William McKinley was shot and fatally wounded by an anarchist. 1941 Nazi Germany made the wearing of the yellow Star of David badges compulsory for all its Jewish citizens. **1965** India invaded West Pakistan. **1975** A massive earthquake centred on Lice, Turkey, caused nearly 3,000 deaths. **1989** Due to a computer error, 41,000 Parisians received letters charging them with murder, extortion, and organised prostitution instead of traffic violations.

Marquis de Lafayette, French soldier and statesman, **1757**; John Dalton, British chemist, **1766**; Jane Addams, US sociologist, **1860**; Edward Appleton, British physicist, **1892**; Britt Ekland, Swedish film actress, **1943**; Roger Waters, English bassist, **1947**.

Suleiman I, sultan of Turkey, **1566**; Jean-Baptiste Colbert, French politician, **1683**; Gertrude Lawrence, English actress and singer, **1952**; Hendrik Verwoerd, South African prime minister, assassinated, **1966**.

7 National Day of Brazil. Feast Day of St Anastasius the Fuller, St Cloud or Clodoald, Saints Alcmund and Tilbert, St Grimonia, St Regina or Reine of Alize, St Sozon, and St John of Nicomedia.

1812 The Russians were defeated by Napoleon's forces at the Battle of Borodino, 70 mi west of Moscow. **1838** Grace Darling and her father rescued the crew of the Forfarshire, a steamer wrecked off the Northumberland coast; she subsequently became a national heroine. **1901** The Peace of Peking was signed, ending the Boxer Rising in China. **1904** Francis Younghusband led a British expedition to Tibet, where a treaty was signed with the Dalai Lama. **1973** Jackie Stewart became world champion racing driver for the third consecutive year. **1986** Bishop Desmond Tutu was appointed Archbishop of Capetown, the first black head of South African Anglicans. **1991** Peace talks on the Yugoslav civil war opened in The Hague, the Netherlands, under EC sponsorship.

Queen Elizabeth I, **1533**; John McDougall Stuart, Australian explorer, **1815**; Elia Kazan, US stage and film director, **1909**; Anthony Quayle, English actor, **1913**; Peter Lawford, English actor, **1923**; Sonny Rollins, US saxophonist, **1929**; Buddy Holly, US rock singer, **1936**.

⫶⟩ Catherine Parr, 6th wife of Henry VIII, **1548**; Armand Sully-Prudhomme, French poet, **1907**; William Hunt, British painter, **1910**; Keith Moon, English rock drummer, **1978**; Christy Brown, Irish novelist, **1981**; Liam O'Flaherty, Irish novelist, **1984**.

8 Feast Day of St Corbinian, St Disibod, St Eusebius, Saints Adrian and Natalia, St Kingsmark or Cynfarch Oer, St Sergius I, pope, St Zeno, St Nestabus, and St Nestor.

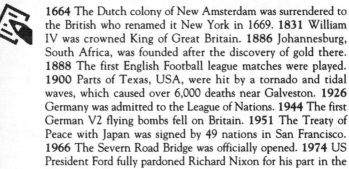

1664 The Dutch colony of New Amsterdam was surrendered to the British who renamed it New York in 1669. **1831** William IV was crowned King of Great Britain. **1886** Johannesburg, South Africa, was founded after the discovery of gold there. **1888** The first English Football league matches were played. **1900** Parts of Texas, USA, were hit by a tornado and tidal waves, which caused over 6,000 deaths near Galveston. **1926** Germany was admitted to the League of Nations. **1944** The first German V2 flying bombs fell on Britain. **1951** The Treaty of Peace with Japan was signed by 49 nations in San Francisco. **1966** The Severn Road Bridge was officially opened. **1974** US President Ford fully pardoned Richard Nixon for his part in the Watergate affair.

⫶⟩ King Richard I (the Lion Heart), **1157**; Ludovico Ariosto, Italian poet, **1474**; Antonín Dvořák, Czech composer, **1841**; Siegfried Sassoon, English writer, **1863**; Jean-Louis Barrault, French actor and director, **1910**; Peter Sellers, English actor and comedian, **1925**; Frankie Avalon, US singer, **1940**.

⫶⟩ Francisco Gomez de Quevedo y Villegas, Spanish writer, **1645**; George Bradshaw, British publisher of the first railway guides, **1853**; Richard Strauss, German composer, **1949**; André Derain, French painter, **1954**; Jean Seberg, US actress, **1979**.

9 Feast Day of St Omer or Audomaurus, St Peter Claver, St Ciaran or Kieran of Clonmacnois, St Bettelin, St Joseph of Volokolamsk, St Gorgonius, and St Isaac or Sahak the Great.

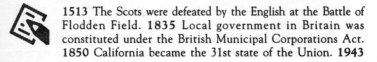

1513 The Scots were defeated by the English at the Battle of Flodden Field. **1835** Local government in Britain was constituted under the British Municipal Corporations Act. **1850** California became the 31st state of the Union. **1943**

Allied forces landed at Salerno, Italy. **1945** Palestinians attempted to hijack an El Al flight but were overpowered by security guards. The Israelis reluctantly handed over the failed hijackers at Heathrow, where the plane made its landing. **1971** Geoffrey Jackson, who had been kidnapped by the Tupamaros in Uruguay eight months previously, was released. **1975** Czech tennis player Martina Navratilova, aged 18, defected to the West, requesting political asylum in the USA. **1985** Massive earthquakes in Mexico left more than 4,700 dead and 30,000 injured.

Cardinal Richelieu, French statesman, **1585**; Luigi Galvani, Italian physiologist, **1737**; Leo Tolstoy, Russian novelist, **1828**; James Hilton, English novelist, **1900**; Otis Redding, US singer and songwriter, **1941**; John Curry, English figure skating champion, **1949**.

King William I (the Conqueror), **1087**; James IV, King of Scotland, **1513**; Giambattista Piranesi, Italian architect, **1778**; Stéphane Mallarmé, French poet, **1898**; Henri Toulouse-Lautrec, French painter, **1901**; Mao Zedong, Chinese leader, **1976**.

10 Feast Day of St Theodard of Maestricht, St Salvius or Salvy of Albi, St Ambrose Barlow, St Aubert of Avranches, Saints Menodora, Metrodora and Nymphodora, St Finian of Moville, St Nemesian, St Nicholas of Tolentino, and St Pulcheria.

1721 The Peace of Nystad was concluded between Russia and Sweden. **1823** Simón Bolívar, known as The Liberator, became the dictator of Peru. **1894** George Smith, a London cab driver, became the first person to be convicted for drunken driving; he was fined 20s (£1). **1919** The Treaty of Saint-Germain was signed; the new boundaries it set brought about the end of the Austrian Empire. **1942** In a single raid, the RAF dropped 100,000 bombs on Dusseldorf. **1945** Former Norwegian Premier Vidkun Quisling, who had collaborated with the Germans during World War II, was sentenced to death. **1981** Picasso's *Guernica* was returned to Spain after 40 years in US custodianship; the artist had refused to show the painting in Spain before the restoration of democracy. **1989** Hungary opened its border to the West allowing thousands of East

JAN FEB MAR APR MAY JUN JUL AUG SEP OCT NOV DEC

Germans to leave, much to the anger of the East German government.

B Giovanni Tiepolo, Italian painter, **1727**; John Soane, English architect, **1753**; Mungo Park, Scottish explorer, **1771**; Franz Werfel, Austrian novelist and poet, **1890**; Robert Wise, US film director, **1914**; Arnold Palmer, US golfer, **1929**; José Feliciano, US singer, **1945**.

D Louis IV, King of France, **954**; Mary Wollstonecraft, British feminist, **1797**; Huey Long, US politician, assassinated, **1935**; Charles Cruft, British dog expert, **1938**; Balthazar Johannes Vorster, South African Nationalist politician, **1983**.

---

11 Feast Day of St Theodora of Alexandria, St Peter of Chavanon, Saints Protus and Hyacinth, St Deiniol, St Patiens of Lyon, and St Paphnutius.

1709 The Duke of Marlborough and Prince Eugene of Austria defeated the French, under Marshal Villars, at the Battle of Malplaquet. **1777** American troops led by George Washington were defeated by the British at the Battle of Brandywine Creek, in the American War of Independence. **1841** The London to Brighton commuter express train began regular service, taking just 105 minutes. **1855** In the Crimean War, Sebastopol was taken by the Allies after capitulation by the Russians. **1922** A British mandate was declared in Palestine. **1951** Stravinsky's *The Rake's Progress* was performed for the first time, in Venice; the libretto was by W H Auden. **1973** A military junta, with US support, overthrew the elected government of Chile. **1978** Georgi Markov, a Bulgarian defector, was fatally stabbed by a poisoned umbrella point wielded by a Bulgarian secret agent in London.

B Pierre de Ronsard, French poet, **1524**; James Thomson, Scottish poet, **1700**; O Henry, US short story writer, **1862**; James Hopwood Jeans, British mathematician and scientist, **1877**; D H Lawrence, English writer, **1885**; Barry Sheene, British racing motor cyclist, **1950**.

D Giovanni Domenico Cassini, Italian-French astronomer, **1712**; David Thomas Graham, Scottish chemist, **1869**; Jan Christian Smuts, South African statesman, **1950**; Nikita Khrushchev,

Russian leader, **1971**; Salvador Allende Gossens, Chilean politician, **1973**; Peter Tosh, Jamaican reggae star, **1987**.

12

Feast Day of St Guy of Anderlecht, St Ailbhe, and St Eanswida.

1609 Henry Hudson sailed the sloop *Half Moon* into New York Harbour and up to Albany to discover the river named after him. **1878** Cleopatra's Needle, the obelisk of Thothmes II, was erected on London's Embankment. **1910** Alice Stebbins Wells, a former social worker, became the world's first policewoman, appointed by the Los Angeles Police Department. **1914** The Allies were victorious at the First Battle of Marne, in World War I. **1919** Italian writer and nationalist Gabriele D'Annunzio led an unofficial army and seized Fiume from Yugoslavia. **1940** The Lascaux Caves, France, containing prehistoric wall paintings, were discovered. **1943** Benito Mussolini, imprisoned by the Allies, was rescued by German parachutists. **1974** A military coup deposed Emperor Haile Selassie of Ethiopia, the Lion of Judah.

Richard Jordan Gatling, US inventor, **1818**; Herbert Henry Asquith, British statesman, **1852**; Maurice Chevalier, French actor and entertainer, **1888**; Louis MacNeice, British poet, **1907**; John Cleveland 'Jesse' Owens, US athlete, **1913**; Wesley Hall, West Indies cricketer and politician, **1937**.

François Couperin, French composer, **1733**; Jean-Philippe Rameau, French composer, **1764**; Gebhard Leberecht von Blücher, Prussian general and field-marshal, **1819**; Peter Mark Roget, English lexicographer, **1869**; Steve Biko, South African civil rights leader, **1977**; Anthony Perkins, US actor, **1992**.

13

Feast Day of St John Chrysostom, St Maurilius of Angers, St Amatus or Amé, abbot, and St Eulogius of Alexandria.

1759 The British defeated the French at the Battle of Quebec, completing the British conquest of North America. **1788** New York became the capital of the USA (until 1789). **1845** The Knickerbocker Club, the first baseball club, was founded in New York. **1914** The first Battle of the Aisne, during World War I, began. **1942** The Germans began their attack on Stalingrad.

1943 General Chiang Kai-shek was re-elected president of the Republic of China. 1956 Little Richard recorded 'Tutti Frutti' in Los Angeles with cleaned-up lyrics. 1957 *The Mousetrap* became Britain's longest running play, reaching its 1,998th performance. 1989 Britain's biggest ever banking computer error gave customers an extra £2 billion in a period of 30 minutes; 99.3 per cent of the money was reportedly returned.

William Betty, British boy actor, 1791; Arnold Schoenberg, Austrian composer, 1874; John Joseph Priestley, English author, 1894; Claudette Colbert, French actress, 1905; John Smith, British politician, 1938; Jacqueline Bisset, English actress, 1944.

Andrea Mantegna, Italian painter, 1506; Michel Eyquem de Montaigne, French essayist, 1592; Charles James Fox, English statesman, 1806; Alexis-Emmanuel Chabrier, French composer, 1894; Leopold Stokowski, US conductor, 1977; Joe Pasternak, US film producer, 1991.

14

Feast Day of St Maternus of Cologne and St Notburga.

1402 The English defeated the Scots at the Battle of Homildon Hill. 1759 A *Journey Through Europe, or the play of Geography*, the earliest dated English board game, went on sale, priced 8s (40p). 1812 Napoleon entered Moscow in his disastrous invasion of Russia. 1891 The first penalty kick was taken in an English League football game was taken by Heath of Wolverhampton Wanderers against Accrington. 1901 Theodore Roosevelt became the 26th US president, 12 hours after the death of President McKinley who had been shot by an anarchist on 6 Sept. 1923 Miguel Primo de Riviera became dictator of Spain. 1959 The Soviet *Lunik II* became the first spacecraft to land on the Moon. 1991 The South African government, the ANC, and the Inkatha Freedom Party signed a peace accord aimed at ending the factional violence in the black townships.

Peter Lely, Dutch painter, 1617; Baron von Humboldt, German traveller and naturalist, 1769; Jan Garrigue Masaryk, Czech statesman, 1886; Peter Scott, British artist and ornithologist, 1909; Jack Hawkins, British film actor, 1910; Kepler Wessels,

Australian cricketer, 1957.

Dante Alighieri, Italian poet, 1321; James Fenimore Cooper, US novelist, 1851; Augustus Pugin, English architect, 1852; Arthur Wellesley, 1st Duke of Wellington, English soldier and politician, 1852; Isadora Duncan, US dancer, 1927; Princess Grace of Monaco (Grace Kelly), 1982.

15 National day of Costa Rica. The Battle of Britain day. Feast Day of St Nicetus the Goth, St Nicomedes, St Aachard or Aichardus, St Mirin, and St Catherine of Genoa.

1784 The first ascent in a hydrogen balloon in England was made by the Italian aeronaut Vincenzo Lunardi. 1812 The Russians set fire to Moscow in order to halt the French occupation. 1830 The Manchester and Liverpool railway opened; during the ceremony, William Huskisson, MP, became the first person to be killed by a train. 1915 Military tanks, designed by Ernest Swinton, were first used by the British Army, at Flers, in the Somme offensive. 1917 Alexander Kerensky proclaimed Russia a republic. 1935 The Nuremburg laws were passed in Germany, outlawing Jews and making the swastika the country's official flag. 1964 The *Sun*, which became Britain's biggest selling newspaper, was first published. 1974 The civil war between Christians and Muslims in Beirut began. 1985 Tony Jacklin's European golf team won the Ryder Cup from the USA who had long dominated the competition.

Trajan, Roman emperor, 53; Titus Oates, British priest and conspirator, 1649; William Taft, 27th US president, 1857; Agatha Christie, English detective novelist, 1890; Jean Renoir, French film director, 1894; Jessye Norman, US soprano 1945; Freddie Mercury, British rock singer, 1946.

Isambard Kingdom Brunel, British engineer, 1859; John Hanning Speke, British explorer, 1864; José Echegaray, Spanish dramatist and scientist, 1916; Geoffrey Fisher, former Archbishop of Canterbury, 1972; Gustav VI, King of Sweden, 1973; Robert Penn Warren, US novelist, 1989.

16 The national day of Mexico. Feast Day of St Cornelius, pope, St Cyprian, St Ludmila, St Ninian, Saints Abundius and

JAN FEB MAR APR MAY JUN JUL AUG SEP OCT NOV DEC

Abundantius, St Edith of Wilton, and St Euphemia.

1847 The house in which Shakespeare was born in Stratford-upon-Avon became the first building in Britain to be purchased for preservation. **1859** David Livingstone discovered Lake Nyasa. **1906** The US Buick and Oldsmobile car manufacturers merged to become General Motors. **1941** The Shah of Iran, Reza Khan Pahlavi, abdicated. **1963** Malaysia became independent and a mob of over 100,000 burned down the British Embassy. **1969** Biba, considered London's trendiest store in the 'swinging 60s', opened on Kensington High Street. **1976** The Episcopal Church in the USA approved the ordination of women to the priesthood. **1987** For the first time in South Africa, Othello was performed with a black actor, John Khani, playing the Moor. **1991** All Iran-Contra charges against Oliver North were dropped.

King Henry V, **1387**; Alexander Korda, British film director and producer, **1893**; Lauren Bacall, US actress, **1924**; Charles Haughey, Irish politician, **1925**; B B King, US blues singer, **1926**; Peter Falk, US actor, **1927**; Andy Irvine, British rugby footballer, **1951**.

Tomás de Torquemada, Spanish Inquisitor-General, **1498**; Gabriel Daniel Fahrenheit, German physicist, **1736**; Louis XVIII, King of France, **1824**; Leo Amery, British statesman and journalist, **1955**; Walter Greenwood, English novelist, **1974**; Maria Callas, US opera singer, **1977**.

17 Feast day of St Francis of Camporosso, St Hildegard, St Columba of Cordova, Saints Socrates and Stephen, St Satyrus of Milan, St Theodora, St Lambert of Maastricht, St Robert Bellarmine, and St Peter Arbues.

1787 The Constitution of the United States of America was signed. **1862** General McClellan repulsed General Lee's invasion of the North at Antietam, ending one of the decisive battles in the American Civil War. **1900** The Commonwealth of Australia, a federation of six colonies, was proclaimed. **1908** Lt Selfridge, on a test flight with Orville Wright, was killed when the plane crashed, becoming the first passenger to die in an air crash. **1931** The first long-playing record was demonstrated in New York by RCA-Victor, but the venture failed because of the high price of the players. **1939** Poland was invaded by the USSR. **1944** The British airborne invasion of Arnhem, Holland began as part of 'Operation Market Garden'. **1991** Estonia, Latvia, Lithuania, North and South Korea, the Marshall Islands, and Micronesia were admitted to the United Nations.

Francisco Gomez de Quevado y Villegas, Spanish poet and satirist, **1580**; William Carlos Williams, US poet, **1883**; Frederick Ashton, British choreographer, **1906**; Stirling Moss, English racing driver, **1929**; Anne Bancroft, US actress, **1931**; Maureen Connolly, US tennis player, **1934**.

Philip IV, King of Spain, **1665**; Tobias George Smollett, Scottish novelist, **1771**; William Henry Fox Talbot, English photographic pioneer, **1877**; Count Folke Bernadotte, Swedish diplomat, assassinated, **1948**; Laura Ashley, Welsh designer and fabric retailer, **1985**.

18 National Day of Chile. Feast Day of St John Massias, St Joseph of Cupertino, St Richardis, St Ferreolus of Limoges, St Ferreolus of Vienne, and St Methodius of Olympus.

1851 The *New York Times* was first published. **1879** Blackpool's famous illuminations were switched on for the first time. **1910** The Chilean revolt against Spanish rule began. **1914** The Irish Home Rule Bill went into effect. **1918** The Battle of Megiddo, in Palestine, began. **1927** CBS, the Columbia Broadcasting System, was inaugurated in the USA. **1931** Japan seized Manchuria and set up a puppet state called Manchukuo – it was returned to China in 1945 after World War II. **1934** The USSR was admitted to the League of Nations. **1939** William Joyce, whose upper-class accent earned him the nickname Lord Haw, made his first Nazi propaganda broadcast from Germany to the UK. **1981** France abolished execution by guillotine. **1991** The Yugoslav navy began a blockade of seven port cities on the Adriatic coast in Dalmatia.

Dr Samuel Johnson, English writer and lexicographer, **1709**; Jean Bernard Léon Foucault, French physicist, **1819**; Greta Garbo, Swedish film actress, **1905**; Jack Cardiff, British film director, **1914**; Frankie Avalon, US singer and actor, **1939**; Peter Shilton, English footballer, **1949**.

Leonhard Euler, Swiss mathematician, **1783**; William Hazlitt, British essayist and critic, **1830**; Dag Hammarskjöld, Swedish UN secretary-general, **1961**; Sean O'Casey, Irish dramatist, **1964**; John Douglas Cockcroft, English nuclear physicist, **1967**; Jimi Hendrix, US rock guitarist, **1970**.

19

Feast Day of St Januarius of Benevento, St Peleus and his Companions, St Emily de Rodat, St Mary of Cerevellon, St Goericus or Abbo, St Theodore of Canterbury, St Susanna of Eleutheropolis, and St Sequanus or Seine.

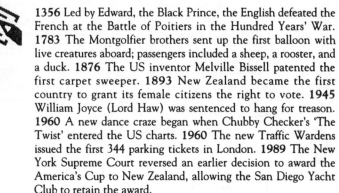

1356 Led by Edward, the Black Prince, the English defeated the French at the Battle of Poitiers in the Hundred Years' War. **1783** The Montgolfier brothers sent up the first balloon with live creatures aboard; passengers included a sheep, a rooster, and a duck. **1876** The US inventor Melville Bissell patented the first carpet sweeper. **1893** New Zealand became the first country to grant its female citizens the right to vote. **1945** William Joyce (Lord Haw) was sentenced to hang for treason. **1960** A new dance craze began when Chubby Checker's 'The Twist' entered the US charts. **1960** The new Traffic Wardens issued the first 344 parking tickets in London. **1989** The New York Supreme Court reversed an earlier decision to award the America's Cup to New Zealand, allowing the San Diego Yacht Club to retain the award.

Lajos Kossuth, Hungarian statesman, **1802**; George Cadbury, English chocolate manufacturer and social reformer, **1839**; William Golding, English novelist, **1911**; Jeremy Irons, English actor, **1948**; Rosemary Casals, US tennis player, **1948**; Twiggy (Lesley Hornby), English model and actress, **1949**.

Meyer Amschel Rothschild, German banker, **1812**; James Garfield, 20th US president, **1881**; Thomas John Barnardo, British philanthropist, **1905**; David Low, British cartoonist, **1963**; Chester Carlson, US inventor of the xerography photocopying process, **1968**; Roy Kinnear, English comedy actor, **1988**.

20

Feast Day of Saints Fausta and Evilasius, St Candida of Carthage, St Vincent Madelgarius, and Saints Theodore, Philippa, and their Companions.

451 The Romans defeated the Huns under Attila at Châlon-sur-Marne. 1519 Ferdinand Magellan, with a fleet of five small ships, sailed from Seville on his expedition around the world. 1854 The Russian army was defeated by the Allied armies at the Battle of Alma in the Crimean War; the first six Victoria Crosses to be awarded to the British Army were won at this battle. 1928 The Fascist Party took over the supreme legislative body in Rome, replacing the Chamber of Deputies. 1961 Argentinian Antonio Abertondo started the first successful non-stop swim across the Channel and back, completed in 43 hr 5 min. 1966 The liner *Queen Elizabeth II* (QE2) was launched at Clydebank, Scotland. 1984 The US embassy in Beirut was attacked by a suicide bomber; explosives within a lorry were set off, killing 40 people.

Alexander the Great, 356 BC; Henry Arthur Jones, British dramatist, 1851; Upton Sinclair, US novelist, 1878; Jelly Roll Morton, US pianist and composer, 1885; John Dankworth, English bandleader and jazzman, 1927; Sophia Loren, Italian film actress, 1934.

Robert Emmet, Irish nationalist, executed, 1803; Jakob Karl Grimm, German philologist, 1863; Annie Besant, British socialist and feminist activist, 1933; Jean Sibelius, Finnish composer, 1957; George Seferis, Greek poet-diplomat, 1971.

21

National day of Malta Feast day of St Theodore of Chernigov, The Martyrs of Korea, St Michael of Chernigov, St Matthew, and St Maures of Troyes.

1529 The Turkish army under Suleiman the Magnificent was defeated at Vienna. 1745 Bonnie Prince Charles and his Jacobite army defeated the English at the Battle of Prestonpans in Scotland. 1784 *The Pennsylvania Packet and General Advertiser*, the first successful US daily newspaper, was published. 1915 Stonehenge was sold at auction to Mr C H Chubb for £6,600. Mr Chubb presented it to the nation three years later. 1917 Latvia proclaimed its independence. 1938

JAN FEB MAR APR MAY JUN JUL AUG SEP OCT NOV DEC

The Anglo-French plan to cede Sudetenland to Germany was accepted by the Czech cabinet. **1949** The Republic of Ireland beat England 2–0 at Goodison Park – England's first home defeat by a foreign football team. **1974** Over 8,000 people were killed by floods caused by hurricanes in Honduras. **1989** Hurricane Hugo struck the US coastal states of Georgia and South Carolina, causing widespread damage and loss of life.

Girolamo Savonarola, Italian political reformer and martyr, **1452**; John Loudon McAdam, Scottish engineer, **1756**; Edmund William Gosse, English author, **1849**; H G Wells, English writer, **1866**; Larry Hagman, US actor, **1931**; Stephen King, US novelist, **1948**.

Virgil, Roman poet, **19 BC**; King Edward II, murdered, **1327**; Sir Walter Scott, Scottish novelist, **1832**; Arthur Schopenhauer, German philosopher, **1860**; Haakon VII, King of Norway, **1957**; William Plomer, South African author, **1973**; Walter Brennan, US film actor, **1974**.

22 Feast day of St Felix II, pope, St Landus or Lô, St Bodo, St Emmeramus, St Maurice of Agaunum, St Thomas of Villanova, The Theban Legion, St Phocas the Gardener, and St Salaberga.

1735 Sir Robert Walpole became the first prime minister to occupy 10 Downing Street. **1792** France was declared a Republic. **1862** US President Lincoln issued the Emancipation Proclamation, ordering the freeing of slaves. **1869** Wagner's opera *Das Rheingold* was first performed in Munich. **1914** Three British cruisers, *Aboukir*, *Hogue*, and *Cressy*, were torpedoed and sunk by German U-boats. **1955** Argentinian leader Juan Perón was deposed in a military coup. **1955** Independent TV began operating; Britain's first commercial and first woman newsreader were transmitted. **1972** Idi Amin gave the 8,000 Asians in Uganda 48 hours to leave the country. **1980** The Solidarity movement in Poland was created, with Lech Walesa as its elected leader. **1985** A severe earthquake hit Mexico, killing 2,000 people. **1989** An IRA bomb attack on the Royal Marines School of Music killed ten and injured twelve of the bandsmen.

Anne of Cleves, 4th wife of Henry VIII, **1515**; Michael Faraday, English chemist and physicist, **1791**; Christabel

Pankhurst, English suffragette, **1880**; Erich von Stroheim, Austrian actor and film director, **1885**; John Houseman, US actor and producer, **1902**; Fay Weldon, British author, **1931**; Catherine Oxenberg, US film actress, **1961**.

Nathan Hale, American revolutionary patriot, hanged, **1776**; Axel Springer, German publisher, **1985**; Jaco Pastorius, US bass guitarist, **1987**; Louis Kentner, English pianist, **1987**; Irving Berlin, US composer, **1989**.

23 National day of Saudi Arabia. Feast day of Saints Andrew, John, Peter and Antony, and St Adamnan or Eunan of Iona.

480 BC The Persians were defeated by the Greeks at the Battle of Salamis. **1779** In the American War of Independence, a French and American fleet commanded by John Paul Jones, captured the British ship Serapis in the Battle of Flamborough Head. **1803** The British under Arthur Wellesley (later Duke of Wellington) defeated Scindia and the Rajah of Berar at Assaye in India. **1846** German astronomer Johann Galle discovered the planet Neptune. **1848** Chewing gum was first commercially produced in the USA by John Curtis in his home, and was called 'State of Maine Pure Spruce Gum'. **1912** *Cohen Collects a Debt*, the first of US film producer Mack Sennet's silent Keystone Cops films, was released. **1940** The George Cross and the George Medal for civilian acts of courage were instituted. **1973** Juan Perón was re-elected President of Argentina; he had been ousted in 1955. **1974** The world's first Ceefax teletext service was begun by the BBC.

Augustus, 1st Roman Emperor, **63 BC**; Ferdinand VI, King of Spain, **1713**; Mickey Rooney, US film actor, **1920**; John Coltrane, US saxophonist, **1926**; Ray Charles, US singer, **1930**; Julio Iglesias, Spanish singer, **1943**; Bruce Springsteen, US rock singer, **1949**; Jeff Squire, rugby footballer, **1951**.

Nicholas François Mansart, French architect, **1666**; Prosper Merimée, French novelist, **1870**; Wilkie Collins, English novelist, **1889**; Sigmund Freud, Austrian psychoanalyst, **1939**; Pablo Neruda, Chilean poet, **1973**; Bob Fosse, US director, **1987**.

24

Feast day of St Pacifico of San Severino, St Robert Flower of Knaresborough, St Geremarus or Germer, and St Gerard of Csanad.

1776 The St Leger horse race was run for the first time at Doncaster. **1852** French engineer Henri Giffaud made the first flight in a dirigible balloon, from Paris to Trappe. **1930** Noel Coward's *Private Lives* was first staged in London. **1953** *The Robe*, the first Cinemascope film, premiered in Hollywood. **1960** The first nuclear-powered aircraft carrier, the USS *Enterprise*, was launched at Newport, Virginia. **1975** British mountaineers Dougal Haston and Doug Scott became the first to reach Mt Everest's summit via the south-west face. **1980** The Iraqis blew up the Abadan oil refinery, turning the Iran–Iraq conflict into a full scale war. **1991** The Shiite Muslim Revolutionary Justice Organization freed British hostage Jack Mann, kidnapped in May 1989.

B

Geronimo Cardano, Italian physician and mathematician, **1501**; Horace Walpole, 4th Earl of Orford, English writer, **1717**; F Scott Fitzgerald, US novelist, **1896**; Howard Walter Florey, pathologist, **1898**; Svetlana Beriosova, British ballerina, **1932**; Gerry Marsden, English rock musician, **1942**.

D

Pépin III (the Short), King of the Franks, **768**; Pope Innocent II, **1143**; Paracelsus, Swiss physician, alchemist, and scientist, **1541**; Isobel Baillie, Scottish oratorio singer, **1983**.

25

Feast Day of St Sergius of Radonezh, St Vincent Strambi, St Aunacharius or Aunaire, St Albert of Jerusalem, St Firminus of Amiens, St Ceolfirth, St Fibar or Bairre.

1066 King Harold II defeated the King of Norway, Harald Hardrada, at the Battle of Stamford Bridge. **1513** Vasco Balboa, Spanish explorer, became the first European to sight the Pacific Ocean after crossing the Darien isthmus. **1818** The first blood transfusion using human blood, as opposed to earlier attempts with animal blood, took place at Guy's Hospital in London. **1888** London's Royal Court Theatre, in Sloane Square, opened. **1909** The French battleship *Liberté* exploded in Toulon Harbour, killing 226 people. **1915** The Battle of Loos, in World War I, began; it would continue into Oct. **1954** François

Duvalier ('Papa' Doc) was elected president of Haiti. **1972** Norway voted against joining the EC in a referendum.

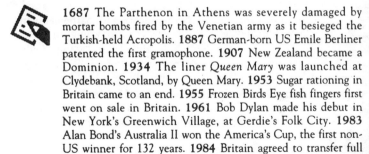

Jean Philippe Rameau, French composer, **1683**; William Faulkner, US novelist, **1897**; Mark Rothko, US painter, **1903**; Dmitri Shostakovich, Russian composer, **1906**; Colin Davis, British conductor, **1927**; Michael Douglas, US actor, **1944**; Christopher Reeve, US film actor, **1952**.

Samuel Butler, English writer, **1680**; Johann Strauss the Elder, Austrian composer, **1849**; Emily Post, US writer, **1960**; Erich Maria Remarque, German novelist, **1970**; Walter Pidgeon, US film actor, **1984**.

26 Feast day of Saints Cosmas and Damian, St Nilus of Rossano, St Colman of Lann Elo, St Teresa Couderc, and St John of Meda.

1687 The Parthenon in Athens was severely damaged by mortar bombs fired by the Venetian army as it besieged the Turkish-held Acropolis. **1887** German-born US Emile Berliner patented the first gramophone. **1907** New Zealand became a Dominion. **1934** The liner *Queen Mary* was launched at Clydebank, Scotland, by Queen Mary. **1953** Sugar rationing in Britain came to an end. **1955** Frozen Birds Eye fish fingers first went on sale in Britain. **1961** Bob Dylan made his debut in New York's Greenwich Village, at Gerdie's Folk City. **1983** Alan Bond's Australia II won the America's Cup, the first non-US winner for 132 years. **1984** Britain agreed to transfer full sovereignty of Hong Kong to China in 1997. **1988** Canadian sprinter Ben Johnson was stripped of his gold medal in the 100 metres at the Seoul Olympics after failing a drugs test.

Théodore Géricault, French painter, **1791**; Ivan Petrovich Pavlov, Russian physiologist, **1849**; T S Eliot, US-born British poet and playwright, **1888**; George Gershwin, US composer, **1898**; Ian Chappell, Australian cricketer **1943**; Bryan Ferry, English rock singer, **1945**; Olivia Newton-John English singer, **1948**.

Daniel Boone, US frontiersman, **1820**; James Keir Hardie, Scottish Labour Party pioneer, **1915**; Béla Bartók, Hungarian composer, **1945**; Alberto Moravia, Italian writer, **1990**.

27 Feast day of St Elzear of Sabran, St Barrog or Barnoch, and St Vincent de Paul.

 1821 Mexico achieved independence through the efforts of General Hubride, who declared himself Emperor Augustin I. 1826 The Stockton and Darlington Railway, the first passenger rail service, opened, with its first steam locomotive travelling at 10 mph. 1922 Constantine I, King of Greece, abdicated following the Greek defeat in Turkey. 1938 The 80,000-ton liner *Queen Elizabeth* was launched by the Queen Mother. 1939 Warsaw, the capital of Poland, surrendered to the German forces. 1968 The musical *Hair*, which took advantage of the end of British stage censorship by including a scene cast in the nude, had its first London performance.

B Samuel Adams, US revolutionary leader, 1722; George Cruikshank, English caricaturist and illustrator, 1792; Louis Botha, South African politician, 1862; Vincent Youmans, US composer, 1898; Alvin Stardust, rock singer, 1942; Michele Dotrice, English actress, 1948.

D Ivan Alexandrovich Goncharov, Russian novelist, 1891; Edgar Degas, French painter, 1917; Engelbert Humperdinck, German composer, 1921; Aristide Maillol, French painter and sculptor, 1944; Clara Bow, US film actress, 1965; Gracie Fields, English singer and comedian, 1979.

28 Feast Day of St Eustochium of Bethlehem, St Annemund or Chamond, St Faustus of Riez, St Ferreolus of Vienne, St Lioba, St Wenceslaus of Bohemia, and St Exuperius or Soupire of Toulouse.

 490 BC The Greeks defeated the Persians at the Battle of Marathon. 1745 At the Drury Lane Theatre, London, *God Save the King*, the national anthem, was sung for the first time. 1794 Britain, Russia, and Austria formed the Alliance of St Petersburg against France. 1864 The First International was founded in London, when Karl Marx proposed the formation of an International Working Men's Association. 1865 Elizabeth Garrett Anderson became the first qualified woman physician in Britain. 1894 Simon Marks and Tom Spencer opened their Penny Bazaar in Manchester, the first of what would become a

nation-wide chain of stores. **1978** Pope John Paul I, pope for only 33 days, was found dead.

Caravaggio, Italian painter, **1573**; Prosper Merimée, French writer, **1803**; Georges Clemenceau, French politician, **1841**; Peter Finch, British film actor, **1916**; Michael Soames, English dancer, **1917**; Marcello Mastroianni, Italian actor, **1924**; Brigitte Bardot, French film actress, **1934**.

Andrea del Sarto, Italian painter, **1530**; Herman Melville, US novelist, **1891**; Louis Pasteur, French chemist, **1895**; Émile Zola, French Novelist, **1902**; W H Auden, English poet, **1973**; William Douglas-Home, British playwright, **1992**.

29 Feast day of Saints Rhipsime, Gaiana and Companions, St Theodota of Philippolis, and St Michael, St Raphael, and St Gabriel, archangels.

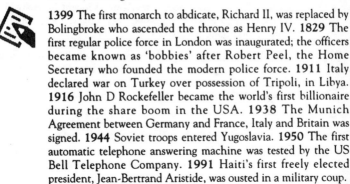

1399 The first monarch to abdicate, Richard II, was replaced by Bolingbroke who ascended the throne as Henry IV. **1829** The first regular police force in London was inaugurated; the officers became known as 'bobbies' after Robert Peel, the Home Secretary who founded the modern police force. **1911** Italy declared war on Turkey over possession of Tripoli, in Libya. **1916** John D Rockefeller became the world's first billionaire during the share boom in the USA. **1938** The Munich Agreement between Germany and France, Italy and Britain was signed. **1944** Soviet troops entered Yugoslavia. **1950** The first automatic telephone answering machine was tested by the US Bell Telephone Company. **1991** Haiti's first freely elected president, Jean-Bertrand Aristide, was ousted in a military coup.

Miguel de Cervantes, Spanish playwright and novelist, **1547**; Horatio Nelson, Viscount, English admiral, **1758**; Enrico Fermi, US physicist, **1901**; Jerry Lee Lewis, US singer and pianist, **1935**; Lech Walesa, Polish leader, **1943**; Sebastian Coe, English athlete, **1956**.

Winslow Homer, US painter, **1910**; Rudolf Diesel, German engineer, **1913**; Willem Einthoven, Dutch physiologist, **1927**; Winifred Holtby, English novelist, **1935**; Bruce Bairnsfather, British cartoonist, **1959**; Carson McCullers, US author, **1967**.

JAN FEB MAR APR MAY JUN JUL AUG SEP OCT NOV DEC

30 National Day of Botswana. Feast day of St Jerome, St Simon of Crépy, St Gregory the Enlightener, and St Honorius of Canterbury.

1791 The first performance of Mozart's *Magic Flute* took place in Vienna. **1888** Jack the Ripper murdered two more women – Liz Stride, found behind 40 Berner Street, and Kate Eddowes in Mitre Square, both in London's East End. **1902** Rayon, or artificial silk, was patented. **1928** Alexander Fleming announced his discovery of penicillin. **1935** George Gershwin's opera *Porgy and Bess* was first performed in Boston. **1939** The USSR and Germany agreed on the partition of Poland. **1952** Cinerama, invented by Fred Waller, was first exhibited in New York. **1987** Keith Best, MP, was sentenced to four months in prison for trying to obtain British Telecom shares by deception.

B Lord Raglan, British field-marshal, **1788**; David Fyodorovich Oistrakh, Russian violinist, **1908**; Deborah Kerr, British actress, **1923**; Truman Capote, US author, **1924**; Angie Dickinson, US actress, **1931**; Johnny Mathis, US singer, **1937**.

D James Brindley, British canal engineer, **1772**; Richard Austin Freeman, British crime writer, **1943**; James Dean, US film actor, **1955**; Simone Signoret, French film actress, **1985**; Virgil Thomson, US composer, **1989**.

OCTOBER ▬▬▬▬▬

1 National day of China, Nigeria, and Cyprus. Feast day of St Romanus the Melodist, St Melorus or Mylor, St Bavo or Allowin, St Thérèse of Lisieux.

331 BC Alexander the Great defeated Darius III at Arbela. **1795** Belgium became part of the French Republic. **1843** The *News of the World*, Britain's most popular Sunday newspaper, was first published. **1908** The first Model T, produced in Detroit, Michigan, was introduced by Henry Ford. **1918** The Arab forces of Emir Faisal, with British officer T E Lawrence, captured Damascus from the Turks. **1936** General Francisco Franco took office as Head of Spain's Nationalist Government. **1938** German forces entered Sudetenland, Czechoslovakia, annexed by Hitler under the Munich Agreement. **1949** The

People's Republic of China was proclaimed, with Mao Tse Tung as its chairman. **1971** Disney World, the world's largest amusement resort, was opened in Florida. **1982** Helmut Kohl became federal chancellor of West Germany, succeeding Helmut Schmidt.

King Henry III, **1207**; Paul Dukas, French composer, **1865**; Vladimir Horowitz, US pianist, **1904**; Walter Matthau, US film actor, **1920**; Jimmy Carter, 39th US president, **1924**; Richard Harris, British actor, **1933**; Julie Andrews, English actress and singer, **1935**.

Pierre Corneille, French dramatist, **1684**; John Blow, British composer, **1708**; Edwin Landseer, English painter, **1873**; Wilhelm Dilthey, German philosopher, **1911**; Louis Seymour Bazett Leakey, English anthropologist, **1972**; Roy Harris US composer, **1979**.

2

Feast day of The Guardian Angels, St Leger or Leodegarius, and St Eleutherius of Nicomedia.

1187 Saladin, the Muslim sultan, captured Jerusalem after its 88-year occupation by the Franks. **1608** The first telescope was demonstrated by the Dutch lens maker, Hans Lipperschey. **1836** Charles Darwin returned from his five-year survey of South American waters aboard the HMS *Beagle*. **1870** Rome became the capital of the newly unified Italy. **1901** The British Royal Navy's first submarine, built by Vickers, was launched at Barrow. **1909** The first rugby football match was played at Twickenham, between Harlequins and Richmond. **1942** The British cruiser Curacao sank with the loss of 338 lives, after colliding with the liner *Queen Mary* off the coast of Donegal. **1983** Neil Kinnock was elected leader of Britain's Labour Party.

Mikhail Yurevich Lermontov, Russian poet, **1814**; Paul von Hindenburg, German field marshal and politician, **1847**; William Ramsay, Scottish chemist, **1852**; Mohandas Karamchand Gandhi, Indian leader, **1869**; Graham Greene, English novelist, **1904**; Sting, English rock singer, **1951**.

Samuel Adams, US statesman, **1803**; Max Bruch, German composer, **1920**; Marie Stopes, Scottish birth-control campaigner, **1958**; Marcel Duchamp, French painter, **1968**;

Rock Hudson, US film actor, **1985**; Peter Medawar, British immunologist, **1987**.

3

Feast day of St Hesychius, St Thomas Cantelupe of Hereford, St Attilanus, St Gerard of Brogne, St Froilan, St Ewald the Fair, and St Ewald the Dark.

1811 The first women's county cricket match began at Newington, between Hampshire and Surrey. **1888** Gilbert and Sullivan's *Yeomen of the Guard* was performed for the first time, at London's Savoy Theatre. **1906** SOS was established as an international distress signal, replacing the call sign CQD. **1929** The Kingdom of Serbs, Croats, and Slovenes was renamed Yugoslavia. **1952** The first British atomic bomb was detonated on the Monte Bello Islands, off W Australia. **1956** The Bolshoi Ballet performed in Britain, at Covent Garden, for the first time. **1990** East and West Germany were officially reunified, with Berlin as the capital.

B

Pierre Bonnard, French painter, **1867**; Louis Aragon, French poet, **1897**; Michael Hordern, English actor, **1911**; James Herriot, Scottish author, **1916**; Gore Vidal, US author, **1925**; Chubby Checker, US rock singer, **1941**.

D

St Francis, Italian founder of the Franciscan order, **1226**; William Morris, English designer, socialist, and poet, **1896**; Woody Guthrie, US singer and composer, **1967**; Malcolm Sargent, British conductor, **1967**; Jean Anouilh, French dramatist, **1987**.

4

National Day of Lesotho. Feast day of St Petronius of Bologna, St Francis of Assisi, and St Ammon.

The first Chinese Embassy in Washington, DC was opened. **1905** Orville Wright became the first to fly an aircraft for over 33 minutes. **1910** Portugal was proclaimed a republic when King Manuel II was driven from the country by a revolution. **1911** Britain's first public escalator was switched on, at London's Earl's Court underground station. **1957** The USSR's *Sputnik I*, the first space satellite, was launched. **1958** BOAC (now British Airways) began operating the first transatlantic passenger jet service. **1965** Pope Paul VI visited New York to address the UN, becoming the first pope to visit the USA. **1983**

A world record speed of 663.5 mph was achieved by Richard
Noble in his jet-powered car *Thrust II*, in Nevada.

Giambattista Piranesi, Italian architect, 1720; Jean François
Millet, French painter, 1814; Engelbert Dollfuss, Austrian
statesman, 1892; Buster Keaton, US comedian, 1892; Charlton
Heston, US film actor, 1924; Terence Conran, British designer,
1931.

Benozzo Gozzoli, Italian painter, 1497; Rembrandt, Dutch
painter, 1669; John Rennie, Scottish civil engineer, 1821;
Arthur Whitten Brown, pioneer aviator, 1948; Janis Joplin, US
singer, 1970.

5

Feast day of St Flora of Beaulieu, St Maurus, St Magenulf or
Meinulf, St Apollinaris of Valence, and St Galla.

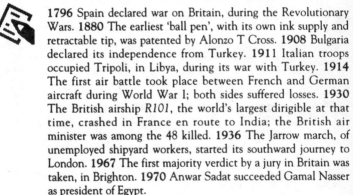

1796 Spain declared war on Britain, during the Revolutionary
Wars. 1880 The earliest 'ball pen', with its own ink supply and
retractable tip, was patented by Alonzo T Cross. 1908 Bulgaria
declared its independence from Turkey. 1911 Italian troops
occupied Tripoli, in Libya, during its war with Turkey. 1914
The first air battle took place between French and German
aircraft during World War I; both sides suffered losses. 1930
The British airship *R101*, the world's largest dirigible at that
time, crashed in France en route to India; the British air
minister was among the 48 killed. 1936 The Jarrow march, of
unemployed shipyard workers, started its southward journey to
London. 1967 The first majority verdict by a jury in Britain was
taken, in Brighton. 1970 Anwar Sadat succeeded Gamal Nasser
as president of Egypt.

Denis Diderot, French philosopher, 1713; Chester Alan Arthur,
21st US president, 1830; Donald Pleasence, English actor,
1919; Glynis Johns, British actress, 1923; Vaclav Havel, Czech
dramatist and president, 1936; Bob Geldof, Irish musician,
1954.

Philip III ('the Bold'), King of France, 1285; Joachim Patinir,
Dutch painter, 1524; Jacques Offenbach, French composer,
1880; Jean Vigo, French film director, 1934; Nelson Riddle,
US composer and arranger, 1985.

6

Feast day of St Mary Frances of Naples, St Faith of Agen, St Nicetas of Constantinople, and St Bruno.

1769 English naval explorer Captain James Cook, aboard the *Endeavour*, landed in New Zealand. 1883 The *Orient Express* completed its first run from Paris to Constantinople (now Istanbul) in nearly 78 hours. 1908 Austria annexed Bosnia and Herzegovina. 1927 Warner Brothers' The *Jazz Singer*, the first talking feature film (starring Al Jolson), premiered in New York. 1928 Nationalist General Chiang Kai-shek became president of China. 1968 The first three places in the US Grand Prix were taken by British drivers: Jackie Stewart, Graham Hill, and John Surtees. 1978 London Underground's first woman driver started work. 1981 One day after the 11th anniversary of his election to office, Egyptian President Anwar Sadat was assassinated by Muslim extremists.

B

Nevil Maskelyne, Astronomer Royal, 1732; Le Corbusier, Swiss architect, 1887; Janet Gaynor, US film actress, 1906; Thor Heyerdahl, Norwegian ethnologist, 1914; Richie Benaud, Australian cricketer and commentator, 1930; Melvyn Bragg, English writer and TV presenter, 1939.

D

William Tyndale, English Bible translator, 1536; William Henry Smith, English newsagent, bookseller and statesman, 1891; Alfred Tennyson, English poet, 1892; George du Maurier, English novelist, 1896; Denholm Elliott, English actor, 1992; Cyril Cusack, Irish actor, 1993.

7

Feast day of St Justina of Padua, St Mark, pope, St Artaldus or Arthaud, and St Osyth.

1571 The Battle of Lepanto, between Christian allied naval forces and the Ottoman Turks attempting to capture Cyprus from the Venetians, took place. 1806 The first carbon paper was patented by its English inventor, Ralph Wedgwood. 1919 The Dutch airline KLM, the oldest existing airline, was established. 1949 The German Democratic Republic, or East Germany, was formed. 1958 The first photograph of the far side of the Moon was transmitted from the USSR's *Lunik I*. 1985 The Italian liner *Achille Lauro* was seized by Palestinian terrorists; they surrendered two days later, having killed one US passenger. **1988** Grey whales trapped under ice in Alaska became the focus of an international rescue effort.

B William Laud, Archbishop of Canterbury, **1573**; Niels Bohr, Danish physicist, **1885**; Desmond Tutu, Archbishop of Cape Town, **1931**; Clive James, Australian critic and TV presenter, **1939**; Yo Yo Ma, Chinese cellist, **1955**; Jane Torvill, English ice skater, **1957**.

D Edgar Allan Poe, US novelist and poet, **1849**; Oliver Wendell Holmes, US writer, **1894**; Marie Lloyd, English music hall comedienne, **1922**; Radclyffe Hall, English author, **1943**; Clarence Birdseye, US deep-freezing inventor, **1967**; Bette Davis, US actress, **1989**; Agnes de Mille, US choreographer, **1993**.

8 Feast day of St Simeon Senex, St Pelagia (or Margaret) the Penitent, St Demetrius, St Keyne, St Thaïs, St Marcellus, and St Reparata of Caesarea.

1085 St Mark's Cathedral in Venice was consecrated. **1871** The Great Fire of Chicago started. It burned until the 11th, killing over 250 people and making 95,000 homeless. **1905** A permanent waving machine was first used on a woman's hair, by Charles Nessler. **1915** The Battle of Loos, in World War I, ended. **1939** Western Poland was incorporated in the Third Reich. **1965** London's Post Office Tower, Britain's tallest building, opened. **1967** A breathalyser was used on a motorist for the first time, in Somerset. **1973** LBC (London Broadcasting), Britain's first legal commercial radio station, began transmitting.

B John Cowper Powys, English novelist, **1872**; Alfred Munnings, British painter, **1878**; Juan Perón, Argentine dictator, **1895**; Betty Boothroyd, British MP, the Speaker,**1929**; Merle Park, British ballerina, **1937**; Jesse Jackson, US politician, **1941**.

D Jan Massys, Flemish painter, **1575**; Henry Fielding, English novelist, **1754**; Franklin Pierce, 14th US president, **1869**; Kathleen Ferrier, English contralto, **1953**; Clement Attlee, British statesman, **1967**; Willy Brandt, former German federal chancellor, **1992**.

9 National Day of Uganda. Feast day of St Demetrius of Alexandria, Saints Eleutherius and Rusticus, Saints Andronicus and Athanasia, St Denis or Dionysius of Paris, St Dionysius the Aeropagite, St Savin, St Publia, St Louis Bertrán, and St Ghislain or Gislenus.

1470 Henry VI was restored to the throne after being deposed in 1461. 1779 The first Luddite riots, against the introduction of machinery for spinning cotton, began in Manchester. 1875 The Universal Postal Union was established, with headquarters in Berne, Switzerland. 1888 The massive marble Washington Monument, designed by Robert Mills, was opened. 1934 Alexander, King of Yugoslavia, and French Foreign Minister Louis Barthou were assassinated by Croatian terrorists in Marseilles. 1967 Ernesto 'Che' Guevara, Argentinian-born guerilla leader and revolutionary, was murdered in Bolivia.

Camille Saint-Saëns, French composer, 1835; Alastair Sim, British actor, 1900; Jacques Tati, French film director, 1908; Don McCullin, British war photographer, 1935; John Lennon, rock singer and songwriter, 1940; Steve Ovett, English athlete, 1955.

Gabriel Fallopius, Italian anatomist, 1562; Pope Pius XII, 1958; André Maurois, French writer, 1967; Clare Booth Luce, US writer and politician, 1987; Jackie Millburn, English footballer, 1988.

10 Feast day of St Francis Borgia, St Daniel, St Cerbonius, Saints Eulampius and Eulampia, St Paulinus of York, St Maharsapor, and St Gereon.

732 The Franks, under Charles Martel, defeated the Saracens at the Battle of Tours. 1886 The dinner jacket was first worn in New York by its creator at the Tuxedo Park Country Club, after which it was named. 1903 Mrs Emmeline Pankhurst formed the Women's Social and Political Union to fight for women's emancipation in Britain. 1911 China's Imperial Dynasty was forced to abdicate, and a republic was proclaimed, under Sun Yat-Sen. 1935 George Gershwin's *Porgy and Bess* opened in New York City. 1961 Following a volcanic eruption, the entire population of the South Atlantic island of Tristan da Cunha

was evacuated to Britain. **1973** US Vice President Spiro Agnew resigned after being fined US $10,000 for income tax evasion.

Jean Antoine Watteau, French painter, **1684**; Henry Cavendish, English physicist, **1731**; Giuseppe Verdi, Italian composer, **1813**; Thelonious Monk, US jazz pianist and composer, **1918**; Harold Pinter, British dramatist, **1930**; Charles Dance, British actor, **1946**.

Fra Filippo Lippi, Italian painter, **1469**; Edith Piaf, French singer, **1963**; Eddie Cantor, US actor and entertainer, **1964**; Ralph Richardson, English actor, **1983**; Orson Welles, US actor and producer, **1985**; Yul Brynner, US film actor, **1985**.

11 Feast day of St Mary Soledad, Saints Andronicus, Tarachus, and Probus, St Agilbert, St Alexander Sauli, St Nectarius of Constantinople, St Bruno the Great of Cologne, St Gummarus or Gomaire, and St Canice or Kenneth.

1521 Pope Leo X conferred the title of 'Defender of the Faith' (Fidei Difensor) on Henry VIII for his book supporting Catholic principles. **1689** Peter the Great, Tsar of Russia, assumed control of the government. **1899** The Anglo-Boer War began. **1923** Rampant inflation in Germany caused the mark to drop to an exchange rate of 10,000,000,000 to the pound. **1968** The US spacecraft *Apollo 7* was launched from Cape Kennedy, with a crew of three. **1980** The Soviet *Salyut* 6 returned to earth; its cosmonauts had been in space for a record 185 days. **1982** The *Mary Rose*, which had been the pride of Henry VIII's fleet until it sank in the Solent in 1545, was raised.

Arthur Phillip, English admiral, **1738**; George Williams, founder of the YMCA, **1821**; François Mauriac, French author, **1885**; Richard Burton, Welsh actor, **1925**; Bobby Charlton, English footballer, **1937**; Dawn French, English actress and comedienne, **1957**.

Huldrych Zwingli, Swiss religious reformer, **1531**; Meriwether Lewis, US explorer, **1809**; James Joule, English physicist, **1889**; Anton Bruckner, Austrian composer, **1896**; 'Chico' Marx, US comedian, **1961**; Jean Cocteau, French poet, dramatist, and film director, **1963**; Jess Thomas, US operatic tenor, **1993**.

JAN FEB MAR APR MAY JUN JUL AUG SEP **OCT** NOV DEC

12 Feast day of St Maximilian of Lorch, Saints Felix and Cyprian, St Edwin, St Wilfrid of York, and St Ethelburga of Barking.

1492 Columbus sighted his first land in discovering the New World, calling it San Salvador. **1901** US President Theodore Roosevelt renamed the Executive Mansion 'The White House'. **1928** The first iron lung was used, at Boston Children's Hospital, Massachusetts. **1948** The first Morris Minor, designed by Alec Issigonis, was produced at Cowley, Oxfordshire. **1968** The 19th Olympic Games opened in Mexico City. **1984** During the Tory Party Conference at the Grand Hotel in Brighton, an IRA bomb exploded in the hotel in an attempt to murder the British Cabinet. **1986** Queen Elizabeth II became the first British monarch to visit China.

King Edward VI, **1537**; Elmer Ambrose Sperry, US inventor, **1860**; James Ramsay McDonald, British statesman, **1866**; Ralph Vaughan Williams, English composer, **1872**; Aleister Crowley, British occultist, **1875**; Luciano Pavarotti, Italian operatic tenor, **1935**.

Piero della Francesca, Italian painter, **1492**; Elizabeth Fry, English prison reformer, **1845**; Robert Stephenson, English civil engineer, **1859**; Robert E Lee, US Confederate general, **1870**; Anatole France, French author, **1924**; Tom Mix, US western film actor, **1940**; Leon Ames, US film actor, **1993**.

13 Feast day of Saints Januarius and Martial, St Gerald of Aurillac, St Edward the Confessor, St Coloman, St Comgan, St Faustus of Cordova, and St Maurice of Carnoët.

1307 On the orders of Philip IV of France, the arrest of the Templars on charges of heresy took place in Paris. **1792** The cornerstone of the White House, Washington, DC, was laid by President George Washington. **1884** Greenwich was adapted as the universal time meridian of longitude from which standard times throughout the world are calculated. **1894** The first Merseyside 'derby' football match was played at Goodison Park between Liverpool and Everton, with Everton winning 3–0. **1904** Sigmund Freud's *The Interpretation of Dreams* was published. **1923** Ankara replaced Istanbul as the capital of Turkey. **1988** The Cardinal of Turin confirmed reports that the

Shroud of Turin, believed to carry the imprint of Christ's face, had been scientifically dated to the Middle Ages.

Rudolf Virchow, German pathologist, **1821**; Lillie Langtry, British actress, **1853**; Yves Montand, French singer and actor, **1921**; Margaret Thatcher, British politician, **1925**; Paul Simon, US singer and songwriter, **1941**; Marie Osmond, US singer, **1959**.

Claudius I, Roman emperor, **54**; Nicholas de Malebranche, French philosopher, **1715**; Joachim Murat, King of the Two Sicilies, **1815**; Antonio Canova, Italian sculptor, **1822**; Henry Irving, English actor, **1905**; Clifton Webb, US actor, **1966**.

14 National day of Madagascar. Feast day of St Callixtus I, St Angadiama, St Justus of Lyons, St Burchard of Würzburg, St Manaccus, St Manechildis, and St Dominic Lauricatus.

1066 The Battle of Hastings was fought on Senlac Hill, where King Harold was slain as William the Conqueror's troops routed the English army. **1884** Photographic film was patented by US entrepreuner and inventor George Eastman. **1920** Oxford degrees were conferred on women for the first time. **1947** The first supersonic flight (670 mph) was made in California by Charles Yeagar in his Bell XI rocket plane. **1971** The US spacecraft *Mariner 9* transmitted the first close-up TV pictures of Mars to Earth. **1982** The largest mass wedding took place in Seoul, South Korea, when 5,837 couples were married simultaneously.

William Penn, Quaker founder of Pennsylvania, **1644**; Éamon de Valera, Irish statesman, **1882**; Dwight D Eisenhower, 34th US president, **1890**; e e cummings, US poet, **1894**; Lillian Gish, US film actress, **1899**; Cliff Richard, English singer, **1940**.

Erwin Rommel, German field-marshal, **1944**; Errol Flynn, Australian actor, **1959**; Edith Evans, English actress, **1976**; Bing Crosby, US singer and film actor, **1977**; Leonard Bernstein, US conductor and composer, **1990**.

15 Feast day of St Teresa of Avila, St Leonard of Vandoeuvre, St Thecla of Kitzingen, and St Euthymius the Younger.

JAN FEB MAR APR MAY JUN JUL AUG SEP **OCT** NOV DEC

1581 The first major ballet was staged at the request of Catherine de' Medici at the palace in Paris. **1582** The Gregorian calendar was adopted in Italy, Spain, Portugal, and France; 5 Oct became 15 Oct. **1915** In World War I, Bulgaria allied itself with the Central European Powers. **1917** Mata Hari, Dutch spy, was shot in Paris, having been found guilty of espionage for the Germans. **1928** The German airship *Graf Zeppelin*, captained by Hugo Eckener, completed its first transatlantic flight. **1961** The human-rights organization Amnesty International was established in London.

B
Virgil, Roman poet, **70 BC**; Evangelista Torricelli, Italian physicist, **1608**; Friedrich Wilhelm Nietzsche, German philosopher, **1844**; P G Wodehouse, English novelist, **1881**; C P Snow, English scientist and novelist, **1905**; Mario Puzo, US novelist, **1920**; HRH the Duchess of York, **1959**.

D
Antoine de la Mothe Cadillac, French explorer, **1730**; Tadeusz Kościuszko, Polish patriot, **1817**; Raymond Nicolas Landry Poincaré, French statesman, **1934**; Hermann Goering, Nazi leader, **1946**; Cole Porter, US composer and lyricist, **1964**.

16
Feast day of Saints Martinian and Maxima, St Margaret- Mary, St Anastasius of Cluny, St Hedwig, St Bertrand of Comminges, St Becharius, St Mommolinus, St Lull, St Gerard Majella, and St Gall.

1815 Napoleon was exiled to the Atlantic island of St Helena. **1846** The first public surgical operation using ether as an anaesthetic was performed at the Massachusetts General Hospital, Boston. **1902** The first detention centre housing young offenders was opened in Borstal, Kent. **1922** The Simplon II railway tunnel, under the Alps, was completed. **1946** Nazi war criminals, including von Ribbentrop, Rosenberg, and Streicher, were hanged at Nuremberg. **1964** China exploded a nuclear device. **1964** Labour Party leader Harold Wilson became Prime Minister. **1978** Cardinal Karol Wojtyla was elected Pope John Paul II – the first non-Italian pope since 1542. **1987** Southern England was hit by hurricane force winds, causing 19 deaths and hundreds of millions of pounds' worth of damage.

B Noah Webster, US lexicographer, **1758**; Oscar Wilde, Irish dramatist and author, **1854**; Austen Chamberlain, British statesman, **1863**; David Ben Gurion, Israeli statesman, **1886**; Eugene O'Neill, US dramatist, **1888**; Günter Grass, German novelist, **1927**.

D Hugh Latimer, bishop and Protestant martyr, **1555**; Nicholas Ridley, bishop and Protestant martyr, **1555**; Marie Antoinette, Queen of France, **1793**; George Marshall, US general and diplomat, **1959**; Moshe Dayan, Israeli general and politician, **1981**; Cornel Wilde, US film actor, **1989**; Paolo Bortoluzzi, Italian dancer and choreographer, **1993**.

17 Feast day of The Ursuline Martyrs of Valenciennes, Saints Ethelbert and Ethelred, St John the Dwarf, St Anstrudis or Austrude, St Seraphino, St Nothelm, St Ignatius of Antioch, and St Rule.

1651 Charles II, defeated by Cromwell at Worcester, fled to France, destitute and friendless. **1777** British commander General Burgoyne surrendered to General Horatio Gates at Saratoga, a victory for the American colonists. **1914** An earthquake struck Greece and Asia Minor, killing over 3,000 people. **1931** US gangster Al Capone was sentenced to 11 years in prison for income-tax evasion, the only charge that could be sustained against him. **1956** Calder Hall, Britain's first nuclear power station, was opened. **1959** The South African De Beers diamond firm announced that synthetic industrial diamonds had been produced. **1977** A US Supreme Court ruling allowed Concorde to use Kennedy Airport, New York.

B John Wilkes, British political reformer, **1727**; Karen Blixen (Isak Dinesen), Danish author, **1885**; Nathaniel West, US novelist, **1903**; Arthur Miller, US dramatist, **1915**; Rita Hayworth, US film actress, **1918**; Montgomery Clift, US film actor; Ann Jones, English tennis player, **1938**.

D Philip Sidney, English poet and soldier, **1586**; Frédéric Chopin, Polish composer, **1849**; Gustav Robert Kirchoff, German physicist, **1887**; Julia Ward Howe, US author, **1910**; S J Perelman, US humorist, **1979**; William Paton, English

JAN FEB MAR APR MAY JUN JUL AUG SEP **OCT** NOV DEC

pharmacologist, **1993**.

18 Feast day of St Luke, St Gwen of Corwall, and St Justus of Beauvais.

1685 The Edict of Nantes, granting religious freedom to the Huguenots, was revoked by King Louis XIV of France. **1826** Britain's last state lottery was held. **1887** Russia transferred Alaska to the USA for $7.2 million. **1922** The British Broadcasting Company (later Corporation) was officially formed. **1977** Germany's anti-terrorist squad stormed a hijacked Lufthansa aircraft at Mogadishu Airport, Somalia, killing three of the four Palestinian hijackers and freeing all of the hostages. **1989** Following a wave of pro-democracy demonstrations in East Germany, Erich Honecker was replaced as head of state by Egon Krenz. **1989** With the end of Communist rule, Hungary was proclaimed a free republic.

Canaletto, Italian painter, **1697**; Henri Bergson, French philosopher, **1859**; Pierre Trudeau, Canadian politician, **1919**; Chuck Berry, US singer, **1926**; George C Scott, US film actor, **1927**; Martina Navratilova, Czech tennis player, **1956**.

Lord Palmerston, British politician, **1865**; Charles Babbage, English mathematician, **1871**; Charles François Gounod, French composer, **1893**; Thomas Edison, US inventor, **1931**; Elizabeth Arden, cosmetics company founder, **1966**; Pierre Mendès-France, French statesman, **1982**.

19 Feast day of St Paul of the Cross, St Philip Howard, St Ethbin, St Aquilinus of Evreux, St Cleopatra, St Frideswide, St Peter of Alcántara, St John de Brébeuf, St René Goupil, St Varus, and Saints Ptolemy and Lucius.

1781 Lord Cornwallis surrendered to General Washington at Yorktown, Virginia, marking the end of the American War of Independence. **1813** The Allies defeated Napoleon at the Battle of the Nations at Leipzig. **1860** The first company to manufacture internal combustion engines was formed in Florence. **1864** In the American Civil War, General Sheridan was victorious over the Confederates at the Battle of Cedar Creek. **1872** The Holtermann nugget was mined at Hill End,

New South Wales; weighing 630lbs, it was the largest gold-bearing nugget ever found. **1935** The League of Nations imposed sanctions on Italy, following her invasion of Abyssinia (Ethiopia). **1987** Wall Street was struck by 'Black Monday', during which millions were wiped out on stock markets around the world. **1989** After serving 14 years in prison for the IRA Guildford and Woolwich bombings, the 'Guildford Four' had their convictions quashed.

Thomas Browne, English author and physician, **1605**; Leigh Hunt, English poet and essayist, **1784**; Alfred Dreyfus, French army officer, **1859**; Auguste Marie Lumière, French photographic pioneer, **1862**; John Le Carré, English novelist, **1931**; Peter Tosh, Jamaican reggae musician, **1944**.

King John of England, **1216**; Thomas Browne, English author and physician, **1682**; Jonathan Swift, Irish author, **1745**; George Pullman, US engineer and sleeping-car manufacturer, **1897**; Ernest Rutherford, New Zealand physicist, **1937**; Jacqueline du Pré, British cellist, **1987**.

20 Feast day of St Artemius, St Andrew the Calybite of Crete, St Caprasius of Agen, St Bertilla Boscardin, and St Acca.

1714 The coronation of King George I took place. **1818** Britain and the USA established the 49th parallel as the boundary between Canada and the USA. **1822** The *Sunday Times* was first published. **1827** The Battle of Navarino, off the coast of Greece, ended with the combined British, French, and Russian fleets completely destroying the Egyptian and Turkish fleets. **1935** Mao Zedong's Long March ended in Yenan, north China. **1944** The Allies captured Aachen, Germany. **1944** US troops landed at Leyte, in the Philippines. **1968** Jacqueline Kennedy, widow of US president Kennedy, married Greek millionaire Aristotle Onassis. **1973** The Sydney Opera House, designed by Danish architect John Utzon, was opened to the public.

Christopher Wren, English architect, **1632**; Lord Palmerston, British statesman, **1784**; Arthur Rimbaud, French poet, **1854**; James Chadwick, English physicist, **1891**; Anna Neagle, British actress, **1904**; Tom Petty, US guitarist and singer, **1953**.

JAN FEB MAR APR MAY JUN JUL AUG SEP OCT NOV DEC

Thomas Linacre, English physician and humanist, **1524**; Richard Francis Burton, English explorer and scholar, **1890**; Herbert Hoover, 31st US president, **1964**; Bud Flanagan, English comedian, **1968**; Sheila Scott, English aviator, **1988**; Anthony Quayle, English actor, **1989**.

21 Feast day of St Hilarion, St Fintan or Munnu of Taghmon, St Condedus, St Tuda, St John of Bridlington, and St Malchus.

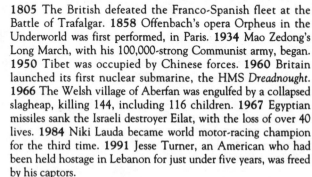

1805 The British defeated the Franco-Spanish fleet at the Battle of Trafalgar. **1858** Offenbach's opera Orpheus in the Underworld was first performed, in Paris. **1934** Mao Zedong's Long March, with his 100,000-strong Communist army, began. **1950** Tibet was occupied by Chinese forces. **1960** Britain launched its first nuclear submarine, the HMS *Dreadnought*. **1966** The Welsh village of Aberfan was engulfed by a collapsed slagheap, killing 144, including 116 children. **1967** Egyptian missiles sank the Israeli destroyer Eilat, with the loss of over 40 lives. **1984** Niki Lauda became world motor-racing champion for the third time. **1991** Jesse Turner, an American who had been held hostage in Lebanon for just under five years, was freed by his captors.

Katsushika Hokusai, Japanese artist and printmaker, **1760**; Samuel Taylor Coleridge, English poet, **1772**; Alfred Nobel, Swedish industrialist, **1833**; Georg Solti, British conductor, **1912**; Dizzie Gillespie, US jazz trumpeter, **1917**; Carrie Fisher, US film actress, **1956**.

Pietro Aretino, Italian writer, **1556**; Edmund Waller, English poet, **1687**; Horatio, Viscount Nelson, English admiral, killed at Trafalgar, **1805**; Jack Kerouac, US poet and novelist, **1969**; Bob Todd, English comedy actor, **1992**.

22 Feast day of St Philip of Heraclea and his Companions, St Mellon or Mallonus, St Abercius, Saints Nunilo and Alodia, and St Donatus of Fiesole.

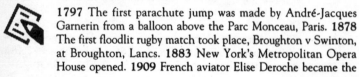

1797 The first parachute jump was made by André-Jacques Garnerin from a balloon above the Parc Monceau, Paris. **1878** The first floodlit rugby match took place, Broughton v Swinton, at Broughton, Lancs. **1883** New York's Metropolitan Opera House opened. **1909** French aviator Elise Deroche became the first woman to make a solo flight. **1910** Dr Hawley Crippen was found guilty of poisoning his wife and was sentenced to be hanged on 23 October 1910. **1935** Haiti was struck by a hurricane, causing over 2,000 deaths. **1962** US President Kennedy announced that Soviet missile bases had been installed in Cuba. **1987** The first volume of the Gutenberg Bible was sold at auction in New York for $5.39m/£3.26m – a record price for a printed book.

Franz Liszt, Hungarian composer, **1811**; Sarah Bernhardt, French actress, **1844**; Doris Lessing, English novelist, **1919**; Robert Rauschenberg, US artist, **1925**; Derek Jacobi, English actor, **1938**; Catherine Deneuve, French film actress, **1943**.

Charles Martel, leader of the Franks, **741**; Thomas Sheraton, English furniture maker, **1806**; Paul Cézanne, French painter, **1906**; Pablo Casals, Spanish cellist, **1973**; Arnold Joseph Toynbee, English historian, **1975**.

23

Feast day of St Severino Boethius, St Severinus or Seurin of Bordeaux, St Elfleda or Ethelfled, St Allucio, St Ignatius of Constantinople, St Theodoret, St Romanus of Rouen, and St John of Capistrano.

1642 The Battle of Edgehill, in the Cotswolds, took place – the first major conflict of the English Civil War. **1922** Andrew Bonar Law took office as British prime minister; he was replaced 22.5.23, making his the shortest term of office in the twentieth century. **1942** The Battle of El Alamein, in Egypt, began. **1946** The first meeting of the United Nations General Assembly took place in New York. **1947** Julie Andrews made her debut in *Starlight Roof*, aged 12. **1956** The Hungarian revolt against Soviet leadership began, in which thousands of demonstrators called for the withdrawal of Soviet forces. **1970** Gary Gabelich achieved the world land speed record of 631.367mph, in his rocket-engine car on Bonneville Salt Flats, Utah. **1987** Former British champion jockey Lester Piggott was sentenced to three years in prison for tax evasion.

Pierre Larousse, French lexicographer, **1817**; Robert Bridges, British poet, **1844**; Louis Riel, French-Canadian rebel, **1844**; Douglas Jardine, English cricketer, **1900**; Pelé, Brazilian

JAN FEB MAR APR MAY JUN JUL AUG SEP **OCT** NOV DEC

footballer, **1940**; Anita Roddick, British entrepreuner and founder of The Body Shop, **1942**.

Marcus Junius Brutus, Roman soldier, **42 BC**; Théophile Gautier, French poet, **1872**; W G Grace, English cricketer, **1915**; John Boyd Dunlop, Scottish inventor of the pneumatic rubber tyre, **1921**; Zane Grey, US novelist, **1939**; Al Jolson, US singer and actor, **1950**.

24 National Day of Zambia and United Nations Day. Feast day of St Martin or Mark, St Martin of Vertou, St Elesbaan, St Felix of Thibiuca, St Antony Claret, St Evergislus, St Aretas, St Senoch, St Maglorius or Maelor, St Proclus of Constantinople, and The Martyrs of Najran.

1648 The Treaty of Westphalia was signed, ending the Thirty Years' War. **1857** The first football club was formed by a group of Cambridge University Old Boys meeting in Sheffield. **1901** Mrs Ann Edson Taylor braved a descent over Niagara Falls in a padded barrel to help pay the mortgage. **1945** The United Nations charter came into force. **1977** Saudi Arabia purchased the transatlantic liner *France* for use as a floating luxury hotel. **1987** Heavyweight boxing champion Frank Bruno knocked out Joe Bugner in Britain's most hyped boxing match held at White Hart Lane, London. **1989** US television preacher Jim Bakker was sentenced to 45 years in prison and fined $500,000/£272,000 for his multi-milion dollar scam.

Anton van Leeuwenhoek, Dutch microscope pioneer, **1632**; Jacques Lafitte, French banker and politician, **1767**; Sybil Thorndike, English actress, **1882**; Tito Gobbi, Italian baritone, **1915**; Robin Day, English TV presenter, **1923**; Bill Wyman, English bass guitarist, **1941**.

Jane Seymour, 3rd wife of King Henry VIII, **1537**; Tycho Brahe, Danish astronomer, **1601**; Vidkun Quisling, Norwegian politician and Nazi collaborator, **1945**; Franz Lehár, Hungarian composer, **1948**; Christian Dior, French couturier, **1957**; Mary McCarthy, US author, **1989**; Jo Grimond, Scottish politician and writer, **1993**; Jiri Hajek, Czech human-rights campaigner, **1993**.

25 Feast day of Saints Crispin and Crispinian, Saints Fronto and George, The Forty Martyrs of England and Wales, Saints Chrysanthus and Daria, St Richard Gwyn, and St Gaudentius of Brescia.

1415 The English army, led by King Henry V, defeated the French at the Battle of Agincourt, during the Hundred Years' War. **1839** *Bradshaw's Railway Guide*, the world's first railway timetable, was published in Manchester. **1854** Lord Cardigan led the Charge of the Light Brigade during the Battle of Balaclava in the Crimean War. **1900** The Transvaal, a region in South Africa which is rich in minerals, especially gold, was annexed by the British. **1961** The British satirical magazine *Private Eye* was first published. **1971** Taiwan was expelled from the UN to allow the admission of the People's Republic of China. **1983** Over 2,000 US troops invaded Grenada.

B Thomas Babington Macaulay, English historian and essayist, **1800**; Johann Strauss the Younger, Austrian composer, **1825**; Georges Bizet, French composer, **1838**; Pablo Picasso, Spanish artist, **1881**; Richard Evelyn Byrd, US aviator and explorer, **1888**; Abel Gance, French film director, **1889**.

D Geoffrey Chaucer, English poet, **1400**; Giorgione, Italian painter, **1510**; Evangelista Torricelli, Italian physicist and inventor of the barometer, **1647**; King George II, **1760**; Frank Norris, US novelist, **1902**; Frederick Rolfe, English writer, **1913**; Vincent Price, US film actor, **1993**.

26 National Day of Iran and of Austria. Feast day of Saints Lucian and Marcian, St Bean, St Rusticus of Narbonne, St Eata, and St Cedd.

1825 The Erie Canal, linking the Niagara River with the Hudson River, was opened to traffic. **1860** Italian unification leader Giuseppe Garibaldi proclaimed Victor Emmanuel King of Italy. **1881** The legendary 'Gunfight at the OK Corral' took place at Tombstone, Arizona. **1905** Sweden and Norway ended their union and Oscar II, the Norwegian king, abdicated. **1927** Duke Ellington and his orchestra recorded the jazz classic, *Creole Love Song*. **1929** T W Evans of Miami, Florida, became the first woman to give birth aboard an aircraft. **1956** The UN's

International Atomic Energy Agency was formed. **1965** Queen Elizabeth presented the Beatles with their MBEs at Buckingham Palace. **1985** A US infant, known as Baby Fae, was given a baboon's heart to replace her malformed one.

B Georges Danton, French revolutionary leader, **1759**; Leon Trotsky, Russian Communist leader, **1879**; François Mitterand, French statesman, **1916**; Mohammed Reza Pahlavi, last Shah of Iran, **1919**; John Arden, English dramatist, **1930**; Bob Hoskins, English actor, **1942**.

D Gilles de Rais, French marshal, **1440**; William Hogarth, English artist and engraver, **1764**; Elizabeth Stanton, US feminist, **1902**; Igor Sikorsky, US aeronautical engineer, **1972**; Roger Hollis, British civil servant and alleged double agent, **1973**.

27 Feast day of St Otteran or Odhran of Iona, and St Frumentius of Ethiopia.

1662 Charles II sold Dunkirk to Louis XIV for 2.5 million livres. **1901** In Paris, a 'getaway car' was used for the first time, when thieves robbed a shop and sped away. **1904** The first section of New York City's subway system was opened. **1917** US troops entered the war in France. **1936** Mrs Wallis Simpson was granted a divorce from her second husband, leaving her free to marry King Edward VIII. **1971** The Republic of Congo changed its name to the Republic of Zaire. **1986** The City of London experienced 'Big Bang' day, due to the deregulation of the money market.

B Captain James Cook, English naval explorer, **1728**; Nicolò Paganini, Italian violinist and composer, **1782**; Theodore Roosevelt, 26th US president, **1858**; Dylan Thomas, Welsh poet, **1905**; Roy Lichtenstein, US painter, **1923**; Sylvia Plath, US poet, **1932**; John Cleese, English actor and comedian, **1939**.

D Ivan III (the Great), Tsar of Russia, **1505**; George Morland, English painter, **1804**; Lise Meitner, Austrian nuclear physicist, **1968**; Eric Maschwitz, English lyricist, **1969**; James M Cain, US novelist, **1977**.

28   Feast day of Saints Anastasia and Cyril, St Faro, St Abraham of
Ephesus, St Salvius or Saire, St Simon, St Jude or Thaddeus,
and St Fidelis of Como.

1636 Harvard University, the first in the USA, was founded.
1746 An earthquake demolished Lima and Callao, in Peru.
1831 English chemist and physicist Michael Faraday
demonstrated the first dynamo. **1886** The Statue of Liberty,
designed by Auguste Bartholdi, was presented by France to the
USA to mark the 100th anniversary of the Declaration of
Independence. **1893** HMS *Havelock*, the Royal Navy's first
destroyer, went on trials. **1914** George Eastman, of Eastman
Kodak Company, announced the introduction of a colour
photographic process. **1971** By a margin of 112 votes, the
House of Commons backed Prime Minister Heath's decision to
apply for EEC membership. **1982** Felipe González became
Spain's first Socialist prime minister, with a sweeping electoral
victory.

B   Evelyn Waugh, English novelist, **1903**; Francis Bacon, British
painter, **1909**; Jonas Salk, US microbiologist, **1914**; Cleo
Laine, British singer, **1927**; Carl Davis, US composer, **1936**;
Hank Marvin, English guitarist, **1941**.

D   John Locke, English philosopher, **1704**; John Smeaton, English
civil engineer, **1792**; Ottmar Mergenthaler, German inventor
of the Linotype, **1899**; Georges Carpentier, French boxer,
1975; Woody Herman, US bandleader, **1987**; Pietro Annigoni,
Italian painter, **1988**.

29   National Day of Turkey. Feast day of The Martyrs of Douay, St
Theuderius or Chef, St Colman of Kilmacduagh, and St
Narcissus of Jerusalem.

1618 Sir Walter Raleigh, English navigator, courtier, and once
favourite of Elizabeth I, was beheaded at Whitehall for treason.
1787 Mozart's opera *Don Giovanni* was first performed, in
Prague. **1863** The International Red Cross was founded by
Swiss philanthropist Henri Dunant. **1929** The Wall Street
crash known as 'Black Tuesday' took place, leading to the Great
Depression. **1964** The union of Tanganyika and Zanzibar was
announced, adopting the name of Tanzania. **1967** Expo-67, an

JAN FEB MAR APR MAY JUN JUL AUG SEP **OCT** NOV DEC

international exhibition, opened in Montreal. **1982** In Australia, Lindy Chamberlain was sentenced to life imprisonment for the murder of her nine-week-old baby who, she claimed, had been carried off by a dingo. **1991** Vietnam formally approved a plan to repatriate forcibly tens of thousands of Vietnamese refugees living in camps in Hong Kong.

James Boswell, Scottish biographer and diarist, **1740**; Wilfred Rhodes, English cricketer, **1877**; Jean Giraudoux, French author, **1882**; Fanny Brice, US singer and entertainer, **1891**; Joseph Goebbels, German Nazi propaganda chief, **1897**; Richard Dreyfuss, US actor, **1947**.

Joseph Pulitzer, US newspaper publisher, **1911**; Frances Hodgson Burnett, English novelist, **1924**; Gustav V, King of Sweden, **1950**; Louis Burt Mayer, US film producer and distributor, **1957**; John Braine, British novelist.

30 Feast day of St Marcellus the Centurion, St Alphonsus Rodriguez, St Germanus of Capua, St Serapion of Antioch, St Asterius of Amasea, and St Ethelnoth.

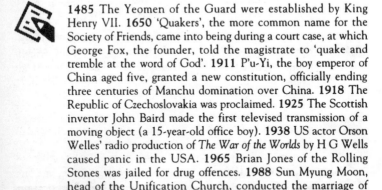

1485 The Yeomen of the Guard were established by King Henry VII. **1650** 'Quakers', the more common name for the Society of Friends, came into being during a court case, at which George Fox, the founder, told the magistrate to 'quake and tremble at the word of God'. **1911** P'u-Yi, the boy emperor of China aged five, granted a new constitution, officially ending three centuries of Manchu domination over China. **1918** The Republic of Czechoslovakia was proclaimed. **1925** The Scottish inventor John Baird made the first televised transmission of a moving object (a 15-year-old office boy). **1938** US actor Orson Welles' radio production of *The War of the Worlds* by H G Wells caused panic in the USA. **1965** Brian Jones of the Rolling Stones was jailed for drug offences. **1988** Sun Myung Moon, head of the Unification Church, conducted the marriage of 6,516 couples in a Seoul factory; the couples had first met the day before.

Richard Brinsley Sheridan, Irish dramatist, **1751**; John Adams, 2nd US president, **1735**; Alfred Sisley, French painter, **1840**; Ezra Pound, US poet, **1885**; Louis Malle, French film director,

1932; Diego Maradona, Argentinian footballer, 1960.

D) Edward Vernon, English admiral, 1757; Edmund Cartwright, English inventor, 1823; Andrew Bonar Law, British statesman, 1923; Pio Baroja, Spanish novelist, 1956; Jim Mollison, Scottish pioneer aviator, 1959; Barnes Neville Wallis, British aeronautical engineer, 1979.

31
All Hallows' Eve (Halloween). Feast day of St Quentin or Quintinus, St Bee or Bega, St Wolfgang, and St Foillan of Fosses.

1517 Martin Luther nailed his theses on indulgences to the church door at Wittenberg, Germany. 1864 Nevada became the 36th state of the Union. 1902 The first telegraph cable across the Pacific Ocean was completed. 1940 The Battle of Britain ended. 1951 Zebra crossings came into effect in Britain. 1952 At Eniwetok Atoll, in the Pacific, the USA detonated the first hydrogen bomb. 1956 British and French troops bombed Egyptian airfields at Suez. 1971 An IRA bomb exploded at the top of the Post Office Tower, London. 1982 The Thames barrier, part of London's flood defences, was raised for the first time.

B Jan Vermeer, Dutch painter, 1632; John Keats, English poet, 1795; Joseph Wilson Swan, English inventor of the electric lamp, 1828; Chiang Kai-shek, Chinese leader, 1887; Dale Evans, US film actress, 1912; Michael Collins, US astronaut, 1930.

D) Dan Leno, British comedian, 1904; Harry Houdini, US escapologist, 1926; Max Reinhardt, Austrian producer and director, 1943; Augustus John, Welsh painter, 1961; Indira Gandhi, Indian politician, assassinated, 1984; River Phoenix, US film actor, 1993.

NOVEMBER ▬▬▬▬

1
National Day of Algeria. Feast day of All Saints, St Benignus of Dijon, Saints Caesarius and Julian, St Austremonius or Stremoine, St Cadfan, St Mary, martyr, St Vigor, St Marcellus of Paris, and Saint Mathurin or Maturinus.

JAN FEB MAR APR MAY JUN JUL AUG SEP OCT NOV DEC

1755 An earthquake reduced two-thirds of Lisbon to rubble and resulted, according to accounts, in the death of 60,000 people. 1848 The first W H Smith railway bookstall opened, at Euston Station, London. 1911 *Woman's Weekly* was first published. 1914 The British ships *Good Hope* and *Monmouth* were sunk by the Germans, at the Battle of Coronel. 1940 A prehistoric painting was discovered in a cave in Lascaux in the Dordogne, France. 1950 Two Puerto Rican nationalists attempted to assassinate US President Truman. 1959 The first stretch of the M1 motorway was opened. 1972 Orissa, India, was struck by a tidal wave which killed 10,000 people and left 5 million homeless.

Benvenuto Cellini, Italian sculptor and goldsmith, 1500; Antonio Canova, Italian sculptor, 1757; Stephen Crane, US novelist, 1871; L S Lowry, English painter, 1887; Victoria de los Angeles, Spanish soprano, 1923; Gary Player, South African golfer, 1935.

George Gordon, British Protestant agitator, 1793; Ezra Pound, US poet, 1972; King Vidor, US film director, 1982; Phil Silvers, US comedian and actor, 1985; Louis Johnson, New Zealand poet, 1988.

2

Feast day of All Souls, St Victorinus of Pettau, and Saint Marcian of Cyrrhus.

1785 The first insubmersible lifeboat was patented by Lionel Lakin, a London coach builder. 1871 The 'Rogues Gallery' was started, when photographs of all prisoners in Britain were first taken. 1899 Ladysmith, in Natal, South Africa, was besieged by the Boers. 1917 The Balfour Declaration, stating British support for the Jewish Zionist goal of a homeland in Palestine, was sent to Lord Rothschild. 1930 Ras Tafari, King of Ethiopia, was crowned Emperor Haile Selassie ('Might of the Trinity'). 1957 With eight simultaneous hits in the UK Top 30 chart, Elvis Presley set an all-time record. 1960 A British jury acquitted Penguin Books of obscenity in the matter of publishing D H Lawrence's *Lady Chatterley's Lover*. 1976 James Earl Carter was elected the 39th President of the USA. 1990 Ivana Trump filed for divorce from US millionaire Donald Trump.

B Daniel Boone, US frontiersman, **1734**; Marie Antoinette, Queen of King Louis XVI of France, **1755**; Joseph Radetzky, Austrian field marshal, **1766**; Luchino Visconti, Italian film director, **1906**; Burt Lancaster, US film actor, **1913**; Keith Emerson, English rock musician, **1944**.

D Richard Hooker, English theologian, **1600**; Jenny Lind, Swedish soprano, **1887**; William Powell Frith, British painter, **1909**; George Bernard Shaw, Irish dramatist, **1950**; James Thurber, US humorous writer and cartoonist, **1961**.

3 National Day of Panama. Feast day of St Rumwald, St Malachy of Armagh, St Amicus, St Winifred or Gwenfrewi, St Martin de Porres, and St Pirminus.

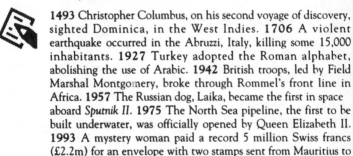

1493 Christopher Columbus, on his second voyage of discovery, sighted Dominica, in the West Indies. **1706** A violent earthquake occurred in the Abruzzi, Italy, killing some 15,000 inhabitants. **1927** Turkey adopted the Roman alphabet, abolishing the use of Arabic. **1942** British troops, led by Field Marshal Montgomery, broke through Rommel's front line in Africa. **1957** The Russian dog, Laika, became the first in space aboard *Sputnik II*. **1975** The North Sea pipeline, the first to be built underwater, was officially opened by Queen Elizabeth II. **1993** A mystery woman paid a record 5 million Swiss francs (£2.2m) for an envelope with two stamps sent from Mauritius to a Bordeaux wine exporter in 1847.

B Vincenzo Bellini, Italian operatic composer, **1801**; Karl Baedeker, German guide-book publisher, **1801**; Charles Bronson, US film actor, **1922**; Roy Emerson, Australian tennis player, **1936**; Larry Holmes, US boxing champion, **1949**; Adam Ant, English rock musician, **1954**.

D Constantius II, Roman emperor of the East, **361**; Annie Oakley, US entertainer and markswoman, **1926**; Henri Matisse, French painter, **1954**; Ralph Hodgson, English poet, **1962**; Leon Theremin, Russian inventor, **1993**.

4 Feast day of saints Vitalis and Agricola, St Birstan or Brynstan of Winchester, St Pierius, St John Zedazneli, St Charles Borromeo, St Joannicus, and St Clarus.

JAN FEB MAR APR MAY JUN JUL AUG SEP OCT **NOV** DEC

1605 Guy Fawkes, a Roman Catholic convert and conspirator in the Gunpowder Plot, was arrested in Parliament's cellar. 1862 US inventor Richard Gatling patented the rapid-fire, or machine, gun. 1914 The first fashion show was organized by Edna Woodman Chase of *Vogue* magazine, and held at the Ritz-Carlton Hotel, New York. 1922 British archaeologist Howard Carter discovered the tomb of the Egyptian pharaoh Tutankhamen. 1946 UNESCO was established, with headquarters in Paris. 1979 Iranian students stormed the US Embassy in Teheran and held over 60 staff and US marines hostage. 1980 Ronald Reagan was elected 40th US president. 1991 Imelda Marcos returned to the Philippines after five years of exile in the USA; the government endorsed her return so that she could be tried on corruption and tax evasion charges.

King William III, 1605; Augustus Montague Toplady, British clergyman and author, 1740; Eden Phillpotts, English novelist and dramatist; G E Moore, British philosopher, 1873; Will Rogers, US humorist and actor, 1879; Art Carney, US actor, 1918.

Felix Mendelssohn, German composer, 1847; Paul Delaroche, French painter, 1856; Joseph Rowntree, British cocoa manufacturer and philanthropist, 1859; Wilfred Owen, English poet, 1918; Gabriel Fauré, French organist and composer, 1924.

5

Guy Fawkes' Night Feast day of Saints Elisabeth and Zachary, St Galation, St Bertilla of Chelles, and St Episteme.

1854 The combined British and French armies defeated the Russians at the Battle of Inkerman during the Crimean War. 1912 The British Board of Film Censors was appointed. 1914 Cyprus was annexed by Britain on the outbreak of war with Turkey. 1919 Rudolph Valentino, the archetypal romantic screen lover, married actress Jean Acker; the marriage lasted less than six hours. 1927 Britain's first automatic traffic lights began functioning, in Wolverhampton. 1968 Richard Nixon was elected 37th US president. 1990 Rabbi Meir Kahane, founder of the militant Jewish Defence League and Israel's extremist anti-Arab Kach party, was assassinated in a New York City hotel.

B James Elroy Flecker, English poet, **1884**; John Haldane, Scottish scientist, **1892**; Vivien Leigh, British actress, **1913**; Lester Piggott, British jockey, **1935**; Elke Sommer, German actress, **1940**; Art Garfunkel, US singer and composer, **1941**.

D Mack Sennett, US film producer, **1960**; Maurice Utrillo, French painter, **1955**; Al Capp, US cartoonist, **1979**; Jacques Tati, French film actor and director, **1982**; Vladimir Horowitz, US pianist, **1989**; Robert Maxwell, British publishing and newspaper proprietor, **1991**.

6 Feast day of St Demetrian of Khytri, St Melaine, St Barlaam of Khutyn, St Leonard of Noblac, St Winnoc, and St Illtud.

1429 Henry VI was crowned King of England. **1860** Abraham Lincoln was elected 16th US president. **1869** Diamonds were discovered at Kimberley, in Cape Province, South Africa. **1924** British Tory leader Stanley Baldwin was elected prime minister. **1932** In general elections held in Germany, the Nazis emerged as the largest party. **1956** Construction of the Kariba High Dam, on the Zambezi River between Zambia and Zimbabwe, began. **1975** UK punk rock group, the Sex Pistols, gave their first public performance at London's St Martin's College of Art; college authorities cut the concert short – after 10 minutes. **1988** Six thousand US Defense Department computers were crippled by a virus; the culprit was the 23-year-old son of the head of the country's computer security agency.

B Alois Senefelder, Austrian inventor of lithography, **1771**; Adolphe Sax, Belgian inventor of the saxophone, **1814**; John Philip Sousa, US bandmaster and composer, **1854**; John Alcock, British pioneer aviator, **1892**; Mike Nichols, US director, **1931**; Sally Field, US actress, **1946**.

D Gustavus II, King of Sweden, **1632**; Heinrich Schütz, German composer, **1672**; William Hone, British satirist and editor, **1842**; Peter Ilyich Tchaikovsky, Russian composer, **1893**; Kate Greenaway, British illustrator, **1901**; Gene Eliza Tierney, US film actress, **1991**.

7 National day of Russia. Feast day of St Herculanus of Perugia, St Engelbert, St Willibrord, and St Florentius of Strasbourg.

JAN FEB MAR APR MAY JUN JUL AUG SEP OCT NOV DEC

1783 The last public hanging in England took place when John Austin, a forger, was executed at Tyburn. 1872 The *Marie Celeste*, the ill-fated brigantine, sailed from New York to be found mysteriously abandoned near the Azores some time later. 1916 Jeanette Rankin, of the state of Montana, became the first woman member of US Congress. 1917 The Bolshevik Revolution, led by Lenin, overthrew Prime Minister Alexander Kerensky's government. 1972 Richard Nixon was re-elected US president. 1988 In Las Vegas, 'Sugar' Ray Lewis knocked out Canadian Donny Londe, completing his collection of world titles at five different weights. 1990 Mary Robinson became the Irish Republic's first woman president.

Marie Curie, French physicist, 1867; Leon Trotsky, Russian Communist leader, 1879; Chandrasekhara Venkata Raman, Indian physicist, 1888; Albert Camus, French writer, 1913; Joan Sutherland, operatic soprano, 1926; Joni Mitchell, Canadian singer, 1943.

Godfrey Kneller, German painter, 1723; Victor McLaglen, English film actor, 1959; Eleanor Roosevelt, US writer and lecturer, 1962; Gene Tunney, US heavyweight boxer, 1978; Steve McQueen, US film actor, 1980; Alexander Dubček, Czech statesman; Adelaide Hall, US singer, dancer, and actress, 1993.

---

8 Feast day of The Four Crowned Martyrs, St Cuby or Cybi, St Godfrey of Amiens, St Deusdedit, St Willehad, and St Tysilio or Suliau.

 1793 The Louvre was opened to the public by the Revolutionary government, although only part of the collection could be viewed. 1895 William Röntgen discovered X-rays during an experiment at the University of Wurzburg. 1923 Hitler led his unsuccessful rising in Munich, known as the Beer Hall Putsch. 1942 Under Eisenhower's command, British and US forces invaded North Africa, in 'Operation Torch'. 1958 *Melody Maker* published the first British album charts. 1987 An IRA bomb went off in Eniskillen, Co Fermanagh, shortly before a Remembrance Day service, killing 11 people. 1991 EC foreign ministers, meeting in Rome, imposed an economic embargo on Yugoslavia in an effort to halt the civil war there.

ʒ Edmond Halley, English astronomer, **1656**; Bram Stoker, Irish writer, **1847**; Herbert Austin, English motor-car manufacturer, **1866**; Margaret Mitchell, US novelist, **1900**; Christiaan Barnard, South African heart transplant pioneer, **1922**; Alain Delon, French film actor, **1935**.

ɔ John Milton, English poet, **1674**; Tom Sayers, English bare-knuckle pugilist, **1865**; Fred Archer, English jockey, **1886**; Victorien Sardou, French dramatist, **1908**; Ivan Alexeyevich Bunin, Russian poet, **1953**; Edgard Varèse, French composer, **1965**.

9 National Day of Cambodia. Feast day of St Theodore the Recruit, St Vitonus or Vanne, and St Benignus or Benen.

1837 Moses Montefiore became the first Jew to be knighted in England. **1859** Flogging in the British army was abolished. **1908** Britain's first woman mayor, Elizabeth Garrett Anderson, was elected at Aldeburgh. **1918** Following a revolution in Germany, Kaiser William abdicated and fled to Holland. **1925** The SS (Schutzstaffel or 'Protection Squad') was formed in Germany. **1965** Capital punishment was abolished in Britain. **1988** Gary Kasparov became world chess champion after beating Anatoly Karpov, who had held the title for ten years, in Moscow.

ʒ Ivan Turgenev, Russian dramatist, **1818**; King Edward VII, **1841**; Giles Gilbert Scott, English architect, **1880**; Katherine Hepburn, US film actress, **1909**; Hedy Lamarr, US film actress, **1913**; Carl Sagan, US astronomer, **1934**.

ɔ Guillaume Apollinaire, French poet, **1918**; James Ramsay MacDonald, British statesman, **1937**; Neville Chamberlain, British statesman, **1940**; Dylan Thomas, Welsh poet, **1953**; Charles de Gaulle, French statesman, **1970**; Yves Montand, French singer and actor, **1991**.

10 Feast day of St Leo the Great, St Justus of Canterbury, St Aedh MacBrice, St Theoctista, and St Andrew Avellino.

1775 The Continental Congress authorised the creation of the 'Continental Marines', now known as the US Marines. **1862** The first performance of Giuseppe Verdi's opera *La Forza del*

JAN FEB MAR APR MAY JUN JUL AUG SEP OCT NOV DEC

Destino was held in St Petersburg. **1871** Henry Morton Stanley, who had been sent to track down missing explorer David Livingstone, met him at Ujiji, on Lake Taganyika. **1938** Kristallnacht, or 'night of (broken) glass', took place when Nazis burned 267 synagogues and destroyed thousands of Jewish homes and businesses in Germany. **1928** Hirohito was crowned Emperor of Japan, at the age of 27. **1989** Bulldozers began demolishing the 28-year-old Berlin Wall, following the government's announcement that it would allow free travel between East and West Germany.

Martin Luther, German Protestant reformer, **1483**; François Couperin, French composer, **1668**; William Hogarth, English painter and engraver, **1697**; Johann Christoph Friedrich von Schiller, German poet and dramatist, **1759**; Jacob Epstein, British sculptor, **1880**; Richard Burton, Welsh actor, **1925**.

Pope Leo I (the Great), **461**; Arthur Rimbaud, French poet, **1891**; Mustapha Kemal Atatürk, Turkish statesman, **1938**; Dennis Wheatley, English novelist, **1979**; Leonid Brezhnev, Soviet political leader, **1982**; Gordon Richards, **1986**.

11 Feast day of St Martin of Tours, St Bartholomew of Grottaferata, St Mannas of Egypt, and St Theodore the Studite.

1918 The armistice was signed between the Allies and Germany in Compeigne, France, effectively ending World War I. **1921** The British Legion held its first Poppy Day to raise money for wounded World War I veterans. **1940** The Willys-Overland Company launched a four-wheel drive vehicle for the US Army, named 'Jeep' after GP (general purpose). **1952** The first video recorder was demonstrated in Beverly Hills, California, by its inventors John Mullin and Wayne Johnson. **1965** Ian Smith, Prime Minister of Rhodesia, unilaterally declared his country's independence from Britain. **1975** Angola gained independence from Portugal.

Louis Antoine de Bougainville, French navigator, **1729**; Fyodor Mikhailovich Dostoevsky, Russian author, **1821**; Edouard Vuillard, French painter, **1868**; Kurt Vonnegut, US novelist, **1922**; Bibi Andersson, Swedish film actress, **1935**; Rodney Marsh, Australian cricketer, **1947**.

Sören Kierkegaard, Danish philosopher, **1855**; Ned Kelly, Australian outlaw, **1880**; Edward German, English composer, **1936**; Jerome Kern, US composer, **1945**; Dimitri Tiomkin, US composer, **1979**; Vyacheslav Mikhailovich Molotov, Russian leader, **1986**.

12 Feast day of St Benedict of Benevento, St Machar or Mochumma, St Astrik or Anastasius, St Nilus the Elder, St Cadwalader, St Lebuin or Liafwine, St Cunibert, St Emilian Cucullatus, St Cumian the Tall, St Josephat of Polotsk, and St Livinus.

1660 English author John Bunyan was arrested for preaching without a licence; refusing to give up preaching, he remained in jail for 12 years. **1847** The first public demonstration of the use of chloroform as an anaesthetic was given by James Simpson, at the University of Edinburgh. **1859** Jules Léotard, the daring young man on the flying trapeze, made his debut at the Cirque Napoléon, in Paris. **1912** The remains of English explorer Robert Scott and his companions were found in Antarctica. **1918** The Republic of Austria was declared, thus ending the Habsburg dynasty. **1944** The RAF bombed and sank the *Tirpitz*, the last of the major German battleships. **1974** For the first time since the 1840s, a salmon was caught in the Thames. **1981** The US shuttle *Columbia* became the first reusable crewed spacecraft, by making its second trip.

Alexander Borodin, Russian composer, **1833**; Auguste Rodin, French sculptor, **1840**; Sun Yat-sen, Chinese nationalist politician, **1866**; Grace Kelly, Princess Grace of Monaco, **1929**; Neil Young, Canadian rock singer and guitarist, **1946**; Nadia Comaneci, Romanian gymnast, **1961**.

Canute II (the Great), king of England and Denmark, **1035**; John Sylvan, French astronomer, **1793**; Elizabeth Gaskell, English novelist, **1865**; Percival Lowell, US astronomer, **1916**; Baroness Orczy, English novelist, **1947**; Rudolf Friml, US composer, **1972**; H R Haldeman, US political aide, **1993**.

13 Feast day of At Arcadius, St Didacus or Diego of Seville, St Abbo of Fleury, St Eugenius of Toledo, St Brice or Britius, St Homobonus, St Nicholas, pope, St Francis Xavia Cabrini, St

Stanislaus Kostka, and St Maxellendis.

1002 The Massacre of the Danes in the southern counties of England took place by order of Ethelred II. **1851** The telegraph service between London and Paris began operating. **1907** The first helicopter rose 2 m/6.5 ft above ground in Normandy. **1914** US heiress Mary Phelps Jacob patented a new female undergarment, known as the 'backless brassiere'. **1916** In World War I, the Battle of Somme ended, having caused the deaths of some 60,000 allied soldiers. **1970** A cyclone and tidal waves struck East Pakistan, killing over 500,000 people. **1985** The Columbian volcano Nevado del Ruiz, dormant since 1845, erupted, killing over 20,000 people. **1987** With a view to encouraging 'safe sex', or AIDS prevention, the BBC screened its first condom commercial (without a brand name).

John Moore, British general, **1761**; Charles Frederick Worth, English couturier, **1825**; Robert Louis Stevenson, Scottish writer, **1850**; Eugene Ionesco, French author and dramatist, **1912**; Adrienne Corri, British actress, **1931**; George Carey, archbishop of Canterbury, **1935**.

Gioacchino Rossini, Italian composer, **1868**; Camille Pissarro, French painter, **1903**; Elsa Schiaparelli, Italian couturière, **1973**; Vittorio de Sica, Italian film director, **1974**; Chesney Allen, British comedian, **1982**.

14 Feast day of St Laurence O'Toole, St Adeotus Aribert, St Nicholas Tavelic, St Dubricius or Dyfrig, St Stephen of Como, and St Peter of Narbonne.

1770 Scottish explorer James Bruce discovered the source of the Blue Nile in NE Ethiopia, then considered the main stream of the Nile. **1896** The speed limit for motor vehicles in Britain was raised from 4 mph to 14 mph. **1925** An exhibition of Surrealist art opened in Paris, including works by Max Ernst, Man Ray, Joan Miró, and Pablo Picasso. **1940** Enemy bombing destroyed Coventry's medieval cathedral. **1952** Britain's first pop singles chart was published by *New Musical Express*. **1963** The island of Surtsey off Iceland was 'born' by the eruption of an underwater volcano. **1973** Bobby Moore made his 108th (and final) international appearance for England, against Italy at Wembley. **1991** Prince Sihanouk, Cambodia's former head of state, returned to Phnom Penh after nearly 13 years in exile to head the country's interim government.

Robert Fulton, US engineer, **1765**; Claude Monet, French painter, **1840**; Jawaarlal Nehru, Indian statesman, **1889**; Elisabeth Frink, English sculptor, **1930**; King Hussein of Jordan, **1935**; HRH the Prince of Wales, **1948**.

Nell Gwyn, English actress and mistress of Charles II, **1687**; Gottfried Wilhelm Leibniz, German philosopher, **1716**; Georg Wilhelm Friedrich Hegel, German philosopher, **1831**; Booker T Washington, US educationalist, **1915**; Manuel de Falla, Spanish composer, **1946**; Tony Richardson, British director, **1991**.

15 Feast day of St Leopold of Austria, Saints Abibus, Gurias, and Samonas, St Fintan of Rheinau, St Malo or Machutus, St Albert the Great, and St Desiderius or Didier of Cahors.

1837 Pitman's system of shorthand was published, under the title *Stenographic Sound-Hand*. **1889** Dom Pedro was overthrown, and Brazil was proclaimed a republic. **1899** Winston Churchill was captured by the Boers while covering the war as a reporter for the *Morning Post*. **1956** *Love Me Tender*, the first film starring Elvis Presley, premiered in New York. **1968** The Cunard liner *Queen Elizabeth* ended her final transatlantic journey. **1983** An independent Turkish Republic of Northern Cyprus was unilaterally proclaimed, recognized only by Turkey. **1985** UK and Irish premiers, Margaret Thatcher and Garret Fitzerald, signed the Anglo-Irish Agreement in Dublin. **1991** In the wake of increased sectarian violence in Northern Ireland, Britain called up 1,400 reserve troops for full-time active duty.

William Pitt the Elder, British statesman, **1708**; William Herschel, English astronomer, **1738**; Erwin Rommel, German field marshal, **1891**; Averell Harriman, US diplomat, **1891**; Petula Clark, British singer and actress, **1934**; Daniel Barenboim, Israeli pianist and conductor, **1942**.

George Romney, English painter, **1802**; Henryk Sienkiewicz, Polish novelist, **1916**; Lionel Barrymore, US actor, **1954**; Tyrone Power, US film actor, **1958**; Jean Gabin, French actor,

1976; Margaret Mead, US anthropologist, **1978**; Luciano Liggio, Italian racketeer, **1993**.

16 Feast day of St Margaret of Scotland, St Agnes of Assisi, St Gertrude of Helfta, St Afan, St Edmund of Abingdon, St Mechtildis of Helfta, St Nikon 'Metanoeite', and St Eucherius of Lyons.

1824 Australian explorer Hamilton Hume discovered the Murray River, the longest river in Australia. **1869** The Suez Canal, which had taken ten years to build, was formally opened. **1913** The first volume of *Remembrance of Things Past*, the classic autobiographical novel by Marcel Proust, was published in Paris. **1918** Hungary achieved independence from the Austro-Hungarian empire and was proclaimed a republic. **1928** In London, obscenity charges were brought against Radclyffe Hall's crusading lesbian novel *The Well of Loneliness*. **1965** The USSR launched *Venus III*, an unmanned spacecraft that successfully landed on Venus. **1993** Amid the tears of its employees and sympathisers, Vladimir Lenin's mausoleum was closed by the Russian authorities; it was the first site in Moscow linked to Lenin to be shut down.

Tiberius, Roman emperor, **42 BC**; John Bright, British political reformer, **1811**; William Frend de Morgan, English artist and novelist, **1839**; George S Kaufman, US dramatist, **1889**; Willie Carson, English jockey, **1942**; Frank Bruno, British boxer, **1961**.

King Henry III, **1272**; Jack Sheppard, English highwayman, **1724**; Louis Riel, Canadian leader of the Métis rebellion, **1885**; Clark Gable, US fim actor, **1960**; William Holden, US film actor, **1981**; Arthur Askey, English comedian, **1983**.

17 Feast day of St Hilda, Saints Acisclus and Victoria, St Anianus or Aignan of Orléans, Saints Alphaeus and Zachaeus, St Elizabeth of Hungary, St Gregory of Tours, St Gregory the Wonderworker, St Dionysius of Alexandria, The Martyrs of Paraguay, and St Hugh of Lincoln.

1800 The US Congress met for the first time, in Washington DC. **1880** The first three British women to graduate received their Bachelor of Arts degrees from the University of London. **1922** The last sultan of Turkey was deposed by Kemal Atatürk. **1922** Siberia voted for union with the USSR. **1970** The USSR's *Luna 17* landed on the Sea of Rains on the moon, and released the first moonwalker vehicle. **1970** Stephanie Rahn became the *Sun* newspaper's first Page Three girl. **1988** Benazir Bhutto was elected prime minister of Pakistan, becoming the first female leader of a Muslim state.

Louis XVIII, King of France, **1755**; Bernard Law Montgomery, British field-marshal, **1887**; Charles Mackerras, Australian conductor, **1925**; Rock Hudson, US film actor, **1925**; Peter Cook, English writer and entertainer, **1937**; Martin Scorsese, US film director, **1942**.

Pico della Mirandola, Italian philosopher, **1497**; Mary I, Queen of England, **1558**; Robert Owen, British socialist, **1856**; Auguste Rodin, French sculptor, **1917**; Heitor Villa-Lobos, Brazilian composer, **1959**; Gladys Cooper, English actress, **1971**.

18

Feast day of St Odo of Cluny, St Romanus of Antioch, and St Mawes or Maudez.

1477 William Caxton's *The Dictes or Sayinges of the Philosophres* was published – the first printed book in England bearing a date. **1626** St Peter's in Rome was consecrated. **1918** Latvia was proclaimed an independent republic. **1928** The first experimental sound cartoon, *Steamboat Willie*, starring Mickey Mouse, was screened in the USA. **1977** President Anwar Sadat became the first Egyptian leader to visit Israel and to address the Knesset (parliament). **1987** A fire broke out at London's King's Cross underground station, killing 30 people. **1991** The Shiite Muslim faction Islamic Jihad freed Church of England envoy Terry Waite (held since Jan 1987) and US university professor Thomas Sutherland (held since June 1985).

Carl von Weber, German composer, **1786**; Louis Daguerre, French photographic pioneer, **1789**; W S Gilbert, English dramatist and librettist, **1836**; Ignacy Paderewski, Polish pianist, composer and statesman, **1860**; Alan Shepard, US astronaut, **1923**; David Hemmings, English and director, **1941**.

Chester Alan Arthur, 21st US president, **1886**; Marcel Proust, French author, **1922**; Niels Henrik Bohr, Danish physicist, **1962**; Joseph Kennedy, US financier and diplomat, **1969**; Gustáv Husák, Czech politician, **1991**.

19

Feast day of St Ermenburga, St Barlaam of Antioch, and St Nerses I.

1493 On his second voyage to the New World, Columbus discovered Puerto Rico. **1850** Alfred Tennyson was appointed Poet Laureate. **1863** President Lincoln delivered his famous Gettysburg address, after the American Civil War. **1942** The Red Army counter-attacked and surrounded the German army at Stalingrad. **1969** Brazilian footballer Pelé scored his 1,000th goal in his 909th first class match. **1987** A record price for a car was reached when a 1931 Bugatti Royale was sold at auction for £5.5 million.

Charles I, King of England and Scotland, **1600**; Ferdinand de Lesseps, French engineer, **1805**; Anton Walbrook, German actor, **1900**; Indira Gandhi, Indian stateswoman, **1917**; Calvin Klein, US fashion designer, **1942**; Jodie Foster, US actress, **1963**.

Nicolas Poussin, French painter, **1665**; Thomas Shadwell, English dramatist and poet, **1692**; Franz Schubert, Austrian composer, **1828**; William Siemens, German metallurgist, **1883**; Basil Spence, British architect, **1976**; Christina Onassis, Greek shipowner, **1988**.

20

Feast day of St Edmund the Martyr, St Maxentia of Beauvais, St Nerses of Sahgerd, St Bernward, St Felix of Valois, and St Dasius.

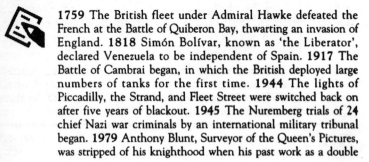

1759 The British fleet under Admiral Hawke defeated the French at the Battle of Quiberon Bay, thwarting an invasion of England. **1818** Simón Bolívar, known as 'the Liberator', declared Venezuela to be independent of Spain. **1917** The Battle of Cambrai began, in which the British deployed large numbers of tanks for the first time. **1944** The lights of Piccadilly, the Strand, and Fleet Street were switched back on after five years of blackout. **1945** The Nuremberg trials of 24 chief Nazi war criminals by an international military tribunal began. **1979** Anthony Blunt, Surveyor of the Queen's Pictures, was stripped of his knighthood when his past work as a double agent was made public. **1980** The *Solar Challenger* was flown for the first time, entirely under solar power.

B

Edwin Powell Hubble, US astronomer, **1889**; Alexandra Danilova, Russian ballerina and choreographer, **1906**; Alistair Cooke, English, journalist and broadcaster, **1908**; Dulcie Gray, English actress, **1920**, Nadine Gordimer, South African novelist, **1923**; Robert Kennedy, US politician, **1925**.

D

Anton Rubinstein, Russian pianist and composer, **1894**; Leo Tolstoy, Russian novelist, **1910**; Queen Alexandra, consort of Edward VII, **1925**; John Rushworth Jellicoe, British admiral, **1935**; Francis William Aston, English physicist, **1945**; Francisco Franco, Spanish dictator, **1975**.

21 Feast day of St Geasius, pope, and St Albert of Louvain.

1783 François de Rozier and the Marquis d'Arlandres made the first human flight when they lifted off from the Bois de Boulogne, Paris, in a hot-air balloon built by the Montgolfier brothers. **1918** The German High Seas Fleet surrendered to the Allies. **1934** Cole Porter's *Anything Goes* was first performed in New York. **1953** The discovery of the Piltdown Man skull by Charles Dawson in Sussex in 1912 was finally revealed as a hoax. **1974** In Birmingham, 20 people were killed and 200 injured by IRA bomb explosions. **1990** Leaders of NATO and Warsaw Pact member states signed the Charter of Paris and a treaty on Conventional Forces in Europe, bringing an end to the Cold War.

B

Voltaire, French philosopher and writer, **1694**; Harpo Marx, US comedian, **1888**; René Magritte, Belgian painter, **1898**; Coleman Hawkins, US jazz saxophonist, **1904**; Natalia Makarova, Russian ballerina, **1940**; Goldie Hawn, US film actress, **1945**.

D

Henry Purcell, English composer, **1695**; James Hogg, Scottish novelist and poet, **1835**; Franz Josef I, Emperor of Austria, **1916**; James Hertzog, South African politician, **1942**; Venkata Raman, Indian physicist, **1970**.

22 National Day of Lebanon. Feast day of St Cecilia or Cecily, and Saints Philemon and Apphia.

JAN FEB MAR APR MAY JUN JUL AUG SEP OCT NOV DEC

1497 Portuguese navigator Vasco da Gama rounded the Cape of Good Hope in his search for a route to India. **1938** The first coelacanth, a prehistoric fish believed to be extinct, was caught off the South African coast. **1946** Biro ball point pens went on sale in Britain, invented by Hungarian journalist László Biro. **1956** The 16th Olympic Games opened in Melbourne. **1963** John F Kennedy, 35th US president, was assassinated in Dallas, Texas, allegedly by Lee Harvey Oswald. **1975** Two days after the death of General Franco, Juan Carlos I was sworn in as King of Spain. **1986** Mike Tyson, aged 20, defeated Trevor Berbick in Las Vegas, becoming the youngest-ever heavyweight boxing champion. **1990** Prime Minister Margaret Thatcher, who had led Britain since 1979, announced her resignation.

George Eliot (Mary Ann Evans), English novelist, **1819**; Wassily Kandinsky, Russian painter, **1866**; André Gide, French author, **1869**; Charles de Gaulle, French statesman, **1890**; Benjamin Britten, English composer, **1913**; Billie Jean King, US tennis champion, **1943**; Boris Becker, German tennis champion, **1967**.

Edward Teach (Blackbeard the pirate), English navigator, **1718**; Robert Clive, British general and administrator, **1774**; Arthur Sullivan, English composer, **1900**; Jack London, US novelist, **1916**; Mae West, US film actress, **1980**; Sterling Holloway, US film actor, **1992**.

23 Feast day of St Clement I, pope, St Alexander, prince, St Columbanus, St Amphilochius, St Trudo or Trond, St Gregory of Girgenti, and St Felicitas.

1670 Molière's *Le Bourgeois Gentilhomme* was performed for the first time in Paris. **1852** Britain's first pillar boxes were erected, at St Helier, Jersey. **1889** The first juke box was installed in the Palais Royal Saloon in San Francisco. **1906** Italian operatic tenor Enrico Caruso was fined $10 for sexual harassment. **1921** US President Warren Harding banned doctors from prescribing beer, eliminating a loophole in the prohibition law. **1963** The first episode of the BBC TV serial *Dr Who* was broadcast, with William Hartnell as Dr Who and Anna Ford as his female companion. **1980** A violent earthquake struck Southern Italy, killing over 4,000 people.

B Billy the Kid, US outlaw, **1859**; Manuel de Falla, Spanish composer, **1876**; Boris Karloff, English film actor, **1887**; Michael Gough, English actor, **1917**; Lew Hoad, Australian tennis player, **1934**; Shane Gould, Australian swimmer, **1956**.

D Abbé Prévost, French author, **1763**; Dr Hawley Harvey Crippen, US murderer, executed, **1910**; Arthur Wing Pinero, British dramatist, **1934**; P C Wren, British novelist, **1941**; André Malraux, French novelist, **1976**; Merle Oberon, British film actress, **1979**.

24 Feast day of Saints Flora and Mary, St Chrysogonus, and St Colman of Cloyne.

1642 Dutch navigator Abel Tasman discovered Van Dieman's Land which he named after his captain, but it was later renamed Tasmania. **1859** Darwin's *The Origin of Species* was published. **1963** Lee Harvey Oswald, charged with the assassination of John F Kennedy, was shot while in police custody by Jack Ruby, a stripclub owner. **1989** Czech politician Alexander Dubček made his first public appearance in over 20 years, speaking at a pro-democracy rally in Prague. **1993** The last 14 bottles of Scotch whisky salvaged from the SS *Politician*, wrecked in 1941 and the inspiration of the book and film, *Whisky Galore*, were sold at auction for £11,462 at Christie's.

B Baruch Spinoza, Dutch philosopher, **1632**; Laurence Sterne, Irish novelist, **1713**; Henri de Toulouse-Lautrec, French painter, **1864**; Scott Joplin, US ragtime pianist and composer, **1868**; Billy Connolly, Scottish comedian, **1942**; Ian Botham, English cricketer, **1955**.

D John Knox, Scottish religious reformer, **1572**; Erskine Childers, Irish nationalist and novelist, **1922**; Georges Clemenceau, French statesman, **1929**; George Raft, US film actor, **1980**; Freddie Mercury, English rock singer, **1991**; Anthony Burgess, British novelist and critic, **1993**.

25 Feast day of St Moses the Martyr and St Mercurius of Caesarea.

1884 Evaporated milk was patented by John Mayenberg of St Louis, Missouri. **1937** An inter-regional spelling competition became the first British quiz programme to be broadcast. **1941**

JAN FEB MAR APR MAY JUN JUL AUG SEP OCT NOV DEC

HMS *Barham* was sunk, with the loss of 868 lives. **1952** The longest-running play, *The Mousetrap* by Agatha Christie, opened in London, at the Ambassador's Theatre. **1969** In protest against Britain's involvement in Biafra and support of US involvement in Vietnam, John Lennon returned his MBE. **1975** Surinam, formerly called Dutch Guiana, became a fully independent republic. **1991** Winston Silcott became the first of the 'Tottenham Three', convicted for the 1985 killing of a policeman in Tottenham, North London, to have his conviction overturned.

Andrew Carnegie, US industrialist and philanthropist, **1835**; Carl Benz, German engineer and car manufacturer, **1844**; Augusto Pinochet, Chilean dictator, **1915**; Ricardo Montalban, US film actor, **1920**; Imran Khan Niaz, Pakistani cricketer, **1952**.

Isaac Watts, English hymn writer, **1748**; Bojangles (Bill Robinson), US tapdancer and entertainer, **1949**; Myra Hess, British pianist, **1965**; Upton Sinclair, US novelist, **1968**; Yukio Mishima, Japanese novelist, **1970**; Anton Dolin, British dancer and choreographer, **1983**.

26 Feast day of St Conrad of Constance, St Peter of Alexandria, St John Berchmans, St Basolus or Basle, St Siricius, St Leonard of Porto Maurizio, and St Silvester Gozzolini.

1703 England was hit by severe gales, known as the Great Storm, in which 8,000 people died. **1789** The American holiday of Thanksgiving was celebrated nationally for the first time. **1906** President Theodore Roosevelt returned to Washington after a trip to Central America, becoming the first US president to travel abroad while in office. **1942** The Soviet forces counter-attacked at Stalingrad, ending the siege and forcing General von Paulus's Sixth Army to retreat. **1949** India became a federal republic within the Commonwealth. **1966** French President Charles de Gaulle opened the world's first tidal power station in Brittany. **1990** Lee Kuan Yew, Singapore's prime minister for 31 years, announced that he was stepping down.

William Cowper, English poet, **1731**; William George Armstrong, English inventor, **1810**; Emlyn Williams, Welsh

JAN

actor and dramatist, **1905**; Cyril Cusack, Irish actor, **1910**; Charles Schultz, US cartoonist, **1922**; Tina Turner, US rock singer, **1938**.

FEB

Isabella I, Queen of Castile and Aragon, **1504**; John McAdam, Scottish engineer, **1836**; Nicolas Soult, French general, **1851**; Leander Jameson, British colonial administrator, **1917**; Tommy Dorsey, US trombonist and bandleader, **1956**; Arnold Zweig, German novelist, **1968**.

27

MAR

Feast day of St James Intercisus, St Cungar of Somerset, Saints Barlaam and Josaphat, St Maximus of Riez, St Fergus of Strathern, St Virgil of Salzburg, and St Secundinus or Sechnall.

APR

1095 Pope Urban began to preach the First Crusade at Clermont, France. **1582** William Shakespeare, aged 18, married Anne Hathaway. **1914** Britain's first policewomen went on duty, at Grantham, Lincolnshire. **1940** In Romania, the pro-fascist group Iron Guard murdered 64 people, including former prime minister Jorga. **1967** French President Charles de Gaulle rejected British entry into the Common Market. **1970** The Gay Liberation Front held its first demonstration in London.

MAY

JUN

Anders Celsius, Swedish astronomer and thermometer inventor, **1701**; Fanny Kemble, English actress, **1809**; Chaim Weizmann, Israeli chemist and Zionist leader, **1874**; Konosuke Matsushita, Japanese industrialist, **1894**; Alexander Dubček, Czech statesman, **1920**; Jimi Hendrix, US guitarist and singer, **1942**.

JUL

AUG

Horace, Roman poet, **8 BC**; Alexandre Dumas fils, French novelist and dramatist, **1895**; Eugene O'Neill, US dramatist, **1953**; Arthur Honegger, Swiss composer, **1955**; Ross McWhirter, British editor, **1975**.

SEP

OCT

28

Feast day of St Stephen the Younger, St Catherine Labouré, St Simeon Metaphrastes, St James of the March, and St Joseph Pignatelli.

NOV

1520 Portuguese navigator Ferdinand Magellan sailed through the Straits at the tip of South America and reached an ocean which he named the Pacific. **1660** The Royal Society was chartered in London. **1905** The Irish political party Sinn Fein

DEC

was founded by Arthur Griffith in Dublin. **1909** In France, a law was passed allowing women eight weeks' maternity leave. **1948** Edwin Land's first polaroid cameras went on sale in Boston. **1960** Mauritania gained independence. **1978** Amid growing fundamentalist opposition, the Iranian government banned religious rallies. **1993** The Northern Ireland peace process and Prime Minister John Major's credibility were dealt a blow when secret government contacts with the IRA were publicly disclosed.

Jean Baptiste Lully, Italian/French composer, **1632**; William Blake, English poet and artist, **1757**; Friedrich Engels, German Socialist, **1820**; Alberto Moravia, Italian writer, **1907**; Claude Lévi-Strauss, French anthropologist, **1908**; Randy Newman, US singer and songwriter, **1943**.

Giovanni Lorenzo Bernini, Italian sculptor, **1680**; Washington Irving, US author, **1859**; Enrico Fermi, Italian physicist, **1954**; Enid Blyton, English children's book author, **1968**; Kenneth Connor, English actor, **1993**.

29 Feast day of St Radbod, St Brendan of Birr, St Saturninus, martyr, and St Saturninus or Sernin of Toulouse.

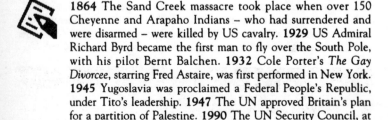

1864 The Sand Creek massacre took place when over 150 Cheyenne and Arapaho Indians – who had surrendered and were disarmed – were killed by US cavalry. **1929** US Admiral Richard Byrd became the first man to fly over the South Pole, with his pilot Bernt Balchen. **1932** Cole Porter's *The Gay Divorcee*, starring Fred Astaire, was first performed in New York. **1945** Yugoslavia was proclaimed a Federal People's Republic, under Tito's leadership. **1947** The UN approved Britain's plan for a partition of Palestine. **1990** The UN Security Council, at the urging of the USA, authorised the use of force against Iraq if it did not withdraw totally from Kuwait by 15 January 1991.

Gaetano Donizetti, Italian composer, **1797**; Christian Johann Doppler, Austrian physicist, **1803**; Louisa May Alcott, US author, **1832**; C S Lewis, English scholar and writer, **1898**; Jacques Chirac, French statesman, **1932**; John Mayall, British vocalist and guitarist, **1949**.

D Thomas Wolsey, English cardinal and politician, **1530**; Maria
Theresa, Empress of Austria. **1780**; Giacomo Puccini, Italian
composer, **1924**; Graham Hill, English racing driver, **1975**;
Natalie Wood, US film actress, **1981**; Ralph Bellamy, US film
actor, **1991**.

30 National Day of Scotland. Feast day of St Andrew the Apostle,
St Sapor, and St Cuthbert Mayne.

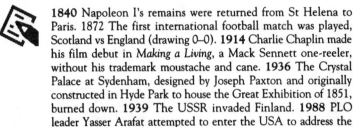

1840 Napoleon I's remains were returned from St Helena to
Paris. **1872** The first international football match was played,
Scotland vs England (drawing 0–0). **1914** Charlie Chaplin made
his film debut in *Making a Living*, a Mack Sennett one-reeler,
without his trademark moustache and cane. **1936** The Crystal
Palace at Sydenham, designed by Joseph Paxton and originally
constructed in Hyde Park to house the Great Exhibition of 1851,
burned down. **1939** The USSR invaded Finland. **1988** PLO
leader Yasser Arafat attempted to enter the USA to address the
UN General Assembly, but was refused a visa.

B Andrea Palladio, Italian architect, **1508**; Philip Sidney, English
poet and soldier, **1554**; Jonathan Swift, Irish author, **1667**;
Mark Twain, US author, **1835**; Winston Churchill, British
statesman, **1874**; Gary Lineker, English footballer, **1960**.

D Oscar Wilde, Irish dramatist, **1900**; Edward John Eyre,
Australian explorer, **1901**; Beniamino Gigli, Italian operatic
tenor, **1957**; Zeppo Marx, US actor and comedian, **1979**; Cary
Grant, US film actor, **1986**; James Baldwin, US writer, **1987**.

DECEMBER

1 World Aids day. Feast day of St Edmund Campion, St Agericus
or Airy, St Eligius or Elroy, St Alexander Briant, St Anasanus,
St Tudwal, and St Ralph Sherwin.

1640 The Spanish were driven out of Portugal and the country
regained its independence. **1919** US-born Lady Nancy Astor
became the first woman to take her seat in the House of
Commons, as MP for the Sutton division of Plymouth. **1925**
The Locarno Pact was signed in London, guaranteeing peace
and frontiers in Europe. **1939** *Gone with the Wind* premiered in

JAN FEB MAR APR MAY JUN JUL AUG SEP OCT NOV DEC

New York. **1942** The Beveridge Report on Social Security, which formed the basis of the welfare state in Britain, was issued. **1953** The first issue of Hugh Heffner's *Playboy* magazine was published; the centre-spread nude featured Marilyn Monroe. **1989** Pope John Paul II and Mikhail Gorbachev met in Rome, ending 70 years of hostility between the Vatican and the USSR. **1991** France won its first Davis Cup tennis title in 59 years by defeating the USA at the finals in Lyons, France.

Madame Tussaud, French wax-modeller, **1761**; Alicia Markova, British ballet dancer, **1910**; Woody Allen, US film actor, writer and director, **1935**; Lee Trevino, US golfer, **1939**; Richard Pryor, US comedian and actor, **1940**; Bette Midler, US comedienne and singer, **1945**.

King Henry I, **1135**; Lorenzo Ghiberti, Italian sculptor and goldsmith, **1455**; Vincent d'Indy, French composer, **1931**; J B S Haldane, English scientist and writer, **1964**; David Ben Gurion, Israeli statesman, **1973**; James Baldwin, US writer, **1987**.

2 Feast day of St Chromatius of Aquilea, St Silvanus of Constantinople, St Nonnus and St Bibiana or Viviana.

1697 The rebuilt St Paul's Cathedral, work of Sir Christopher Wren, was opened. **1805** Napoleon (crowned Emperor exactly one year earlier) defeated the Austrians and Russians at the Battle of Austerlitz. **1823** US President James Monroe proclaimed the Monroe Doctrine, warning that any further European colonial ambitions in the western hemisphere would be considered threats to US peace and security. **1901** In the USA, King Camp Gillette patented a safety razor with a double-edged disposable blade. **1942** The first nuclear chain reaction took place at the University of Chicago, under physicists Enrico Fermi and Arthur Compton. **1988** In Bangladesh, a cyclone killed thousands of people and left five million homeless. **1990** West German Chancellor Helmut Kohl was elected chancellor of a united Germany.

Georges Seurat, French painter, **1859**; Ruth Draper, US entertainer, **1884**; John Barbirolli, English conductor, **1899**; Peter Carl Goldmark, US inventor of the LP record, **1906**; Maria Callas, US lyric soprano, **1923**; Alexander Haig, US general and politician.

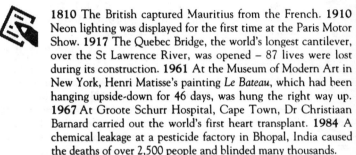

Hernándo Cortés, Spanish conquistador, 1547; Gerhardt Mercator, Belgian cartographer, 1594; Marquis de Sade, French writer and philosopher, 1814; John Brown, US abolitionist, 1859; Philip Larkin, English poet, 1985; Aaron Copland, US composer, 1990; Pablo Escobar, Colombian racketeer, 1993.

3

Feast day of Saints Claudius, Hilaria and their Companions, St Birinus, St Lucius of Britain, St Cassian of Tangier, and St Francis Xavier.

1810 The British captured Mauritius from the French. 1910 Neon lighting was displayed for the first time at the Paris Motor Show. 1917 The Quebec Bridge, the world's longest cantilever, over the St Lawrence River, was opened – 87 lives were lost during its construction. 1961 At the Museum of Modern Art in New York, Henri Matisse's painting *Le Bateau*, which had been hanging upside-down for 46 days, was hung the right way up. 1967 At Groote Schurr Hospital, Cape Town, Dr Christiaan Barnard carried out the world's first heart transplant. 1984 A chemical leakage at a pesticide factory in Bhopal, India caused the deaths of over 2,500 people and blinded many thousands.

Niccolò Amati, Italian violin-maker, 1596; Joseph Conrad, British novelist, 1857; Anton von Webern, Austrian composer, 1883; Andy Williams, US singer, 1930; Jean-Luc Godard, French film director, 1930; Franz Klammer, Austrian skier, 1953.

Frederick VI, King of Denmark, 1839; Robert Louis Stevenson, Scottish novelist, 1894; Mary Baker Eddy, US founder of Christian Science, 1910; Pierre Auguste Renoir, French painter, 1919; Oswald Mosley, English fascist leader, 1980; Lewis Thomas, US physician and biologist, 1993; Frank Zappa, US composer and guitarist, 1993.

4

Feast day of St Maruthas, St Bernard of Parma, St Sola, St Osmund, St Anno, St Barbara, virgin-martyr, and St John of Damascus.

1154 The only Englishman to become a pope, Nicholas Breakspear, became Adrian IV. 1791 Britain's oldest Sunday paper, the *Observer*, was first published. **1798** William Pitt the Younger first introduced income tax in Britain, to finance the wars with revolutionary France. **1808** Napoleon abolished the Inquisition in Spain. **1829** Under British rule, suttee (whereby a widow commits suicide by joining her husband's funeral pyre) was made illegal in India. **1947** The first performance of Tennessee Williams' *A Streetcar Named Desire* starring Marlon Brando and Jessica Tandy, in New York. **1961** Birth control pills became available on the NHS. **1991** News correspondent Terry Anderson, the longest-held Western hostage in Lebanon (2,454 days in captivity), was freed by Islamic Jihad.

B Thomas Carlyle, Scottish author, **1795**; Edith Cavell, English nurse, **1865**; Rainer Maria Rilke, German poet, **1875**; Francisco Franco, Spanish dictator, **1892**; Ronnie Corbett, British comedian, **1930**; Jeff Bridges, US film actor, **1949**.

D Cardinal Richelieu, French politician, **1642**; John Gay, English poet and dramatist, **1732**; Luigi Galvani, Italian physiologist, **1798**; Jack Payne, British bandleader, **1969**; Benjamin Britten, English composer, **1976**.

5 The national day of Thailand. Feast day of St Christian, St Sabas, St Justinian or Iestin, St Crispina, St Nicetius of Trier, St Sigiramnus or Cyran, and St John Almond.

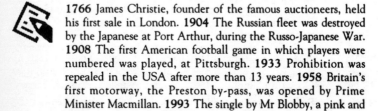

1766 James Christie, founder of the famous auctioneers, held his first sale in London. **1904** The Russian fleet was destroyed by the Japanese at Port Arthur, during the Russo-Japanese War. **1908** The first American football game in which players were numbered was played, at Pittsburgh. **1933** Prohibition was repealed in the USA after more than 13 years. **1958** Britain's first motorway, the Preston by-pass, was opened by Prime Minister Macmillan. **1993** The single by Mr Blobby, a pink and yellow spotted BBC television star, reached number one in the charts.

B Christina Georgina Rossetti, English poet, **1830**; Fritz Lang, Austrian film director, **1890**; Walt Disney, US filmmaker and animator, **1901**; Otto Preminger, Austrian film director, **1906**; Little Richard, US rock 'n' roll pioneer, **1935**; José Carreras, Spanish operatic tenor, **1946**.

Wolfgang Amadeus Mozart, Austrian composer, **1791**; Alexandre Dumas père, French novelist, **1870**; Henry Tate, English businessman and philanthropist, **1899**; Claude Monet, French painter, **1926**; Jan Kubelik, Czech violinist, **1940**; Robert Aldrich, US film director, **1983**.

6 National Day of Finland. Feast day of St Gertrude the Elder, St Abraham of Kratia, St Nicholas of Bari, St Asella, and Saints Dionysia, Majoricus and their Companions.

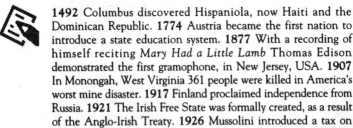

1492 Columbus discovered Hispaniola, now Haiti and the Dominican Republic. **1774** Austria became the first nation to introduce a state education system. **1877** With a recording of himself reciting *Mary Had a Little Lamb* Thomas Edison demonstrated the first gramophone, in New Jersey, USA. **1907** In Monongah, West Virginia 361 people were killed in America's worst mine disaster. **1917** Finland proclaimed independence from Russia. **1921** The Irish Free State was formally created, as a result of the Anglo-Irish Treaty. **1926** Mussolini introduced a tax on bachelors. **1990** Saddam Hussein announced that he would free all of the 2,000 foreign hostages held in Iraq and occupied Kuwait.

King Henry VI, **1421**; George Monck, English admiral, **1608**; Warren Hastings, British administrator, **1732**; Osbert Sitwell, English writer, **1892**; Ira Gershwin, US lyricist, **1896**; Dave Brubeck, US jazz musician, **1920**.

Jean-Baptiste-Siméon Chardin, French painter, **1779**; Madame du Barry, mistress of King Louis XV of France, **1793**; Anthony Trollope, English novelist, **1882**; Ernst Werner von Siemens, German inventor, **1892**; Roy Orbison, US singer and songwriter.

7 Feast day of St Martin of Saujon, St Ambrose of Milan, St Eutychianus, St Servus, and St Buithe or Boethius.

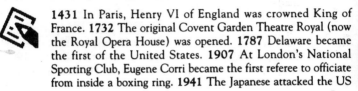

1431 In Paris, Henry VI of England was crowned King of France. **1732** The original Covent Garden Theatre Royal (now the Royal Opera House) was opened. **1787** Delaware became the first of the United States. **1907** At London's National Sporting Club, Eugene Corri became the first referee to officiate from inside a boxing ring. **1941** The Japanese attacked the US

JAN FEB MAR APR MAY JUN JUL AUG SEP OCT NOV DEC

fleet in Pearl Harbor. **1982** The first execution by lethal injection took place at Fort Worth Prison, Texas. **1988** An earthquake in Armenia killed thousands and caused widespread destruction. **1990** A week-long succession of violent clashes between Hindus and Muslims in several Indian cities began, resulting in about 300 deaths and 3,000 arrests.

Giovanni Lorenzo Bernini, Italian sculptor, **1598**; Pietro Mascagni, Italian composer, **1863**; Eli Wallach, US film actor, **1915**; Mario Soares, Portuguese politician, **1924**; Ellen Burstyn, US actress, **1932**; Geoff Lawson, Australian cricketer, **1958**.

Cicero, Roman orator, **43 BC**; William Bligh, captain of the Bounty, **1817**; Ferdinand de Lesseps, French engineer, **1894**; Kirsten Flagstad, Norwegian operatic soprano, **1962**; Thornton Wilder, US novelist, **1975**; Robert Graves, English poet and author, **1985**; Wolfgang Paul, German nuclear physicist, **1993**.

8 Feast day of the Immaculate Conception, St Romaric, St Eucharius, St Sophronius of Cyprus, and St Patapius.

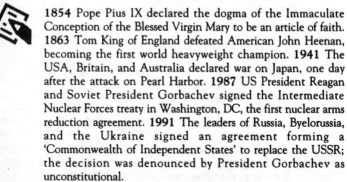

1854 Pope Pius IX declared the dogma of the Immaculate Conception of the Blessed Virgin Mary to be an article of faith. **1863** Tom King of England defeated American John Heenan, becoming the first world heavyweight champion. **1941** The USA, Britain, and Australia declared war on Japan, one day after the attack on Pearl Harbor. **1987** US President Reagan and Soviet President Gorbachev signed the Intermediate Nuclear Forces treaty in Washington, DC, the first nuclear arms reduction agreement. **1991** The leaders of Russia, Byelorussia, and the Ukraine signed an agreement forming a 'Commonwealth of Independent States' to replace the USSR; the decision was denounced by President Gorbachev as unconstitutional.

Horace, Roman poet, **65 BC**; Mary Stuart, Queen of Scots, **1542**; Björnstjerne Björnson, Norwegian poet and dramatist, **1832**; James Thurber, US wit and cartoonist, **1894**; Sammy Davis Jr, US singer, actor, and dancer, **1925**; Jim Morrison, US singer, **1943**.

Thomas de Quincey, English author, **1859**; Herbert Spencer, British philosopher and writer, **1903**; Simon Marks, English

retailer, **1964**; Golda Meir, Israeli politician, **1978**; John
Lennon, British rock singer and songwriter, **1980**.

9

The national day of Tanzania. Feast day of The Seven Martyrs
of Samosata, St Peter Fourier, St Budoc or Beuzec, St Gorgonia,
and St Leocadia.

1783 The first executions at Newgate Prison took place. **1868**
Gladstone was elected prime minister of Britain, beginning the
first of his four terms. **1917** The British captured Jerusalem from
the Turks, during World War I. **1955** Sugar Ray Robinson
knocked out Carl Olson, regaining his world middleweight
boxing title. **1960** The first episode of *Coronation Street* was
screened on ITV. **1987** The first martyrs of the 'intifada' in the
Gaza Strip were created when an Israeli patrol attacked the
Jabaliya refugee camp. **1990** Lech Walesa, leader of the once-
outlawed Solidarity labour movement, was elected president of
Poland.

John Milton, English poet, **1608**; Clarence Birdseye, US
inventor of deep-freezing process, **1886**; Douglas Fairbanks Jr,
US film actor, **1909**; Kirk Douglas, US film actor, **1918**; Robert
Hawke, Australian politician, **1929**; Joan Armatrading, English
singer and songwriter, **1950**.

Anthony Van Dyck, Flemish painter, **1641**; Joseph Bramah,
English inventor of the hydraulic press, **1814**; Juan de la Cierva,
Spanish enginer, **1963**; Edith Sitwell, English poet and author,
1964; Karl Barth, Swiss theologian, **1968**; Bernice Abbott, US
photographer, **1991**; Danny Blanchflower, Irish footballer, **1993**.

10

Feast day of St Gregory, pope, St Edmund Gerhings, St Eustace
White, St John Roberts, St Eulalia of Merida, St Swithin Wells,
Saints Mannas, Hermogenes and Eugrphus, St Polydore
Plaaden, and St Melchiades or Miltiades.

1768 The Royal Academy of Arts was founded in London by
George III, with Joshua Reynolds as its first president. **1845**
Pneumatic tyres were patented by Scottish civil engineer Robert
Thompson. **1898** Cuba became independent of Spain following
the Spanish-American War. **1901** Nobel prizes were first
awarded. **1941** The Royal Naval battleships *Prince of Wales* and

Repulse were sunk by Japanese aircraft in the Battle of Malaya. The leaders of the 12 EC nations ended their two-day summit and agreed on the treaty of Maastricht, pledging closer political and economic union.

César Franck, Belgian composer, **1822**; Emily Dickinson, US poet, **1830**; William Plomer, South African author, **1903**; Olivier Messiaen, French composer and organist, **1908**; Dorothy Lamour, US film actress, **1914**; Kenneth Branagh, British actor and director, **1960**.

Paolo Uccello, Italian painter, **1475**; Leopold I, King of the Belgians, **1865**; Alfred Nobel, Swedish industrialist and philanthropist, **1896**; Damon Runyon, US writer, **1946**; Otis Redding, US soul singer and songwriter, **1967**; Jascha Heifetz, US violinist, **1987**.

11 Feast day of St Daniel the Stylite, St Damasus, pope, Saints Fuscianus, Victoricus and Gentianus, and St Barsabas.

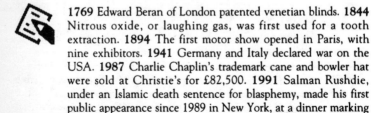

1769 Edward Beran of London patented venetian blinds. **1844** Nitrous oxide, or laughing gas, was first used for a tooth extraction. **1894** The first motor show opened in Paris, with nine exhibitors. **1941** Germany and Italy declared war on the USA. **1987** Charlie Chaplin's trademark cane and bowler hat were sold at Christie's for £82,500. **1991** Salman Rushdie, under an Islamic death sentence for blasphemy, made his first public appearance since 1989 in New York, at a dinner marking the 200th anniversary of the First Amendment (which guarantees freedom of speech).

Pope Leo X, **1475**; Hector Berlioz, French composer, **1803**; Carlo Ponti, Italian film director and producer, **1913**; Alexander Solzhenitsyn, Russian author, **1918**; Kenneth MacMillan, Scottish choreographer, **1929**; Brenda Lee, US pop singer, **1944**.

Llewlyn ap Gruffydd, last native Prince of Wales, **1282**; Bernardino Pinturicchio, Italian painter, **1513**; Olive Schreiner, South African novelist, **1920**; Ed Murrow, US journalist and broadcaster, **1965**.

12 National Day of Kenya. Feast day of St Jane Frances de Chantel, St Corentin or Cury, Saints Epimachus and Alexander, St Edburga of Minster, St Vicelin, and St Finnian of Clonard.

 1896 Guglielmo Marconi gave the first public demonstration of radio at Toynbee Hall, London. 1915 The first all-metal aircraft, the German *Junkers J1*, made its first flight. 1925 The world's first motel, in San Luis Obispo, California, opened. 1955 Bill Haley and the Comets recorded 'See You Later Alligator' at Decca Recording Studios, New York. 1955 British engineer Christopher Cockerell patented the first hovercraft. 1989 US billionairess Leona Helmsley, dubbed the 'Queen of Greed', was fined $7 million and sentenced to four years in prison for tax evasion.

B Gustave Flaubert, French novelist, 1821; Edvard Munch, Norwegian painter, 1863; Edward G Robinson, US film actor, 1893; Frank Sinatra, US singer and actor, 1915; Dionne Warwick, US singer, 1941; Emerson Fittipaldi, Brazilian racing driver, 1960.

D Robert Browning, English poet, 1889; Douglas Fairbanks, Sr, US film actor, 1939; Peter Fraser, New Zealand politician, 1950; Tallulah Bankhead, US actress, 1968; Anne Baxter, US film actress, 1985.

13 Feast day of St Lucy, St Aubert of Cambrai, St Othilia or Odilia, St Eustratius of Sebastea, and St Judocus or Josse.

 1577 Francis Drake began his journey from Plymouth in the *Golden Hind* that was to take him around the world. 1642 Dutch navigator Abel Tasman discovered New Zealand. 1903 Moulds for ice cream cones were patented by Italo Marcione of New York. 1904 The Metropolitan Underground railway in London went electric. 1967 A military coup replaced the monarchy in Greece, sending King Constantine II into exile. 1973 Due to the Arab oil embargo and the coalminers' slowdown, the British government ordered a three-day work week.

B Heinrich Heine, German poet and journalist, 1797; John Piper, English painter and writer, 1903; Laurens van der Post, South African writer and explorer, 1906; Balthazar Johannes Vorster,

JAN FEB MAR APR MAY JUN JUL AUG SEP OCT NOV DEC

South African politician, **1915**; Christopher Plummer, US film actor, **1929**; Howard Brenton, English dramatist, **1942**.

Maimonides, Jewish philosopher, **1204**; Donatello, Italian sculptor, **1466**; Dr Samuel Johnson, English lexicographer, **1784**; Wassily Kandinsky, Russian painter, **1944**; Grandma Moses, US primitive painter (aged 101), **1961**; Mary Renault, English novelist, **1983**.

14   Feast day of St John of the Cross, Saints Fingar or Gwinnear and Phiala, St Spiridion, St Venantius Fortunatus, and St Nicasius of Reims.

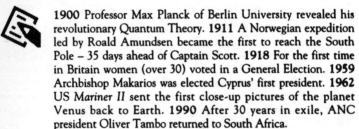

1900 Professor Max Planck of Berlin University revealed his revolutionary Quantum Theory. 1911 A Norwegian expedition led by Roald Amundsen became the first to reach the South Pole – 35 days ahead of Captain Scott. 1918 For the first time in Britain women (over 30) voted in a General Election. 1959 Archbishop Makarios was elected Cyprus' first president. 1962 US *Mariner II* sent the first close-up pictures of the planet Venus back to Earth. 1990 After 30 years in exile, ANC president Oliver Tambo returned to South Africa.

Nostradamus, French physician and astrologer, **1503**; Tycho Brahe, Danish astronomer and mathematician, **1546**; Roger Fry, English painter and critic, **1866**; King George VI, **1895**; Lee Remick, US actress, **1935**; Stan Smith, US tennis player, **1946**.

George Washington, 1st US president, **1799**; Prince Albert, consort of Queen Victoria, **1861**; Stanley Baldwin, British politician, **1947**; Stanley Spencer, English painter, **1959**; Andrei Sakharov, Russian physicist and human-rights campaigner, **1989**.

15   Feast day of St Nino, St Valerian, St Mary di Rosa, and St Paul of Latros.

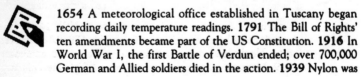

1654 A meteorological office established in Tuscany began recording daily temperature readings. 1791 The Bill of Rights' ten amendments became part of the US Constitution. 1916 In World War I, the first Battle of Verdun ended; over 700,000 German and Allied soldiers died in the action. 1939 Nylon was first produced commercially in Delaware, USA. **1961** Nazi official Adolph Eichmann was found guilty of crimes against the Jewish people and sentenced to death, after a trial in Jerusalem. **1982** Gibraltar's frontier with Spain was opened to pedestrian use after 13 years. **1992** Bettino Craxi, the leader of Italy's Socialist Party, was informed that he was under investigation in a burgeoning corruption scandal that had racked the northern city of Milan.

Nero, Roman emperor, **37**; George Romney, English painter, **1734**; Gustave Eiffel, French engineer, **1832**; John Paul Getty, US oil billionaire, **1892**; Edna O'Brien, Irish novelist, **1936**; Dave Clark, English pop drummer, **1942**.

Jan Vermeer, Dutch painter, **1675**; Izaak Walton, English author of *The Compleat Angler*, **1683**; Sitting Bull, chief of the Sioux Indians, **1890**; Fats Waller, US jazz pianist, **1943**; Charles Laughton, English actor, **1962**; Walt Disney, US filmmaker and animator, **1966**.

16 Feast day of St Irenion, Saints Ananiah, Azariah, and Michael, and St Adelaide.

1653 Oliver Cromwell became Lord Protector of England. **1773** The Boston Tea Party, a protest against British taxation, took place off Griffin's Wharf in Boston harbour. **1809** Napoleon divorced his wife Joséphine, because she had not produced children. **1838** The Zulu chief Dingaan was defeated by a small force of Boers at Blood River – celebrated in South Africa as 'Dingaan's Day'. **1850** The first immigrant ship, the Charlotte Jane, arrived at Lyttleton, New Zealand. **1944** The Battle of the Bulge, in the Ardennes, began with a strong counter-attack by the Germans under General von Rundstedt. **1990** Jean-Bertrand Aristide, a leftist priest, was elected president in Haiti's first democratic elections. **1991** The UN General Assembly voted to repeal its 1975 resolution equating Zionism with racism.

Catherine of Aragon, 1st wife of King Henry VIII, **1485**; Jane Austen, English novelist, **1775**; Jack Hobbs, English cricketer, **1882**; Noël Coward, English dramatist, actor and composer, **1889**; Margaret Mead, US anthropologist, **1901**; Liv Ullmann,

JAN FEB MAR APR MAY JUN JUL AUG SEP OCT NOV DEC

Norwegian actress, **1938**.

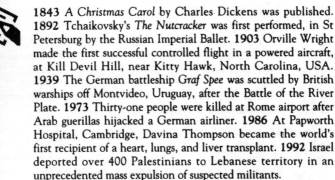

Wilhelm Grimm, German philologist and folklorist, **1859**; Camille Saint-Saëns, French composer, **1921**; Glenn Miller, US trombonist and bandleader, **1944**; William Somerset Maugham, British novelist, **1965**; Kakuei Tanaka, Japanese politician, **1993**.

17

Feast day of St Lazarus, St Sturmi, St Begga, St Wivina, and St Olympias.

1843 *A Christmas Carol* by Charles Dickens was published. **1892** Tchaikovsky's *The Nutcracker* was first performed, in St Petersburg by the Russian Imperial Ballet. **1903** Orville Wright made the first successful controlled flight in a powered aircraft, at Kill Devil Hill, near Kitty Hawk, North Carolina, USA. **1939** The German battleship *Graf Spee* was scuttled by British warships off Montvideo, Uruguay, after the Battle of the River Plate. **1973** Thirty-one people were killed at Rome airport after Arab guerillas hijacked a German airliner. **1986** At Papworth Hospital, Cambridge, Davina Thompson became the world's first recipient of a heart, lungs, and liver transplant. **1992** Israel deported over 400 Palestinians to Lebanese territory in an unprecedented mass expulsion of suspected militants.

Domenico Cimarosa, Italian composer, **1749**; Humphry Davy, English chemist and inventor, **1778**; William Lyon MacKenzie King, Canadian statesman, **1874**; Erskine Caldwell, US novelist, **1903**; Tommy Steele, British singer and actor, **1936**; Peter Snell, New Zealand athlete, **1938**.

Simón Bolívar, South American revolutionary leader, **1830**; Alphonse Daudet, French novelist, **1897**; Elizabeth Garrett Anderson, first English woman physician, **1917**; Harold Holt, Australian politician, **1967**; Sy Oliver, US composer, **1988**.

18

Feast day of Saints Rufus and Zosimus, St Flannan, St Winebald, St Gatian, and St Samthan

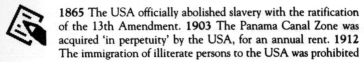

1865 The USA officially abolished slavery with the ratification of the 13th Amendment. **1903** The Panama Canal Zone was acquired 'in perpetuity' by the USA, for an annual rent. **1912** The immigration of illiterate persons to the USA was prohibited

by Congress. **1912** The discovery of the Piltdown Man in East Sussex was announced; it was proved to be a hoax in 1953. **1969** The death penalty for murder was abolished in Britain. **1970** Divorce became legal in Italy. **1979** The sound barrier on land was broken for the first time by Stanley Barrett, driving at 739.6 mph, in California.

Joseph Grimaldi, English clown, **1779**; Paul Klee, Swiss painter, **1879**; Willy Brandt, German statesman, **1913**; Betty Grable, US film actress, **1916**; Keith Richards, British guitarist, **1943**; Steven Spielberg, US film director, **1947**.

Antonio Stradivari, Italian violin maker, **1737**; John Alcock, English aviator, **1919**; Dorothy L Sayers, English author, **1957**; Bobby Jones, US golfer, **1971**; Ben Travers, British dramatist, **1980**; Paul Tortelier, French cellist, **1990**.

19 Feast day of St Timothy, St Gregory of Auxerre, St Anastasius I of Antioch, and St Nemesius of Alexandria.

1154 Henry II became King of England. **1562** The Battle of Dreux was fought between the Huguenots and the Catholics, beginning the French Wars of Religion. **1842** Hawaii's independence was recognised by the USA. **1955** 'Blue Suede Shoes' was recorded by Carl Perkins in Memphis, Tennessee. **1957** An air service between London and Moscow was inaugurated. **1984** Ted Hughes was appointed Poet Laureate. **1984** Britain and China signed an agreement in Beijing, in which Britain agreed to transfer full sovereignty of Hong Kong to China in 1997. **1991** Bob Hawke was deposed as Australia's prime minister by his parliamentary colleagues and replaced by Paul Keating.

William Edward Parry, English Arctic explorer, **1790**; Albert Abraham Michelson, US physicist, **1852**; Ralph Richardson, English actor, **1902**; Leonid Brezhnev, Soviet leader, **1906**; Jean Genet, French dramatist and essayist, **1910**; Edith Piaf, French singer, **1915**.

Vitus Bering, Danish navigator, **1741**; Emily Brontë, English novelist, **1848**; Joseph Turner, English painter, **1851**; Robert Andrews Millikan, US physicist, **1953**; Alexei Nikolaievich Kosygin, Soviet politician, **1980**; Stella Gibbons, English

JAN FEB MAR APR MAY JUN JUL AUG SEP OCT NOV DEC

author, **1989**.

20

Feast day of St Dominic of Silos, St Ammon and his Companions, St Ursicinus, and St Philogonius.

1860 South Carolina seceded from the American Union, and joined the Confederacy. **1915** The ANZACS, Australian and New Zealand forces with British troops were evacuated from Gallipoli, after their expedition against the Turks went seriously wrong. **1933** *Flying Down to Rio*, the first film to feature Fred Astaire and Ginger Rogers, was first shown in New York. **1957** Elvis Presley, at the height of his stardom, received his draft papers. **1989** General Noriega, Panama's former dictator, was overthrown by a US invasion force invited by the new civilian government. **1990** Soviet Foregn Minister Shevardnadze resigned, complaining of conservative attacks on his policies.

Robert Menzies, Australian politician, **1894**; James Leasor, English author, **1923**; Geoffrey Howe, British politician, **1926**; Uri Geller, Israeli psychic/illusionist, **1946**; Jenny Agutter, English actress, **1952**; Billy Bragg, English rock singer, **1958**.

Erich Ludendorff, German general, **1937**; James Hilton, English novelist, **1954**; John Steinbeck, US novelist, **1968**; Artur Rubinstein, US pianist, **1982**; Bill Brandt, British photographer, **1983**.

21

Feast day of St Thomas the Apostle, Saints Themistocles and Dioscorus, St John Vincent, St Anastasius II of Antioch, St Peter Canisius, and St Glycerius.

1620 The Pilgrim Fathers, aboard the *Mayflower*, landed at Plymouth Rock, Massachusetts. **1879** Ibsen's *A Doll's House* was first performed in Copenhagen, with a revised happy ending. **1925** Eisenstein's film *Battleship Potemkin* was first shown in Moscow. **1937** Walt Disney's *Snow White and the Seven Dwarfs* was shown in Los Angeles, the first full-length animated talking picture. **1958** Charles de Gaulle became President of France. **1988** A Pan Am jet blew up in mid-flight and crashed in Lockerbie, Scotland, killing all 259 passengers aboard and 11 people on the ground; the terrorist bomb had been concealed within a radio. **1990** In a German television interview, Saddam

Hussein declared that he would not withdraw from Kuwait by the UN deadline.

B Benjamin Disraeli, British politician, 1804; Joseph Stalin, Soviet leader, 1879; Heinrich Böll, German author, 1917; Jane Fonda, US film actress, 1937; Frank Zappa, US rock singer and composer, 1940; Chris Evert, US tennis player, 1954.

D Giovanni Boccaccio, Italian author, 1375; James Parkinson, British neurologist, 1824; F Scott Fitzgerald, US novelist, 1940; George Patton, US military leader, 1945; Jack Hobbs, English cricketer, 1963.

22 Feast day of St Flavian of Tuscany, St Zeno, St Chaeremon and Others, and St Ischyrion.

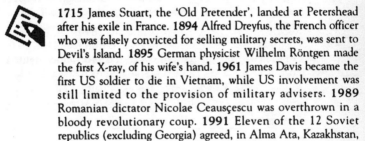

1715 James Stuart, the 'Old Pretender', landed at Petershead after his exile in France. 1894 Alfred Dreyfus, the French officer who was falsely convicted for selling military secrets, was sent to Devil's Island. 1895 German physicist Wilhelm Röntgen made the first X-ray, of his wife's hand. 1961 James Davis became the first US soldier to die in Vietnam, while US involvement was still limited to the provision of military advisers. 1989 Romanian dictator Nicolae Ceauşçescu was overthrown in a bloody revolutionary coup. 1991 Eleven of the 12 Soviet republics (excluding Georgia) agreed, in Alma Ata, Kazakhstan, on the creation of a Commonwealth of Independent States.

B John Crome, English painter, 1768; John Nevil Maskelyne, English stage magician, 1839; Giacomo Puccini, Italian composer, 1858; Peggy Ashcroft, English actress, 1907; Noel Edmonds, English TV presenter, 1948; Maurice and Robin Gibb, Australian pop musicians, 1949.

D George Eliot, English novelist, 1880; Beatrix Potter, English author and artist, 1943; Harry Langdon, US silent film comedian, 1944; Richard Dimbleby, British broadcaster, 1965; Samuel Beckett, Irish author and dramatist, 1989.

23 Feast day of The Ten Martyrs of Crete, St Dagobert II of Austria, St John of Kanti, Saints Victoria and Anatolia, St Frithebert, St Servulus, and St Thorlac.

JAN FEB MAR APR MAY JUN JUL AUG SEP OCT NOV DEC

1834 English architect Joseph Hansom patented his 'safety cab', better known as the Hansom cab. 1888 Following a quarrel with Paul Gauguin, Dutch painter Vincent Van Gogh cut off part of his own earlobe. 1922 The BBC began daily news broadcasts. 1948 General Tojo and six other Japanese military leaders were executed, having been found guilty of crimes against humanity. 1953 Soviet secret police chief Lavrenti Beria and six of his associates were shot for treason following a secret trial. 1986 Dick Rutan and Jeana Yeager made the first non-stop flight around the world without refueling, piloting the US plane *Voyager*. 1965 A 70-mph speed limit was introduced in Britain. 1990 Elections in Yugoslavia ended, leaving four of its six republics with non-Communist governments.

Richard Arkwright, English inventor, 1732; Alexander I, tsar of Russia, 1777; Samuel Smiles, Scottish author, 1812; J Arthur Rank, British film magnate, 1888; Maurice Denham, English actor, 1909; Helmut Schmidt, German statesman, 1918.

Michael Drayton, English poet, 1631; Thomas Robert Malthus, English economist, 1834; George Catlin, US painter and explorer, 1872; Charles Dana Gibson, US artist and illustrator, 1944; Henry Cotton, British golfer, 1987; Ernst Krenek, US composer, 1991.

24 Feast day of St Gregory of Spoleto, Saints, Tharsilla and Emiliana, St Adela, St Irmina, St Delphinus, and St Sharbel Makhlouf.

1814 The War of 1812 between the USA and Britain was brought to an end with the signing of the Treaty of Ghent. 1828 William Burke who, with his partner William Hare, dug up the dead and murdered to sell the corpses for dissection, went on trial in Edinburgh. 1871 Verdi's *Aida* was first performed in Cairo. 1914 The first air raid on Britain was made when a German airplane dropped a bomb on the grounds of a rectory in Dover. 1951 Libya achieved independence as the United Kingdom of Libya, under King Idris. 1965 A meteorite landed on Leicestershire; it weighed about 100lbs. 1979 Afghanistan was invaded by Soviet troops as the Kabul government fell.

King John, 1167; Ignatius of Loyola, Spanish founder of the Jesuits, 1491; Matthew Arnold, English poet and critic, 1822;

Howard Hughes, US tycoon, **1905**; Ava Gardner, US film actress, **1922**; Colin Cowdrey, English cricketer, **1932**.

Vasco da Gama, Portuguese explorer and navigator, **1524**; W M Thackeray, English novelist, **1863**; Leon Bakst, Russian painter and stage designer, **1924**; Alban Berg, Austrian composer, **1935**; Frank Richards, English writer, **1961**; Karl Doenitz, German naval commander, **1980**.

25   Christmas Day. Feast day of The Martyrs of Nicomedia, St Eugenia, St Alburga, and St Anastasia of Sirmium.

800 Charlemagne was crowned first Holy Roman Emperor in Rome by Pope Leo III. **1066** William the Conqueror was crowned king of England at Westminster Abbey. **1914** During World War I, British and German troops observed an unofficial truce, even playing football together on the Western Front's 'no man's land'. **1926** Hirohito succeeded his father Yoshihito as emperor of Japan. **1941** Hong Kong surrendered to the Japanese. **1972** The Nicaraguan capital Managua was devastated by an earthquake which killed over 10,000 people. **1989** Dissident playwright Vaclav Havel was elected president of Czechoslovakia. **1991** Unable to maintain control over a disintegrating Soviet Union, Mikhail Gorbachev announced his resignation as president.

Isaac Newton, English scientist, **1642**; Maurice Utrillo, French painter, **1883**; Humphrey Bogart, US film actor, **1899**; Anwar Sadat, Egyptian statesman, **1918**; Sissy Spacek, US film actress, **1949**; Annie Lennox, British pop singer, **1954**.

Karel Čapek, Czech dramatist, **1938**; W C Fields, US actor and screenwriter, **1946**; Charlie Chaplin, English actor and director, **1977**; Joan Miró, Spanish artist, **1983**; Nicolae Ceauşescu, Romanian politician, executed, **1989**.

26   Boxing Day (Handsel Day in Scotland). Feast day of St Stephen, St Dionysius, pope, St Archelaus of Kashkar, St Vicentia Lopez, St Zosimus, pope, and St Tathai or Athaeus.

1898 Marie and Pierre Curie discovered radium. **1908** Texan boxer 'Galveston Jack' Johnson knocked out Tommy Burns in Sydney, Australia, to become the first black boxer to win the

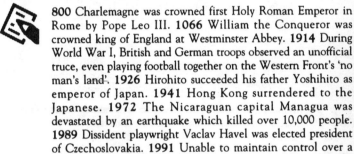

JAN FEB MAR APR MAY JUN JUL AUG SEP OCT NOV DEC

world heavyweight title. **1943** The German battlecruiser *Scharnhorst* was sunk in the North Sea, during the Battle of North Cape. **1956** Fidel Castro attempted a secret landing in Cuba to overthrow the Batista regime; all but 11 of his supporters were killed. **1959** The first charity walk took place, along Icknield Way, in aid of the World Refugee Fund. **1991** The Soviet Union's parliament formally voted the country out of existence.

B Thomas Gray, English poet, **1716**; Charles Babbage, English mathematician, **1792**; Henry Miller, US novelist, **1891**; Mao Zedong, Chinese Communist leader, **1893**; Richard Widmark, US film actor, **1914**; Jane Lapotaire, English actress, **1944**.

D John Wilkes, British politician and journalist, **1797**; Heinrich Schliemann, German archaeologist, **1890**; Charles Pathé, French film pioneer, **1957**; Harry S Truman, 33rd US president, **1972**; Jack Benny, US comedian, **1974**.

27 Feast day of St John the Evangelist, St Fabiola, Saints Theodore and Theophanes Graptoi, and St Nicarete.

1703 The Methuen Treaty was signed between Portugal and England, giving preference to the import of Portuguese wines into England. **1831** Charles Darwin set sail in the *Beagle* on his voyage of scientific discovery. **1904** James Barrie's *Peter Pan* premiered in London. **1927** Defeated in his struggle for power against Stalin, Leon Trotsky was expelled from the Communist Party. **1965** The BP oil rig Sea Gem capsized in the North Sea, with the loss of 13 lives. **1978** With the adoption of a new constitution, Spain became a democracy after 40 years of dictatorship.

B Johannes Kepler, German astronomer, **1571**; George Cayley, British aviation pioneer, **1773**; Louis Pasteur, French chemist and microbiologist, **1822**; Sydney Greenstreet, English film actor, **1878**; Marlene Dietrich, German singer and actress, **1901**; Gerard Depardieu, French film actor, **1948**.

D Charles Lamb, English essayist and critic, **1834**; Max Beckmann, German painter, **1950**; Lester Pearson, Canadian statesman, **1972**; Houari Boumédienne, Algerian politician, **1978**; Hoagy Carmichael, US composer, singer, and pianist,

1981; Hervé Guibert, French novelist and photographer, 1992.

28

Feast day of the Holy Innocents, St Antony of Lérins, and St Theodore the Sanctified.

1065 Westminster Abbey was consecrated under Edward the Confessor. **1836** Mexico's independence was recognised by Spain. **1879** The central portion of the Tay Bridge collapsed as a train was passing over it, killing 75 people. **1908** An earthquake killed over 75,000 at Messina in Sicily. **1926** The highest recorded cricket innings score of 1107 runs was hit by Victoria, against New South Wales, in Melbourne. **1937** The Irish Free State became the Republic of Ireland when a new constitution established the country as a sovereign state under the name of Eire. **1950** The Peak District became Britain's first designated National Park. **1989** Alexander Dubček, who had been expelled from the Communist Party in 1970, was elected speaker of the Czech parliament.

B

Woodrow Wilson, 28th US president, 1856; Arthur Stanley Eddington, English astronomer, 1882; Earl Hines, US jazz pianist, 1905; Lew Ayres, US film actor, 1908, Maggie Smith, English actress, 1934; Nigel Kennedy, English violinist, 1956.

D

Queen Mary II, 1694; Rob Roy, Scottish clan chief, 1734; Gustave Eiffel, French engineer, 1923; Maurice Ravel, French composer, 1937; Max Steiner, US film music composer, 1971; Sam Peckinpah, US film director, 1984.

29

Feast day of St Thomas of Canterbury, St Ebrulf or Evroult, St Trophimus of Arles, and St Maroellus Akimetes.

1170 St Thomas à Becket, the 40th Archbishop of Canterbury, was murdered in his own cathedral by four knights acting on Henry II's orders. **1860** HMS *Warrior*, Britain's first seagoing iron-clad warship, was launched. **1890** The massacre at Wounded Knee, the last major battle between Native American Indians and US troops, took place. **1895** The Jameson Raid from Mafikeng into Transvaal, which attempted to overthrow Kruger's Boer government, started. **1911** Sun Yat-sen became the first president of a republican China, following the Revolution. **1989** Following Hong Kong's decision to forcibly repatriate some Vietnamese refugees, thousands of Vietnamese 'boat people' battled with riot police.

Marquise de Pompadour, mistress of King Louis XV, **1721**; Charles Goodyear, US inventor, **1800**; William Gladstone, English statesman, **1809**; Pablo Casals, Spanish cellist, **1876**; Jon Voight, US film actor, **1938**; Marianne Faithfull, English singer and actress, **1946**.

Thomas Sydenham, English physician, **1689**; Jacques Louis David, French painter, **1825**; Christina Georgina Rossetti, English poet, **1894**; Rainer Maria Rilke, German poet, **1926**; James Fletcher Henderson, US jazz pianist and composer, **1952**; Harold Macmillan, British politician, **1986**.

30

Feast day of St Sabinus of Spoleto, St Anysia, St Anysius, and St Egwin.

1460 At the Battle of Wakefield, in the Wars of the Roses, the Duke of York was defeated and killed by the Lancastrians. **1879** Gilbert and Sullivan's *The Pirates of Penzance* was first performed, at Paignton, Devon. **1880** The Transvaal was declared a republic by Paul Kruger, who became its first president. **1887** A petition to Queen Victoria with over one million names of women appealing for public houses to be closed on Sundays was handed to the home secretary. **1919** Lincoln's Inn, in London, admitted the first female bar student. **1922** The Union of Soviet Socialist Republics was formed. **1947** King Michael of Romania abdicated in favour of a Communist Republic. **1988** Colonel Oliver North subpoenaed President Reagan and Vice President Bush to testify at the Irangate hearings.

André Messager, French composer, **1853**; Rudyard Kipling, English author and poet, **1865**; Carol Reed, English film director, **1906**; Bo Diddley, US rhythm and blues singer, **1928**; Tracey Ullman, English comedienne, **1959**; Ben Johnson, Canadian athlete, **1961**.

Robert Boyle, Irish physicist and chemist, **1691**; Amelia Bloomer, US social reformer, **1894**; Grigoriy Efimovich Rasputin, Siberian mystic, **1916**; Trygve Lie, Norwegian politician and diplomat, **1968**; Richard Rodgers, US composer, **1979**.

31 New Year's Eve. Feast day of St Silvester I, pope, St Melania the Younger, and St Columba of Sens.

1687 The first Huguenots set sail from France for the Cape of Good Hope, where they would later create the South African wine industry with the vines they took with them on the voyage. **1695** The window tax was imposed in Britain, which resulted in many being bricked up. **1891** New York's new Immigration Depot was opened at Ellis Island, to provide improved facilities for the massive numbers of arrivals. **1923** The chimes of Big Ben were first broadcast by the BBC. **1960** The farthing coin, which had been in use in Great Britain since the 13th century, ceased to be legal tender. **1990** Titleholder Gary Kasparov of the USSR won the world chess championship match against his countryman Anatoly Karpov.

B Charles Edward Stuart, the Young Pretender, **1720**; Henri Matisse, French painter, **1869**; George Marshall, US general, **1880**; Anthony Hopkins, Welsh actor, **1937**; Ben Kingsley, British actor, **1943**; Donna Summer, US singer, **1948**.

D John Flamsteed, first Astronomer Royal, **1719**; Gustave Courbet, French painter, **1877**; Miguel de Unamuno, Spanish writer, **1936**; Malcolm Campbell, British racing driver, **1948**; Maxim Litvinov, Soviet leader, **1951**; Rick Nelson, US rock and country singer, **1985**.

JAN FEB MAR APR MAY JUN JUL AUG SEP OCT NOV DEC